THREE WHO DARED

Recent Titles in
Contributions to Women's Studies

THREE WHO DARED

Prudence Crandall, Margaret Douglass, Myrtilla Miner—Champions of Antebellum Black Education

Philip S. Foner
and
Josephine F. Pacheco

Contributions in Women's Studies, Number 47

GREENWOOD PRESS
Westport, Connecticut • London, England

Library of Congress Cataloging in Publication Data

Foner, Philip Sheldon, 1910-
  Three who dared.

  (Contributions in women's studies, ISSN 0147-104X ;
no. 47)
  Bibliography: p.
  Includes index.
  1. Afro-Americans—Education—History—19th century.
2. Crandall, Prudence. 3. Douglass, Margaret.
4. Miner, Myrtilla, 1815-1864. 5. Slavery—United
States—Anti-slavery movements. 6. Women educators—
United States—Biography. I. Pacheco, Josephine F.
II. Title. III. Series.
LC2801.F57 1984   370'.8996073   83-12830
ISBN 0-313-23584-8

Library of Congress Catalog Card Number: 83-12830
ISBN: 0-313-23584-8
ISSN: 0147-104X

First published in 1984

Greenwood Press
A division of Congressional Information Service, Inc.
88 Post Road West, Westport, Connecticut 06881

Printed in the United States of America

10 9 8 7 6 5 4 3 2 1

Contents

Acknowledgments

We are indebted to the following institutions for their kind assistance in preparing this work: Boston Public Library, Library of Congress, New York Public Library, Connecticut Historical Society, State Library of Connecticut, Virginia State Library, Cornell University Library, Smith College Library, and University of Rochester Library. In addition, we wish to thank Henry Foner, Louise Lowe, Anita Pacheco, Armando C. Pacheco, and Vernon Spence for reading chapters and giving valuable advice. Thanks are due also to Dr. Robert H. Fennell, Jr., of the University of Colorado Medical School for his careful attention to Myrtilla Miner's medical history. Arlene Belzer has improved the book through her skill as an editor.

Introduction

This is the story of three women in antebellum America who endured persecution and hardship because they undertook to teach black children. They lived in different parts of the United States—in Connecticut, Virginia, and Washington, D.C.—but their experiences were similar. They learned that people would go to great lengths to prevent the education of blacks. Of the three schools they established, only the one in the nation's capital was more or less permanent, but all three of the schools had an impact on American life. They provided antislavery agitators with clear proof of the handicaps blacks suffered, regardless of where they lived. None of the women under discussion taught slaves, but opponents of slavery used the hostility toward the schools as proof of American inhumanity to an oppressed group, whether slave or free.

Of the three women under consideration, only Myrtilla Miner anticipated hostility and violence, for she planned a school in the District of Columbia, where slavery continued, even though the slave trade had ended as a result of the Compromise of 1850; Washington was a very Southern city. Opposition to Margaret Douglass seemed inevitable, for she operated her school in Norfolk, Virginia, in the heart of the slave system, in a state where the education of any blacks, slave or free, was forbidden by law. The persecution of Prudence Crandall was the least likely, for she lived in Connecticut, where there were few blacks and where slavery had ceased to exist. All three women found out that prejudice was not limited by geography.

Miner and Crandall had similar backgrounds, for both were descendents of New England Puritans, but Douglass prided herself on being a Southern gentlewoman. Crandall and Miner had loyal supporters, largely among religious leaders of antislavery conviction, who constantly reassured them by praising their endeavors and giving financial support where necessary. Margaret Douglass was entirely alone, except for her daughter. Her story is probably the most pathetic of the three, for she felt—and was—totally isolated from her community. We know a good deal about the lives of Crandall and Miner, largely because they operated within a circle of friends and defenders. Douglass appears briefly in history as a woman of uncommon bravery and then disappears. She was an important symbol but not a well-rounded historical figure. The three women form a unity, however, because they demonstrated unusual courage and deserve to take their places with the many other brave women of nineteenth-century America.

Denying an education to blacks in pre-Civil War America had particular impact because schools were becoming increasingly significant in American life. The growing interest in education reflected a general agreement on the importance of an educated electorate: "the people must rule but . . . in order to rule properly they must be educated."[1] In 1834 an Ohioan warned that "these children all about your streets" would be the future rulers of the country. "Is it not important that they be well educated?" The same year the *Southern Literary Messenger*, published in Richmond, Virginia, expressed a similar attitude: "The promotion and the general well-being of society by a cultivation of the heart and intellect is impliedly required of Americans, from the nature and structure of our government."[2] Americans disagreed on the type of education that was desirable and also on who deserved it. Those young people who would not be participating in the political processes of voting and holding office did not need much education, if any at all. But acknowledgment of the need for an educated electorate led to the establishment, especially in the northeastern, Middle Atlantic, and midwestern states, of common schools (equivalent to today's primary schools), seminaries, and academies.

The common schools received their support in some cases from state or local governments or in other instances from levies on students' parents. Seminaries and academies were usually private undertakings financed by tuition, and they probably tried to enroll more students than could be taught effectively because they wanted to bring in more money. Schools varied greatly in quality, and all too often they were uncomfortable, ill equipped, and staffed by poorly trained teachers. Furthermore, they were ephemeral, appearing in response to community interest and disappearing when enthusiasm waned. For example, between 1821 and 1860, New York incorporated 240 academies, but one out of every twelve disappeared after the first year, and half survived fifteen years or less.[3] When schools closed or there were disagreements about them within the community, teachers were in danger of receiving none of the meager salary promised. We shall see that Myrtilla Miner suffered from the irregularities of schools in New York State.

All teachers were grossly underpaid, but the wages of female teachers were abysmally low. In 1847, when Horace Mann surveyed teachers' monthly pay, he found that in Massachusetts male teachers received an average of $24.51, whereas females earned $8.08. In Connecticut men earned $16.00 to $6.50 for women. In New York men teachers' wages were $14.96 to women's $6.69. The pattern was the same in all the states surveyed.[4] Nevertheless, in spite of the wage differential, women were anxious to get teaching positions because teaching was one of the few respectable professions open to females. It may well be that women were able to secure teaching positions because frugal local governments, looking for a bargain, hired women simply because they would accept lower wages.[5] Another reason may have been the general perception of women as morally superior.

Since the purpose of schooling was to make good citizens, teachers had the preeminent responsibility of developing high moral standards in young people. The nineteenth century perceived women as more moral than men; therefore, women were especially qualified to inculcate those standards in young minds. Women's role in life, according to nineteenth-century standards, was to use the home for training children in morality, uplifting men, and perpetuating pious motherhood. It was natural, therefore, to see the school as an extension of the home, where imparting moral precepts could continue. Such a belief paved the way for the general acceptance of females as teachers and the recognition of teaching as an honorable profession. The "innately high character" of women should be carried into the classroom. An 1836 book of lectures to young ladies said, "The profession of teaching is, then, one which is open to those of our sex who are disposed to gain for themselves an honorable standing and support, to be useful to the world, and to cultivate the talents which God has given them."[6]

The increase in the number of female teachers presented a considerable problem, for the desire for an educated electorate did not apply to women. They did not have the vote. But if women were to serve as teachers, then there would have to be an increase in the training available for them. There is no doubt about the "feminization of the teaching profession during the two decades prior to the Civil War." By 1860 females made up 77.8 percent of the teachers in the state of Massachusetts. It has been estimated that one out of every five Massachusetts women served, at one time or another, as a schoolteacher.[7] The argument could then be made that even though women did not vote and hold political office, they taught future citizens. Hence it was necessary to increase young women's education beyond the social graces, needlework, and music. The result was the establishment of a few academies where young females received rigorous training in the same sorts of courses as young males. The best example of these academies is Mary Lyon's Mt. Holyoke Female Seminary, established in 1837, where the curriculum was the same as at men's colleges and where Lyon undertook to demonstrate that women had no more difficulty learning than did men.[8] Myrtilla Miner would use Lyon as her model when she established her school in Washington. Catharine Beecher, of the famous and large Beecher family, devoted her life to the development of schools for females, and though her antifeminist bias might not have endeared her to Miner, we shall see that Miner used her arguments in stressing the importance of education for women.

Much more accessible to the average female teacher were the normal schools, institutes, and "short courses" that became the major sources of education for teachers, both male and female. Such programs began under the leadership of New Englanders Horace Mann and Henry Barnard and then spread to New York, Pennsylvania, and New Jersey. New York's first normal school was established in Albany in 1844.[9] It is probably true, however, that most teachers were not able to attend the full three-year course of a normal school. Many began the program but had to drop out because of lack of funds, and as we have seen, the pitifully small wages they received made it unlikely that teachers could save enough money to return to school on a full-time basis. Consequently, a more usual source of training was the summer institute or short course that lasted only a few weeks and yet gave the student some indication of the process of education.[10] Taking advantage of even a short course was not easy for women because of their extremely low wages. Nevertheless, the trend in the first half of the nineteenth century was toward better and more widespread education for women. By 1860 the percentage of illiterate white females in New England was only 5.4 percent, in the Middle Atlantic states 6.5 percent, and in the South Atlantic states 17.8 percent.[11]

The increasing availability of at least a basic education for women widened their horizons and led some of them to seek further advancement. A goodly number were inspired to open schools of their own and to take pride in the fact that they were not dependent on others, and Margaret Douglass, though she regarded herself as a gentlewoman, was pleased to call herself a "workwoman." It is impossible to separate the advancement of education for women from their increasing self-consciousness. Literacy meant greater accessibility of information about what women were deprived of, whether it was decent wages or civil rights. Teachers provided models for other women to follow, for they were usually the only professional women in a community. The acceptance of women as teachers might have meant the "feminization" of the profession,[12] but for Miner and Douglass, opening a school was an assertion of independence and an expression of self-assurance. Feminization did not always mean acquiescence; Prudence Crandall's determination in face of adversity demonstrated quite the opposite. Much of the instruction in the schools was certainly designed to make women acquiescent and dependent, but it may be unfair to say that "in qualitative terms, educational experiences probably had a negative effect on the self-images of young women."[13] Our story will demonstrate the opposite.

Southern women had fewer educational opportunities than did their Northern sisters. In 1850 in the South Atlantic states, 22.7 percent of white females could neither read nor write; on the eve of the Civil War, the percentage was still 17.8. The South Central states had an even higher percentage of illiterates: in 1850, 25.7 percent, and in 1860, 20.0 percent.[14] The South lagged far behind the North in providing schooling for all young people, male and female. In spite of the scarcity of schools, especially those funded by state or local governments, some Southerners followed with great interest the development of new ideas in education in the North. They corresponded with Horace Mann and Henry Barnard about possible solutions to the educational problems of the South.[15] In other words, thoughtful Southerners believed that the South could profit from Northern ideas. But by about 1845 and certainly by 1850, many Southerners distrusted the North, feared the use of Yankee textbooks, and refused to accept the Yankee schoolmasters that had been an important part of Southern education since the eighteenth century.[16] Nevertheless, in 1847 a school in Mississippi accepted New Yorker Myrtilla Miner as a teacher, and Miner knew other Northerners who were teaching not far away. Clearly, some Southerners placed quality of teaching above ideological purity. In general, however, Southerners distrusted education while at the same time it was assuming greater importance in the North and the Middle West.

Southern distrust of the North was largely due to the increasing pressure of antislavery agitation. Not only were Southerners defensive about the institution of slavery, they were alarmed at what blacks might learn about antislavery activities. Consequently, the South made it more and more difficult for blacks, whether slave or free, to learn to read. That seemed the ultimate protection against antislavery publications. Some blacks learned to read, and some were even taught by their owners in order to make them more useful, but the masters or mistresses were breaking the law when they did so. Furthermore, Southern states passed laws forbidding the teaching of free blacks as well as slaves.

In the North and the Middle West there was little concern for the education of blacks because they did not belong to the body politic, usually not having the right to vote or hold political office. Therefore, the pressure for the development of schools for an informed electorate did not apply to blacks, and in the North the attitude toward the instruction of blacks was either hostile or indifferent. Since blacks were usually poor, they did not have the resources to open schools for their children when public schools were not provided.

There was, however, one motive for educating blacks, whether they were slave or free, whether they lived in the North or the South. That was the concept of morality. If blacks were to follow a moral course, if they were to be obedient and acquiescent, surely the teachings of Christianity were of preeminent importance. Furthermore,

at the heart of Protestant Christianity was the importance of reading
the Bible. Was it essential to instruct blacks sufficiently so that they
would be able to study the Bible? This was the justification for the
development of schools, especially Sunday schools, for blacks.

Sunday schools began in England in the latter part of the eighteenth century and almost immediately appeared in the United States.
The first American Sunday school was in Virginia, with classes for
both whites and blacks, though they were separate. The movement
spread rapidly, and within a century there were more than 2.5 million
Sunday school pupils in the United States.[17] The American Sunday
School Union (ASSU) said that its classes taught "cleanliness and
subordination" and "habits of sobriety, temperance, and reverence
for the Sabbath." It claimed that it had done "specific, visible,
tangible service to the State."[18] Its great success was in teaching both
adults and children to read. A reading primer printed by the American Sunday School Union sold 100,000 copies between 1850 and
1854.[19]

Americans in general recognized the Sunday school as a valuable
institution for blacks and whites. Stonewall Jackson taught in a
Sunday school for blacks while he was a professor at Virginia Military
Institute in Lexington, Virginia.[20] Students at Lane Theological
Seminary in Cincinnati maintained "three large Sabbath schools and
Bible classes among the colored people."[21] As might be expected,
most teachers were women, for Sunday schools were even more the
natural extension of the home than were day schools. The movement
probably could not have survived without the devoted service of
churchwomen.[22]

As tension over antislavery agitation increased within the South,
Sunday schools for blacks came under attack. It did not seem advisable to close them entirely, for Southerners perceived religious
indoctrination as essential, but teachers in Southern Sunday schools
learned that they had to instruct their black pupils orally so they
could not learn to read.[23] Margaret Douglass found, however, that
this policy was not always followed.

If education for Southern blacks was almost nonexistent, blacks
in the rest of the country did not find schools readily available. They
longed for education, but state and local governments were unre-
sponsive. In Ohio, for example, from 1829 to 1849 the public schools
excluded Negro children entirely.[24] When state governments pro-

vided schools, they were almost always segregated: "They were usually poorer than [those for] whites, worse taught and worse equipped, and wretchedly housed."[25] Whites in the North and West opposed both public and private education for blacks. In Ohio, white teachers instructing black pupils ran the risk of mob violence.[26] When the Noyes Academy in Canaan, New Hampshire, opened its doors to black students, people reacted with such anger that with the help of men from neighboring towns "and nearly one hundred yoke of oxen" they removed the school building from its foundations and moved it to the town common, where it could not be used.[27] A proposal to establish a black college in New Haven, Connecticut, encountered such bitter opposition from the townspeople that it had to be abandoned. It would, they claimed, destroy the prosperity of the city, bring in blacks of low character, "lower moral standards, and frighten away summer visitors and students for Yale and the girls' schools."[28] It is not surprising, therefore, that Prudence Crandall, of Canterbury, Connecticut, found it impossible to open her school to black students—or even one black student.

Although the members of the antislavery movement were divided on many subjects, all agreed on the importance of education for a subjugated people. The antebellum period witnessed many attempts to establish educational institutions under the sponsorship of antislavery organizations such as the Pennsylvania Abolition Society and antislavery leaders such as Gerrit Smith and Lewis and Arthur Tappan.[29] The admission of blacks to Oberlin College helped to emphasize the lack of facilities for training them so they could attain college level. Recognition of the centrality of education was the basis for antislavery support for the schools of Prudence Crandall and Myrtilla Miner and the sponsorship of Margaret Douglass as she reported on her persecution. Slavery was not ending in the United States, but those working for its abolition could feel that through their efforts in the area of education they were making an immediate contribution, if not to slaves, then to their brothers and sisters who were free.

NOTES

1. Rush Welter, *Popular Education and Democratic Thought in America* (New York: Columbia University Press, 1962), p. 68.

2. Quoted in Alice Felt Tyler, *Freedom's Ferment* (New York: Harper and Row, 1944, 1962), p. 233.

3. Harry G. Good and James D. Teller, *A History of American Education*, 3d ed. (New York: Macmillan, 1973), pp. 107, 108, 111.

4. Ibid., p. 150.

5. Merle Curti, *The Social Ideas of American Educators* (New York: Charles Scribner's Sons, 1935), p. 173.

6. Jill K. Conway, "Perspectives on the History of Women's Education in the United States," *History of Education Quarterly* 14 (Spring 1974): 4; Almira H. Phelps, *The Female Student, or Lectures to Young Ladies on Female Education* (New York: Leavitt, Lord, and Company, 1836), p. 420, quoted in Glenda Riley, "Origins of the Argument for Improved Female Education," *History of Education Quarterly* 9 (Winter 1969): 467.

7. Maris A. Vinovskis and Richard M. Bernard, "Beyond Catharine Beecher: Female Education in the Antebellum Period," *Signs: Journal of Women in Culture and Society* 3 (Summer 1978): 868.

8. Tyler, *Freedom's Ferment*, p. 253; Sydney R. MacLean, "Mary Lyon," *Notable American Women 1607-1950: A Biographical Dictionary*, ed. Edward T. James, Janet Wilson James, and Paul S. Boyer (Cambridge: Harvard University Press, 1971), 2: 443–47.

9. Good and Teller, *History of American Education*, p. 138.

10. Paul H. Mattingly, "Educational Revivals in Antebellum New England," *History of Education Quarterly* 11 (Spring 1971): 40, 42–43.

11. Vinovskis and Bernard, "Beyond Catharine Beecher," p. 863.

12. Ibid., pp. 865–66; Phillida Bunkle, "Sentimental Womanhood and Domestic Education, 1830-1870," *History of Education Quarterly* 14 (Spring 1974): 22.

13. Vinovskis and Bernard, "Beyond Catharine Beecher," p. 866.

14. Ibid., p. 863.

15. William R. Taylor, "The Patrician South and the Common Schools," *The American Experience in Education*, ed. John Barnard and David Burner (New York: New Viewpoints, Franklin Watts, 1975), pp. 76–80.

16. Ibid., pp. 70–71; for an example of the importance of a Northern schoolmaster in the South see Hunter Dickinson Farish, ed., *Journal and Letters of Philip Vickers Fithian, 1773–1774: A Plantation Tutor of the Old Dominion* (Williamsburg, Va.: Colonial Williamsburg, Inc., 1943).

17. Clarence H. Benson, *A Popular History of Christian Education* (Chicago: Moody Press, 1943), pp. 129–31, 161.

18. Quotation from the annual report of the ASSU of 1831 in William Bean Kennedy, *The Shaping of Protestant Education: An Interpretation of the Sunday School and the Development of Protestant Educational Strategy in the United States, 1789–1860* (New York: Association Press, 1966), p. 23.

19. Ibid., p. 24.

20. Howard K. Beale, "The Education of Negroes before the Civil War," *The American Experience in Education*, ed. Barnard and Burner, p. 91.

21. Theodore D. Weld to Lewis Tappan, March 18, 1834, *The Liberator*, April 12, 1834.

22. Kennedy, *The Shaping of Protestant Education*, p. 63.

23. Beale, "The Education of Negroes," p. 91.

24. Frederick A. McGinnis, *The Education of Negroes in Ohio* (Wilberforce, Ohio: Curless Printing Co., 1962), p. 35.

25. W. E. Burghardt Du Bois, *The Negro Common School* (Atlanta: University Press, 1901), p. 21.

26. McGinnis, *The Education of Negroes in Ohio*, p. 38.

27. Leon F. Litwack, *North of Slavery: The Negro in the Free States, 1790–1860* (Chicago: The University of Chicago Press, 1961), pp. 117–20.

28. Ibid., p. 125.

29. Carter Godwin Woodson, *The Education of the Negro Prior to 1861* (New York: G. P. Putnam's Sons, 1915), p. 146; Carleton Mabee, *Black Education in New York State from Colonial to Modern Times* (Syracuse: Syracuse University Press, 1979), pp. 166–68.

THREE WHO DARED

1

PRUDENCE
CRANDALL

PHILIP S. FONER

I

"There is now hanging in my parlour," Samuel Joseph May, Unitarian clergyman and an early supporter and devoted follower of William Lloyd Garrison,[1] wrote in July 1852, "an excellent portrait of Prudence Crandall, the heroic young woman who, in 1833, instituted and attempted to sustain a school for coloured girls in Canterbury, Connecticut." The picture had been painted by James Alexander, one of the leading artists in the United States, at the request of the New England Anti-Slavery Society, "as an expression of their respect for a woman who had dared and endured so much in the cause of a despised and much injured portion of the people of our Republic."[2]

When the portrait was finished, Garrison wrote to Helen Eliza Benson, who lived in Brooklyn, Connecticut, the town adjacent to Canterbury, and who was the daughter of Garrison's closest friend, George E. Benson. Benson, together with his family, had stood beside Prudence Crandall and befriended her against the malice of the town of Canterbury. In his letter, Garrison ventured a prediction that, unlike a number of his other predictions, was to be fully realized. "I am happy to say," he wrote, "that the artist has been very successful in taking the portrait of Miss Crandall; but the story of her persecution will outlive the canvass."[3]

The town of Canterbury lies quietly among the hills of Windham County, Connecticut. On its main street there still stands one house that is larger and handsomer than the rest. On the front lawn there is a signpost that proclaims to the curious, "Prudence Crandall kept a school here for colored girls in 1833."

It was this house that Prudence Crandall purchased in 1831, when, at the request of aristocratic residents of Canterbury, she set up a select school for their daughters. Originally from Hopkinton, Rhode Island, she was then a young woman of twenty-seven and a graduate of the Friends' Boarding School in Providence. She had been teaching "young ladies" in the nearby town of Plainfield when she received her invitation to Canterbury.

Canterbury was a relatively prosperous place. Scattered through the village were small factories that made woolen and cotton goods, hats, axes, carriages, and coffins. The town was able to keep a jewelry store in business and raised the then enormous sum of eight hundred dollars to equip a "social library." Most of the funds had been raised from the town's chief professional men—lawyers, physicians, and ministers.[4]

But the village lacked a school for girls, and since public schools were considered "too advanced," the citizens of Canterbury asked Prudence Crandall to open up "a genteel female seminary for the young ladies of the village." Thus, a private academy for girls, Canterbury Female Boarding School, came into existence.

The school's Board of Visitors, or what today would be called trustees, was composed of Canterbury's "most prominent and wealthy citizens." The Board of Visitors was made up of Andrew T. Judson, one of the leaders of the Democratic party and an eager aspirant for the governorship, Dr. Andrew Harris, physician and surgeon (whose wife was the daughter of General Moses Cleveland, founder of Cleveland, Ohio), Daniel Frost, Jr., temperance movement activist, Rufus Adams, justice of the peace, Samuel L. Hough, William Kinne, Daniel Packer, and the Reverend Dennis Platt. Several of these board members lived close to the school, and the Judson residence was next to it.

According to some reports, Prudence Crandall invested all of her money as well as some she had borrowed to purchase the handsome house for her school, while others claim that the sponsors helped her raise the funds to buy the property. In any case, the school for young ladies opened its doors in November 1831 to the town's unanimous approval. Its reputation quickly spread; young ladies from distant towns applied and were admitted as boarders. By 1833 the school was recognized as one of the best in the state.[5] It was just at this point that Prudence Crandall admitted a black girl as a student. Overnight, the situation in Canterbury changed.

Prudence Crandall had been brought up as a Quaker and inevitably heard discussions of the evils of slavery and of discrimination against free blacks. Four years before she established her school, the Connecticut branch of the American Colonization Society had been founded, and most of Canterbury's "established citizens" joined. The society's program for sending free Negroes to Africa appealed to the conscience of these elements as a comfortable solution to the problem of slavery. They believed that if slave owners could be convinced that emancipated bondsmen would be shipped off immediately to Africa, they might be induced to manumit their slaves gradually, and over the years, by this process, the "peculiar institution" would disappear. Meanwhile, they reasoned, the free blacks in Northern cities, towns, and villages would be sent to Liberia, ridding these communities of a "useless," "dangerous," "criminal" element, which was increasingly dependent upon welfare, and for whom there was no hope of ever achieving equality with whites, since God had ordained that the two races should be separate, with the white superior and the black inferior.

Most who were not actual members of the American Colonization Society in Canterbury were counted as Friends of Colonization in Africa and fully supported the society in opposing any education for blacks beyond training them to be leaders of their race in Africa. Education, in their eyes, would make the blacks only more discontented and a more disturbing element in the community, since they never would be able, no matter how well educated, to achieve equality. At the same time, they would be alienated from the uneducated majority of free blacks. On top of all this, education would encourage the amalgamation of the races.[6]

As the teacher of young ladies whose parents were members of the American Colonization Society or Friends of Colonization, Prudence Crandall was expected to share their low opinion of the black people. But in 1831 William Lloyd Garrison's *The Liberator* appeared on the scene. In announcing the policy of the paper, Garrison said:

I am aware that many object to the severity of my language; but is there not cause for severity? I will be as harsh as truth, and as uncompromising as justice. On this subject I do not wish to think or speak or write with moderation . . . I am in earnest—I will not equivocate—I will not excuse— I will not retreat a single inch—And I will Be Heard.[7]

And "this subject" was the immediate, complete, and unconditional abolition of slavery as well as the right of free blacks to equality in American society—including equality in education. In 1832 the New England Anti-Slavery Society came into existence to implement this program.

Copies of Garrison's *Liberator* began to circulate in Connecticut's towns and villages. According to her own account, however, Prudence Crandall was "entirely unacquainted save by reputation" with "the friends of color, called 'abolitionists,'" at the time she settled in Canterbury.[8] It was not long before *The Liberator*'s militant program captured the imagination of the teacher. As a "help" in the family, the Crandalls had a "nice colored girl" named Marcia, whose intended husband, Charles Harris, was the son of William Harris, a local agent of Garrison's *Liberator*. Marcia lent Prudence a copy of the paper. She described what she read:

In that [paper] the condition of the colored people, both slaves and free, was truthfully portrayed, the double-dealing and manifest deception of the Colonization Society were faithfully exposed, and the question of Immediate Emancipation of the millions of slaves in the United States boldly advocated. Having been taught from early childhood the sin of slavery, my sympathies were greatly aroused.[9]

She described her reactions more concretely:

My feelings began to awaken. I saw the prejudice of the whites against color was deep and inveterate. In my humble opinion it was the strongest, if not the only chain that bound those heavy burdens on the wretched slaves. . . . I contemplated for a while, the manner in which I might best serve the people of color. As wealth was not mine, I saw no means of benefiting them, than by imparting to those of my own sex that were anxious to learn, all the instruction I might be able to give however small the amount.[10]

Prudence Crandall soon had the opportunity to put her resolution into action. Here is how she described what happened a few months later, when the event was still fresh in her memory:

A colored girl of respectability—a professor of religion—and daughter of respectable parents, called on me some time during the month of September [1832], and said in a very earnest manner, "Miss Crandall, I want to get a little more learning, enough if possible to teach colored children, and if you will admit me to your school, I shall forever be under the greatest obligation to you. If you think it will be the means of injuring you, I will not insist on the favor."[11]

The request for the "favor" was from Sarah Harris, daughter of an industrious black farmer in Canterbury and agent for *The Liberator*. Sarah had been to the District School with several of Crandall's pupils, had a reputation for "correct . . . deportment," and was "an accredited member of the Orthodox Congregational Church of Canterbury," to which many leading citizens also belonged.[12]

Prudence Crandall did not answer immediately, "as I thought perhaps, if I gave her permission some of my scholars might be disturbed." In further conversation with Harris, however, she found that the black girl "had a great anxiety to improve in learning." She then made up her mind. As she put it: "Her repeated solicitations were more than my feelings could resist, and I told her if I was injured on her account I would bear it—she might enter as one of my pupils."[13]

In January 1833 Sarah Harris entered the Canterbury Female Boarding School. "By this act I gave great offense," Prudence Crandall recalled many years later. Yet even this was an understatement. To be sure, the white pupils, having known Harris as their classmate in the District School, accepted her. The parents, however, began to complain, and soon the school's patrons informed Crandall that, unless she dismissed Harris, the white pupils would all be withdrawn. "If she stays she will ruin your school," the village authorities warned Crandall, and the wife of an Episcopal clergyman who lived in the village told her that if she "continued that colored girl" in the school, "it could not be sustained." Prudence Crandall's reply is historic: *"Then it might sink then, for I should not turn her out."*[14]

Most of the indignant parents withdrew their daughters, confident that this would bring Crandall to her senses. But the principal of the Boarding and Day School for Young Ladies would not retreat. She decided to meet the boycott with still more boldness. Here, in fact, was the answer to the question of how to "best serve the people of color," a question about which she had been thinking for a while. She made up her mind "that if it were possible I would teach colored girls exclusively."[15]

Having decided, she acted. She sent a letter to Garrison asking what he thought of her plan. After introducing herself and describing her experience up to this point, she asked:

I wish to know your opinion respecting changing white scholars for colored ones. . . . I have been for some months past determined if possible during the remaining part of my life to benefit the people of color. I do not dare tell anyone of my neighbors anything about the contemplated change in my school, and I beg of you, sir, that you will not expose it to any one; for if it was known, I have no reason to expect but it would ruin my present school.[16]

Crandall urged Garrison to reply by return mail: "if you consider it possible to obtain 20 or 25 young ladies of color to enter this school for the term of one year at the rate of $25 per quarter, including board, washing, and tuition." Garrison heartily approved the project, and Crandall came to Boston to map out a strategy with him.[17] Others, nearer home, also supported the planned school for black girls, especially Samuel Joseph May and George E. Benson in nearby Brooklyn, Connecticut. May was convinced that the inevitable impending controversy that would follow the establishment of the school for black girls could have been avoided if only Sarah Harris's admission as a student had been accepted by the parents and the community:

There could not have been a more unexceptionable person than Sarah Harris, save her complexion. If she had been allowed to remain without molestation in the school there would have been no excitement, no agitation of the Anti-Slavery question in connection with it. . . . Her [Prudence Crandall's] fame might have been restricted to the region round about Canterbury.[18]

But once Prudence Crandall decided to establish her school for black girls, May defended her right to do so vigorously and to the end.

George E. Benson, a successful merchant in Providence, had retired to Brooklyn, Connecticut, and dedicated his last years (he died in 1836) to abolition. He threw his full support behind Crandall and was assisted in this by his daughters, all dedicated abolitionists, especially Helen Eliza, whom Garrison was to marry.[19]

From Boston Prudence Crandall went to Providence, where a black woman, Mrs. Hammond, agreed to help get pupils; indeed, her own daughter, Ann Eliza Hammond, aged seventeen, enrolled. Mrs. Hammond took Prudence to three other black families who "seemed to feel much for the education of their children, and I think I shall be able to obtain six scholars from Providence." So Prudence wrote joyfully, and encouraged by this support, she took the boat to New York, where she secured more pupils with the aid of a black minister, Mr. Miller. After her visits, she had prospects for at least twenty black students from New York, Philadelphia, Boston, and Providence. But she also had a premonition of what would soon face her. She had told her plan to Daniel Packer, a resident of a hamlet a few miles to the south of Canterbury and a member of her Board of Visitors. After the discussion, she wrote to Garrison: "He said he thought the object to be praiseworthy, but he was very much troubled about the result. . . . he thinks I shall injure myself in the undertaking."[20]

But Prudence Crandall held her ground. She knew she would be blowing up a public storm. In September 1831 there had been the "New Haven excitement," following the announcement of the third National Convention of Free Blacks in Philadelphia to establish a manual labor college for Negroes at New Haven. The officials of New Haven took prompt action. They met and decided that the founding of such a college was "an unwarrantable and dangerous undertaking," and that they would "resist the movement by every lawful means." Furthermore, the meeting denounced the demand for the "immediate emancipation of the slaves," and called "the contemporaneous founding of colleges for educating colored people, . . . an unwarrantable and dangerous interference with the internal concerns of other states, and ought to be discouraged." In the face of such determined opposition, the promoters of the Negro college decided to abandon the project.[21]

The New Haven excitement did not, however, deter Prudence Crandall. In fact, she notified the remaining white pupils in her school on February 20, 1833, that they were dismissed to make room for black boarding students. Six days later, Crandall reported to Reverend S. S. Jocelyn, a black minister in New Haven, that the news of what she had done had caused the people of Canterbury to "become very much alarmed for fear the reputation of the village will be injured." Crandall explained that the night before they had held a meeting to decide on "what shall be done to destroy the school I have now in contemplation." The town had appointed a committee to visit and urge Crandall to give up the idea of a colored school. The committee was composed of four of "the most powerful men" of the town: Rufus Adams, Richard Fenner, Dr. Andrew Harris, and Daniel Frost, Jr. The committee told Crandall that the people who had appointed it had resolved "to do everything in their power to *destroy* my undertaking," and that "they *could* do it and *should* do it." When one of the four hinted "in a kind of affecting manner," the danger that the school might open the door to interracial marriage, Crandall could take it no longer, and shot back: "Moses had a black wife." On this note the interview ended, after which Crandall wrote that clearly stormy days lay ahead, "and what will be the result of this commotion I cannot tell. . . ."[22]

But she was prepared to meet whatever would come. In *The Liberator* of March 2, 1833, Garrison announced "with a rush of pleasurable emotions" that his paper was carrying "the advertisement of Miss P. Crandall (a white lady of Canterbury, Conn.) for a High School for young colored Ladies and Misses." The advertisement (which was to continue in the paper until the school was disbanded) read in part:

PRUDENCE CRANDALL,
Principal of the Canterbury, (Conn.) Female Boarding School,

RETURNS her most sincere thanks to those who have patronized her School, and would give information that on the first Monday of April next, her School will be opened for the reception of young Ladies and little Misses of color. The branches taught are as follows:—Reading, Writing, Arithmetic, English Grammar, Geography, History, Natural and Moral Philosophy, Chemistry, Astronomy, Drawing and Painting, Music on the Piano, together with the French language.

☞ The terms, including *board*, *washing*, and tuition, are $25 per quarter, one half paid in advance.

☞ Books and Stationary will be furnished on the most reasonable terms.

Canterbury (Ct), Feb. 25, 1833.[23]

II

With the publication of the advertisement for Prudence Crandall's school in *The Liberator* of March 2, 1833, the storm broke. Everywhere Canterburians gathered in groups voicing anger at the idea of a school for blacks in their midst and insisting that the institution be suppressed. If this was not done swiftly, they warned, property values would sink to their lowest levels.[24] As black lawyer and statesman Archibald H. Grimké succinctly put it: "If she had announced that she contemplated opening a college for the spread of contagious diseases among her townspeople, Canterbury could not possibly have been more agitated and horrified."[25]

A major charge against the school was that it was part of an abolitionist plot to further the amalgamation of the races. The fact that Crandall tried to have her black pupils attend the local church, contrary, it was charged, to her promise not to do so, strengthened this fear. Crandall publicly denied the charge: "This is utterly false—*the object, and sole object of this school, is to instruct the ignorant—and fit and prepare teachers, for the people of color, that they may be elevated, and their intellectual and moral wants supplied.*"[26]

She was wasting her breath. Canterbury would have no black school in its midst, no matter what the assurances of its principal. Samuel May and George Benson, who were known as Crandall supporters, drove to Canterbury from Brooklyn; when they arrived they were warned that they might suffer injury because of the rising resentment against the proposed school. They made a hurried departure, but before they left they saw a notice calling a town meeting on March 9 to prevent the school from opening.[27]

The meeting was the result of a feeling of confidence among the town's leaders that public opposition would have the same effect as the meeting eighteen months earlier in New Haven, which had resulted in the abandonment of the planned Negro college. What they did not realize was that the New Haven experience had served to strengthen abolitionist determination that never again would such a disgraceful experience occur. On the day before the scheduled town meeting, Garrison wrote to George E. Benson:

If possible, Miss Crandall must be sustained at all hazards. If we suffer the
school to be put down in Canterbury, other places will partake of the panic,
and also prevent its introduction in their vicinity. We may as well "first and
last," meet this proscriptive spirit, *and conquer it.* We—i.e., all true friends
of the cause—must make this a common concern. The New Haven excitement has furnished a bad precedent, a second must not be given, or I know
not what we can do to raise up the colored population, in a manner which
their intellectual and moral necessities demand.[28]

The March 9 meeting announced that its formal purpose was "to
devise and adopt such measures as would effectually avert the nuisance, or speedily abate it if it should be brought into the village."
It opened with the reading of a preamble and two resolutions prepared in advance. They read:

WHEREAS, it hath been publicly announced that a school is to be opened
in this town, on the first Monday of April next, using the language of the
advertisement, "for young ladies and little misses of color," or in other
words for the people of color, the obvious tendency of which would be to
collect within the town of Canterbury large numbers of persons from other
States whose characters and habits might be various and unknown to us,
thereby rendering insecure the persons, property and reputations of our
citizens. Under such circumstances our silence might be construed into an
approbation of the project;

Thereupon, Resolved, That the locality of a school for the people of color
at any place within the limits of this town, for the admission of persons of
foreign jurisdiction, meets with our unqualified disapprobation, and it is to
be understood, that the inhabitants of Canterbury protest against it in the
most earnest manner.

Resolved, That a committee be now appointed, to be composed of the
Civil Authority and Selectmen, who shall make known to the person con-
templating the establishment of said school, the sentiments and objections
entertained by this meeting in reference to said school—pointing out to her
the injurious effects and incalculable evils resulting from such an establishment within this town, and persuade her to abandon the project.[29]

Speeches in favor of the resolutions followed. The leading oration
was by Andrew Judson, lawyer, politician, and Crandall's next-door
neighbor. He warned that "once open the door, and New England
will become the Liberia of America." He continued with the charge

that "there were powerful conspirators engaged with Miss Crandall in the plot," a conspiracy, he warned, that menaced Canterbury's real estate values. He then reminded the audience that the town had a law which would prevent the school from opening—"the law that related to the introduction of foreigners"—and, to great applause, he promised it would be enforced.

Only one speaker, George S. White, attempted to defend Prudence Crandall as a good Christian and to question Judson's prediction of catastrophe for Canterbury "if colored children were admitted into the town." But White was continually interrupted and forced to cut short his remarks.

As a woman, Prudence Crandall could not attend the meeting. She authorized Reverend Samuel J. May and Arnold Buffum, agent of the New England Anti-Slavery Society, to represent her and present on her behalf an offer to move the school to a less conspicuous part of the town if the citizens would take her house off her hands. But neither May nor Buffum ever got a chance to speak; May recalled that they found "fists doubled in our faces" as Judson launched into a tirade against Crandall's representatives. These men, he cried, had no right to be in the town hall. They were insulting the community by their presence and were interfering in local matters. Since they had not been invited to state their views, "let them, therefore, go back to where they came from." After other men had followed in the same pattern, launching abuse on Crandall's representatives, the moderator declared the resolutions unanimously adopted and adjourned the meeting. May tried as best he could to salvage something from the situation. He jumped on a chair and cried out in a voice that caused half the people in the hall to turn and listen: "Men of Canterbury, I have a word for you! Hear me!" It was no use. Crandall's representatives were summarily escorted from the hall, and Judson proceeded to lock it for the night. Outside the two men attempted to convince the townspeople that they had done Prudence Crandall a great wrong by adopting the resolution, but few would listen, and they finally had to depart.[30]

Thus the meeting ended. One of those present characterized the proceedings as "disgraceful"—a display he had "little expected to witness in the middle of the nineteenth century."[31]

Two days after the town meeting, on March 11, Reverend May visited Judson. (He also addressed two letters to Judson, which were later published as a pamphlet in Brooklyn, Connecticut, under the heading, "The Right of Colored People to Education, Vindicated.") During their conversation, which became quite heated at times, Judson told May exactly what his objections were to the establishment of a "school for nigger girls." The village, he said frankly, would lose its desirability as a place of residence, and the value of the real estate would drop. As a result, the whole town would suffer.

May listened patiently to Judson's remarks and, as he had been instructed by Prudence Crandall, offered to remove the school to a less conspicuous place. The only stipulation he made was that Crandall was to be reimbursed for the money she had already spent. But Judson interrupted him savagely:

Mr. May, we are not merely opposed to the establishment of that school in Canterbury; we mean that there shall not be set up such a school anywhere in the state. The colored people can never rise from their menial condition in our country; they ought not to be permitted to rise here. They are an inferior race of beings and never can or ought to be recognized as the equals of the whites. Africa is the place for them. I am in favor of the colonization scheme. Let the niggers and their descendants be sent back to their fatherland, and there improve themselves if they can. . . . You and your friend Garrison have undertaken what you cannot accomplish. The condition of the colored people of our country can never be improved on this continent. You are fanatical about them. You are violating the constitution of our republic which settled forever the status of the black man in this land. They belong in Africa. Let them be sent back there *or kept as they are here.* The sooner you abolitionists abandon your project, the better for our country, for the niggers, and yourselves.

To this outburst, May replied:

Mr. Judson, there never will be fewer colored people in this country than there are now. Of the vast majority of them, this is their native land as much as yours. It will be unjust, inhuman, in us to drive them out or make them willing to go by our cruel treatment of them. No, sir, there will never be fewer colored people in our country than there are this day . . . and the only question is, whether we will recognize the rights which God gave them as men, and encourage and assist them to become all he has made them capable of being, or whether we will continue wickedly to deny them the privileges we enjoy, condemn to degradation, enslave and imbrute them. . . . Education is one of the primal, fundamental rights of all the children of

men. Connecticut is the last place where this should be denied. But as, in
the providence of God, that right has been denied in a place so near to me,
I feel that I am summoned to its defense.

"That nigger school," said Judson, "will never be allowed in
Canterbury, nor in a town of this state."

"How can you prevent it legally?" asked May. "How but by lynch
law, by violence?"

"We can expel her pupils from abroad," said Judson, "under the
provisions of our pauper and vagrant laws."

"But we will guard against them," answered May, "by giving our
town ample bonds."

"Then," answered Judson, "we will get a law passed by our legislature . . . forbidding the institution of such a school . . . in any
part of Connecticut."

"It would be an unconstitutional law, and I will contend against
it," said May. "If you, sir, pursue the course you have now indicated,
I will dispute every step you take, from the lowest court in Canterbury up to the highest court in the United States."

"You talk big," exploded Judson angrily, "it will cost more than
you are aware to do all that you threaten."

To this May answered:

True, I do not possess the pecuniary ability to do what you have made me
promise . . . but I am sure the lovers of impartial liberty, the friends of
humanity in our land, the enemies of slavery, will so justly appreciate the
importance of sustaining Miss Crandall in her . . . undertaking that I shall
receive from one quarter and another all the funds that I may need to
withstand your attempt to crush the . . . Canterbury school.

In his defense of Crandall's school, May went to the very heart of
the racist argument against black Americans, quoting a statement of
Alexander H. Everett, "one of the ripest scholars, and most distinguished civilians in our land," who, in addressing the Annual Meeting of the Massachusetts Colonization Society on February 9, 1833,
had challenged the concept of Africa used to justify the view that
blacks were "inferior":

But, Sir, we are sometimes told that the African is a degraded member of
the human family—that a man with a dark skin and curled hair is necessarily,

as such, incapable of improvement and civilization, and condemned by the
vice of his physical conformation to vegetate forever in a state of hopeless
barbarism. Mr. President, I reject with contempt and indignation this miserable heresy. In replying to it, the friends of truth and humanity have not
hitherto done justice to the argument. In order to prove that the blacks were
capable of intellectual efforts, they have painfully collected a few imperfect
specimens of what some of them have done in this way, even in the degraded
condition which they occupy at present in Christendom. Sir, this is not the
way to treat the subject. Go back to an earlier period in the history of our
race. See what the blacks were, and what they did; three thousand years
ago, in the period of their greatness and glory, when they occupied the
forefront in the march of civilization—when they constituted, in fact, the
whole civilized world of their time. Trace this very civilization, of which
we are so proud, to its origin, and see where you will find it. We received
it from our European ancestors—they had it from the Greeks and Romans,
and the Jews. But, Sir, where did the Greeks, the Romans, and the Jews
get it? They derived it from Ethiopia and Egypt—in one word—from
Africa. . . .

Well, Sir, who were the Egyptians? They were Africans . . . [and] Her-
odotus, the father of history, tells us that the Egyptians were black. . . . It
seems, therefore, for this very civilization of which we are so proud, and
which is the only ground of our present claim of superiority, we are indebted
to the ancestors of these very blacks, whom we are pleased to consider as
naturally incapable of civilization.

So much for the supposed inferiority of the colored race, and their in-
capacity to make any progress in civilization and improvement.

Finally, May summed up the entire controversy:

The question between us is not simply whether thirty or forty colored girls
shall be well educated at a school to be kept in Canterbury; but whether
the people in any part of our land will recognize and generously protect the
"inalienable rights of man," without distinction of color.

. . . the *greatest* question our nation is now called upon to decide—i.e.,
whether our immense colored population shall henceforth be permitted to
rise among us, *as they may be able*, in intellectual and moral worth; or be
kept down in helpless degradation, until in the providence of a just God
they may throw off the yoke of their oppressors, with vindictive violence.

The spirit that is in the children of men is usually roused by persecution.[32]

"How," asked Henry E. Benson on the day following the town
meeting, "does Miss Crandall bear up under such a mighty oppo-

sition?" He answered: "Unmoved. Not a purpose of her heart is shaken—not a fear awakened within her bosom. Confident that she is determined to press on to the end. No persecution that can assail her, will alter the steadfast purpose of her soul."[33]

The truth of this observation became clear several days later when the committee of fourteen, chosen by the town meeting, and headed by Andrew T. Judson, visited Crandall and informed her that the citizens of Canterbury were opposed to the school. They had learned, the committee declared, that "the school was to become auxiliary in the work of *immediate abolition,* as well as in opposing colonizing efforts." And that *"The Liberator* was to be the mouthpiece of this school." Therefore, they reported, the committee had been authorized, in the name of "responsible individuals," to pay Crandall for the sum she had spent in buying the house, upon condition that "she would abandon the proposed school." However, the committee was compelled to report regretfully to the American Colonization Society: "This she has declined to do." On the contrary, she informed them clearly and firmly that she was determined to proceed with the opening of the school.[34]

And proceed she did. Under the heading MISS CRANDALL'S SCHOOL, *The Liberator* reported in April 1833: "We have received from an authentic source, the heart-cheering information that Miss Crandall has commenced her school, and is resolved to persevere against all opposition." "We trust," Garrison continued, "That our colored friends will stay up her hands by affording her a large number of pupils, and that the school will live until its heathenish opposers repent of their barbarity."[35]

The boarding school for females had reopened on April 1 with fifteen black girls from Philadelphia, New York, Providence, Boston, and Connecticut. These young girls stood bravely by their teacher's side.[36]

In its report to the American Colonization Society, the committee, which had visited Crandall and vainly tried to dissuade her from opening her school, observed that "if there has been *excited feelings,* sure there has been no unlawful or improper *act* done."[37] But it was only a matter of days before such acts followed, a process hastened by the distribution by the committee of an editorial in the *Norwich Republican* that gave the following answer to the question: What do the abolitionists "propose to do by means of this institution?"

Why, to break down the barriers which God has placed between blacks and whites—to manufacture *"Young Ladies of color,"* and to foist upon the community a new species of gentility, in the shape of sable belles. They propose, by softening down the rough features of the African mind, in these wenches, to cook up a palatable morsel for our white bachelors. After the precious concoction is completed, they are then to be taken by the hand, introduced into the best society, and made to aspire to the first matrimonial connections in the country. In a word, they hope to force the two races to amalgamate![38]

Once the school was reopened on April 1, the storekeepers in Canterbury refused to sell supplies to its owner. ("Not a shop in the village will sell her a morsel of food," Henry Benson reported.) The village doctor would not attend ailing students. ("Hippocratic oath be damned!" one commentator noted.) The druggist refused to give medicine. The church doors were closed. On top of such fierce inhumanity, rowdies smashed the school windows and threw manure into the well.[39]

The students needed exercise, and it was Crandall's custom to take them on a walk each day. "When we walk out, horns are blown and pistols fired," one student reported. In addition to verbal insults from all sides, pellets of manure, dead cats, chicken heads, and other missiles were thrown at the students and teacher.[40]

Somehow, Prudence Crandall kept the school going. A friendly black in Norwich brought provisions from a grocer in Packerville, and Prudence's brother, Hezekiah, and her father, Pardon, brought food and other supplies to the school weekly. Sarah Harris's father daily carted buckets of water from his farm two miles away.[41]

For daring to assist his daughter, Prudence's father was assailed with threats of vengeance. "Mr. Crandall," said Judson on behalf of his committee, "you are to be fined $100 for the first offense, $200 for the second, and double it every time (you visit your daughter). . . . And your daughter, the one that established the school for colored females, will be taken up the same way as for stealing a horse or for burglary. Her property will not be taken—but she will be put in jail, not. . . having the liberty of the yard. There is no mercy to be shown about it." Small wonder one of the students wrote: "The place is delightful; all that is wanting to complete the scene is *civilized* men."[42]

Under this pressure, Prudence Crandall's father retreated, and he urged his daughter to give up. But she refused, and she was fully supported by her students. So the Canterbury bigots invoked the law. They arrested Ann Eliza Hammond, the seventeen-year-old student from Providence, under an ancient pauper and vagrancy statute of Connecticut, which called for whipping on "the naked body, not exceeding ten stripes." Upon hearing this, Samuel Joseph May hurried down to Canterbury and deposited with the town treasurer a $10,000 bond, put up by the elder Benson as a guarantee against the vagrancy of any pupil and resultant cost to the town. He also assured Eliza Hammond that

the persecutors would hardly dare to proceed to such an extremity and strengthened her to bear meekly the punishment, if they should in their meanness inflict it; knowing that every blow they should strike her would resound throughout this land, if not over the whole civilized world, and call out an expression of indignation before which Mr. Judson and his associates would quail. But I found her ready for the emergency.[43]

So, too, was her teacher. On April 9, 1833, after describing how she was surrounded on all sides "by those whose enmity and bitterness of feeling can hardly be contemplated," Prudence Crandall wrote: "I have put my hand to the plough and I will *never* no *never* look back."[44]

This determination to continue in the face of the local boycott and other forms of intimidation led Judson and his allies to appeal to the state legislature in Hartford for aid. Their petitions were submitted to a committee, which in May 1833 issued a report and a bill for the legislature's consideration. The report boasted of Connecticut's action in gradually abolishing the "unjust bondage of slavery" and noted with pride that "the constitution and laws" of the state assured its free black population of "all the rights and privileges of other citizens, except that of the elective franchise." It was the duty, the report continued, of the legislature to do nothing to retard "the education of all those of that unfortunate class of beings" who lived in the state, and even "so far as may be within their province, and consistent with the best interests of the people, to foster and sustain the benevolent efforts of individuals directed to that end." But there it drew the line. To permit individuals to educate the "colored people of *other* States, and *other countries*" would be going beyond "the boundaries of our Legislative rights and *duties*."

We are under no obligation, moral or political, to incur the incalculable evils, of bringing into *our own State*, colored emigrants from abroad. . . . It is a fact confirmed by painful and long experience, and one that results from the condition of the colored people, in the midst of a white population, in all States and countries, that they are an appalling source of crime and pauperism.

This being the case, it was the legislature's duty "to protect *our* own *citizens*, against that host of colored emigrants, which would rush in from every quarter, when invited to our colleges and schools," and which, on the basis of past experience, would continue to reside permanently within the state, thus imposing "on our own people burdens which would admit no future remedy and can be avoided only by timely prevention."[45] Such "timely prevention," the report concluded, required passage of a bill by the legislature entitled "An Act for the admission and settlement of Inhabitants in Towns." The vital provision of the bill read:

Be it enacted by the Senate and House of Representatives, in General Assembly convened, That no person shall set up or establish in this State any school, academy, or literary institution, for the instruction or education of colored persons who are not inhabitants of this State, nor instruct or teach in any school, academy, or literary institution whatsoever in this State, or harbor or board, for the purpose of attending or being taught or instructed in any such school, academy or literary institution, any colored person who is not an inhabitant of any town in this State, without the consent, in writing, first obtained of a majority of the civil authority, and also of the select-men of the town in which such school, academy, or literary institution is situated; and each and every person who shall knowingly do an act forbidden as aforesaid, or shall be aiding or assisting therein; shall, for the first offence, forfeit and pay to the treasurer of this State, a fine of one hundred dollars, and for the second offence shall forfeit and pay a fine of two hundred dollars, and so double for every offence of which he or she shall be convicted.[46]

The bill, which became notorious as Connecticut's "Black Law," was passed by the Senate and House of Representatives on May 24, 1833—a mere six weeks after Crandall had reopened her school.

There is no record of any opposition in the debates or of a single vote being cast against the bill.

Now "joy and exultation ran wild in Canterbury." A student in Prudence Crandall's school wrote: "Last evening the news reached us that the new Law had passed. The bell rang, and a cannon was fired for half an hour. Where is justice? In the midst of all this Miss Crandall is unmoved."[47]

At a "Mental Feast," a feature of the school, four of the youngest students, dressed in white, sang the story of their trials, in verses composed by Prudence Crandall:

> Four little children here you see,
>   In modest dress appear;
> Come, listen to our song so sweet,
>   And our complaints you'll hear.
>
> 'Tis here we come to learn to read,
>   And write and cipher too;
> But some in this enlightened land
>   Declare 'twill never do.
>
> The morals of this favored town,
>   Will be corrupted soon.
> Therefore they strive with all their might,
>   To drive us to our homes.
>
> Sometimes when we have walked the streets
>   Saluted we have been,
> By guns, and drums, and cow-bells too,
>   And horns of polished tin.
>
> With warnings, threats and words severe
>   They visit us at times
> And gladly would they send us off
>   To Afric's burning climes.
>
> But we forgive, forgive the men,
>   That persecute us so.
> May God in mercy save their souls
>   From everlasting wo!

Soon they were to add a new verse:

> Our teacher too they put in jail,
> Fast held by bars and locks!
> Did e'er such persecution reign
> Since Paul was in the stocks?[48]

III

On the morning of June 27, 1833, a sheriff entered her house and arrested Prudence Crandall. She was expecting him. She was taken before two justices of the peace, her fellow-townsmen, Rufus Adams and Askel Bacon, both bitter opponents of her school. The charge was that "with force of arms," she "wilfully and knowingly did harbour and board certain coloured persons" who "were not inhabitants of any town in this state."[49]

The phrase "with force of arms," one commentator has observed, would imply to one not familiar with legal phraseology "that she had started a military academy in which to teach them literally to scatter fire-brands, arrows and death!"[50] Actually, as another observer notes, the accurate words should have been "with obstinate determination."[51]

The arraignment did not take long. Prudence Crandall was committed to stand trial at the August session of the Superior Court in Brooklyn. Meanwhile, she would be jailed unless a bond of at least $150 was posted.[52]

Crandall, however, would not post the bond, and in Brooklyn, Reverend May was informed that she would go to prison unless he or someone gave bond. When the sheriff arrived in Brooklyn with Prudence in his custody, May, George W. Benson, and Benson's daughter, Mary, were at the jail awaiting them. May drew Prudence aside and, according to his memoirs, asked her, "If you now hesitate, if you dread the gloomy place so much as to be wished to be saved from it, I will give bonds for you even now." He had the money in his pocket. To which Prudence Crandall answered: "I am only afraid they will *not* put me into jail."[53]

When the time came to imprison her, however, the sheriff made every effort to stall. "We are not her friends," he told May frantically, "we are not in favor of her school; we don't want any more—niggers coming among us. It is your place to stand by Miss Crandall and help her now. You and your—abolition brethren have encouraged her to bring the nuisance into Canterbury, and it is . . . mean in you to desert her now."

May was adamant. "The law which her persecutors have persuaded our legislators to enact is an infamous one, worthy of the dark ages. If you see fit to keep her from imprisonment in the cell of a murderer for having proffered the blessing of a good education to those who, in our country, need it most, you may do so; we *shall* not."[54] The reference to "the cell of a murderer" was to a report that Crandall would be occupying the cell just vacated by a man executed for having murdered his wife.

Judson and his allies knew that Crandall's imprisonment would stir up a storm of indignation; they tried again to persuade May to place bond. In the end, there was no way out for them. After waiting as long as they dared, they jailed Prudence Crandall, thereby committing in May's judgment, "a great blunder." Meanwhile, May visited the jailer, arranged to have the cell thoroughly scrubbed, and removed the old bed and mattress, replacing them with two beds, one from his house and one from Benson's.[55]

On the following day bond was set for Prudence, and she was released. The calculations of May and his fellow abolitionists proved correct. "Comments that were made upon the deed in almost all the newspapers," May writes, "were far from grateful to the feelings of her persecutors."[56] *The Liberator* carried the following headline and story:

SAVAGE BARBARITY!

Miss Crandall Imprisoned!!!

The persecutors of Miss Crandall have placed an indelible seal upon her infamy! *They have cast her into prison!* Yes, *into the* very cell occupied by WATKINS, the MURDERER!! She was arrested on the 27th ult., and examined before Justices Adams and Bacon, leaders in the conspiracy, and by them committed to take her trial at the next session of the Superior Court at Brooklyn, in August.

And for what is she imprisoned? For presuming, in this *republican* and *christian* land, to instruct young ladies of color! Yes, let it be remembered, that Miss Crandall has been *immured in prison in America for attempting to instruct the ignorant and oppressed!!*

In its next issue *The Liberator* reported: "We understand that Miss Crandall has been liberated, some friend having become surety for her appearance at court."[57]

As soon as he heard of Crandall's imprisonment, Arthur Tappan, New York abolitionist merchant, wrote at once to May, whom he had still not met, approving the course he had followed in refusing at first to give bond. "But I am aware, Sir," he continued,

that you can ill afford to bear the expense of the contest you have dared. In this respect I am happily able to help you, and shall consider it a duty and a privilege to do so. I wish you to consider me your banker, assured that I will honor promptly your drafts. Keep your accounts carefully, and let me know whenever you need any money. Spare no necessary expense; employ the best legal counsel; and let this legal question be fully tried, not doubting that under the good providence of a righteous God, the truth and right will ultimately prevail.[58]

After a visit to Canterbury, Tappan was so shocked by the community's hostility to the school and the absence of any local paper willing to publish a single article in its support, that he reached a quick decision. "You are almost helpless without the press," he told May, "You must issue a newspaper, publish it largely, send it to all persons whom you know in the country. Many will subscribe to it and contribute otherwise to its support, and I will pay whatever more it may cost." Before Tappan left Canterbury, May had both a printing office in Brooklyn and more than sufficient funds "to maintain the defense of Miss Crandall and her much hated school."[59]

Tappan, impressed by an article Charles C. Burleigh had published denouncing Connecticut's anti-Negro legislation in William Goodell's *Genius of Temperance*, offered Burleigh the editorship of a newspaper whose aim it would be to defend Prudence Crandall and her school for black girls.[60] Entitled *The Unionist*, its motto was "Righteousness Exalteth a Nation," and it described itself as "The Tyrants foe the people's friend." The initial issue came off the press on August 1, 1833, in Brooklyn, Connecticut, carrying articles and editorials defending Crandall and her school, a theme that the paper stressed weekly for almost two years.[61] A typical article read:

MISS CRANDALL'S SCHOOL. One of the children now in that school is the daughter of a poor woman in the city of New York, who obtains a living by her daily labor. Of course she is unable to give her children an education, and this child is *supported by another woman, who was once a slave*, and purchased her freedom by her own exertions. Another of Miss C's scholars is the daughter of a father who was himself a slave.

Where can we find such thirsting for knowledge among our white population?—Where can we find a man, nay, where can we find a woman who has risen from a state of the lowest degradation by her own unaided exertions, under the weight of all the prejudices which are crushing her in the dust, against the seemingly irresistible tide of public opinion which is ever setting against her—I say where can we find a person with a white skin who has risen from such a situation, and *taught himself* the real worth of man, the real dignity of the human mind, and the exalting, ennobling power of education, to such an extent that, although by no means in affluent circumstances he is willing to spend a portion of his little, all to support at school the child of an indigent neighbor.[62]

Burleigh's brother, William H. Burleigh, not only helped his brother edit *The Unionist*, but also taught at Prudence Crandall's school. Like all who went in and out of the school, he was the daily target of rotten eggs thrown by young rowdies. After one such pelting, he assured Canterburian parents, in his *Unionist* column,

that there can be no danger of their sons ever marrying any of the colored girls of Miss C's school even if they were so inclined. They must become far more refined, in mind and in manners, before they would be able to come in competition with the most ignorant and least refined scholar in school.[63]

The trial of Prudence Crandall began on August 23, 1833, at the Windham County Court, with Judge Joseph Eaton presiding. The prosecution was conducted by none other than Andrew T. Judson, Crandall's original and most persistent opponent, assisted by two attorneys who presented the state's case against the school. Furnished with ample resources by Tappan, May had employed the most distinguished Connecticut lawyers to defend Crandall: William W. Ellsworth, Calvin Goodard, and Henry Strong. Ellsworth, who headed the defense, was the son of Oliver Ellsworth, chief justice of the United States, and himself a distinguished lawyer and Whig congressman from Connecticut.[64]

The prosecution called as witnesses several pupils in Crandall's school, who were from out of the state. On the advice of counsel, they refused to testify because they would implicate themselves, as the "Black Law" subjected all who aided or abetted Crandall to like penalty, and if they acknowledged applying to her to be taught, they would be abetting her in the act of teaching. When the prosecution insisted that they testify, counsel for the defense argued that the law did not provide for such testimony being used against the witness, and the Fifth Amendment to the United States Constitution forbade compelling any person to incriminate himself or herself. The court decided that the pupils should testify, but, again on the advice of counsel, they refused, and were ready, they declared, to go to prison if the court chose to send them there. At this, the court upheld their right not to testify, but ordered the sheriff to travel to Canterbury and bring Eliza Glasko, a pupil who was a resident of Connecticut, to testify as a witness. However, Glasko, on advice of counsel, also refused to testify that she was a pupil in the school on the ground that she would thereby reveal that she was being paid by Crandall for some assistance, and thus would also be abetting her and be subject to punishment under the "Black Law." The court angrily ordered Glasko to prison, and as the sheriff was taking her to jail, she was advised by counsel to testify and returned to the witness stand.

Glasko testified that some of her fellow students were from out of the state. As to the operation of the school, the instruction consisted of such "dangerous subjects" as "the ordinary branches . . . reading, writing, grammar; geography, &c . . . the school was usually opened and closed with prayer—the scriptures were read and explained daily in her school—some portions were committed to memory by the pupils, and considered part of their education."[65]

Blacks of Connecticut, went the prosecution's argument, already had access to district schools, which ought to be enough. As for those who came from other states, without the enactment of a law to prevent their entrance, the South might some day free all its slaves and send them to Connecticut to be educated—an event catastrophic in its implications. (One might add that this was an argument ridiculous in all its aspects.) How, Judson asked, would the other towns of the state like to see colonies of black girls started in their midst, "tempting their sons into marriage?" As for the argument that the law that Crandall had violated was unconstitutional because free blacks were citizens, there was a simple answer: "Where the colored people are not enfranchised they can not be considered as citizens or have the rights of citizens," and in Connecticut, of course, they could not vote. Since the free Negroes of Connecticut were not citizens, the law was constitutional.

Continuing, Judson noted ("graciously," the local press reported): "I am not opposed to their improvement, except so far as it violates the Constitution and endangers the Union." This result, he predicted, was likely to follow if Crandall was not found guilty and her school suppressed.[66]

Crandall's counsel argued that the "Black Law" was unconstitutional, insisting that free blacks were citizens and thus enjoyed in Connecticut every essential right of citizenship, including the right of free movement and education that white citizens enjoyed. Ellsworth appealed eloquently to the jury:

In order to convict my client, you gentlemen must find on your oaths that she has committed a crime. You may find that she has violated an act of the State legislature, but if you also find her protected by higher power, it will be your duty to acquit.[67]

Having already demonstrated from the beginning his hostility to Crandall and her counsel, Judge Eaton, not surprisingly, instructed the jury that "the law is constitutional and obligatory on the people of this State." After this, the jury deliberated for several hours and returned to inform the court they could not agree. Twice again they were further instructed and sent out. Finally, they told the court that there was no possibility that they could reach an agreement. Seven were firm for conviction; five, for acquittal, and no prospect existed that either side would budge from its position. Reluctantly, Judge Eaton discharged the jury.[68]

"The result of the trial," Garrison exulted in his paper, "is a triumph for the friends of human rights." He was confident that the same result would be the outcome of any new trial, and he predicted "that no jury will ever be found in Connecticut to sustain the Constitutionality of their *black law*; by convicting a female of a crime, whose only offense is instructing colored females."[69]

Events soon proved Garrison a poor prophet. The hung jury in the first trial of Prudence Crandall automatically meant the case would be continued at the next term of the county court. Although it was supposed to be held in December, the prosecution began the second trial on October 3, 1833, in the state supreme court sitting in Brooklyn before Chief Justice Daggett, who had publicly voiced support of the "Black Law." Counsel for the prosecution and defense were the same as in the first trial, and practically all of the arguments advanced for and against the law's constitutionality were the same. However, in his charge to the jury, Justice Daggett not only upheld the constitutionality of the "Black Law," but delivered a lengthy analysis of why, in his opinion, "the persons contemplated in this act are *not citizens* of the United States or of their respective states." After disposing of slaves and Indians, he turned to free blacks and said:

Are *free blacks*, citizens? . . . I think Chancellor Kent, whose authority it gives me pleasure to quote, determines the question, by fair implication. Had this authority considered free blacks citizens, he had an ample opportunity to say so. But what he said excludes the idea: "In most of the *United States*, there is a distinction in respect to political privileges, between free white persons and free coloured persons of *African* blood; and in no part of the country do the latter, in point of fact, participate equally with the whites, in the exercise of civil and political rights. The *African* race are essentially a degraded caste, of inferior rank and condition in society. Marriages are forbidden between them and whites, in some of the states, and when not absolutely contrary to law, they are revolting, and regarded as an offence against public decorum. . . . "

To my mind, it would be a perversion of terms, and the well known rule of construction, to say, that slaves, free blacks, or *Indians*, were citizens, within the meaning of that term, as used in the constitution. God forbid that I should add to the degradation of this race of men; but I am bound by my duty, to say, they are not citizens.

I have thus shown you that this law is not contrary to the 2d section of the 4th art. of the constitution of the *United States*; for that embraces only citizens.

This time the jury agreed and returned a verdict of guilty. Prudence Crandall's lawyers immediately filed a motion in arrest of judgment on two technical points: that the superior court had no jurisdiction over the offenses charged; and that the "information" (that is, the particulars of the formal charge) was insufficient.[70]

IV

The appeal of Prudence Crandall's conviction to the Court of Errors was scheduled to be heard on July 22, 1834. Meanwhile, the cause of all the legal actions continued. Late in 1833 Garrison reported: "Miss Crandall's school increases numerically. She has now thirty-two scholars, and can accommodate fifty. A few weeks more will probably give her a full supply."[71]

Meanwhile, too, Prudence Crandall's courage and persistence were winning her support and admiration in the North, in Canada, and in England. The influential *Boston Press* declared:

The Connecticut black law is as direct a violation of the Constitution as Nullification is. The Constitution says—"The citizens of each state shall be entitled to all privileges and immunities of citizens in several states." It makes no exception of black citizens; consequently if free blacks are citizens, they are entitled to the same protection the whites are. If Miss Crandall has a right to receive white scholars from other states, she has an equal right to receive colored ones.[72]

And the Hollowell (New York) *Free Press* editorialized: "Miss Crandall. This lady has again been prosecuted and brought to trial for the *horrid* crime of teaching little black girls to read and write! What an abandoned wretch she must be, to attempt to instruct a *drove* of little *brutes*, and that too in the Christian State of Connecticut."[73]

During a visit to Boston in April 1834 to have her portrait painted at the request of the New England Anti-Slavery Society, Crandall received "a kindly and cordial reception" from many of her abolition friends. She informed the citizens, to great applause, that her "School still continues in a flourishing condition," and that it was her "purpose to continue it with all the fidelity, zeal and perseverance" she had up to then demonstrated. An outstanding feature of the Boston visit was the outpouring of affection, gratitude, and respect "which were made to her by our colored brethren and sisters."

They thronged around her in crowds, and poured their benedictions upon her head, in strong and fervent language. Every effort was made by them to make her visit agreeable. On Saturday afternoon, a large number of colored friends, of both sexes, sat down with her and a few white friends to a splendid entertainment given by Mr. and Mrs. Robinson, in George Street.[74]

The Essex County Anti-Slavery Society Convention voted a resolution on May 26, 1834, that "Miss Prudence and Miss Almira Crandall [Prudence's sister and a teacher in the school] merit the warmest approbation of all friends of the colored race, for their persevering and continuing exertions to educate colored females under a most bitter and unchristian opposition."[75] Influenced by the Crandall courage, an abolitionist announced the opening of "A New School for Colored Females" in Boston, while Rebecca Buffum informed the readers of *The Liberator* that "she has opened a school at No. 29, North Fifth Street, near Arch [in Philadelphia], where she will receive young females without regard to their complexion, for instruction in all the useful branches of an English education."[76]

In August 1833 the *Female Advocate* published an "Appeal to the Females of the United States in Behalf of Miss Prudence Crandall," calling for "some expression of female sympathy and approbation for a *lady*, devoted to the intellectual, moral, and physical emancipation of tenfold the number American females; a lady against whom, for her work of mercy, a *State* has fulminated its persecuting enactment, and thrust into felon's prison!" The *Female Advocate* concluded its appeal with the observation:

If any thing can save our country from the most dismal scenes, to what influence can we look, but to the gentle but firm remonstrance of WOMAN? Why should not her voice be heard? *And why should not the legislature of Connecticut, a state once distinguished for liberality, intelligence, and religion, be respectfully* MEMORIALIZED *by the females of every mountain, glen, and hamlet in the United States, for the repeal of this most disgraceful enactment against* FEMALE *effort for Female improvement.*[77]

The appeal not only produced a flood of letters from women to the Connecticut legislature from different parts of the North, but, when reprinted in the British press, stimulated a similar response from women in England.[78] Moreover, the antislavery women of England and Scotland expressed their admiration and support for Prudence Crandall in a variety of ways. Early in February 1834 Crandall received a clipping from the Glasgow *Chronicle* reporting that a piece of silver plate might be seen at the shop of Alexander Mitchell, in

Argyle Street. The plate, subscribed to by the Ladies Auxiliary of
the Glasgow Emancipation Society, was to be presented to Prudence
Crandall as soon as someone was found who would carry it across
the sea. The words engraved on the silver surface read:

> To
> Miss Crandall
> of Canterbury, Connecticut,
> This small offering is presented,
> With affectionate respect,
> By
> Female Friends in Glasgow;
> In testimony of their high admiration
> of that ardent benevolence, heroic fortitude, and
> unflinching steadiness,
> In the midst of wanton and unequalled persecution,
> Which Almighty God has enabled her to display,
> In her disinterested and noble endeavours,
> Destined to be crowned with honour and triumph,
> To introduce into the privileges, and elevate in the scale
> of social and religious life,
> A long injured class of
> Her beloved Countrywomen.[79]

The silver plate was brought to Crandall by George Thompson,
the British abolitionist, when he visited the United States late in
1834 to experience in person some of the same persecution visited
upon the teacher he was honoring. Captain Charles Stuart also brought
with him in his visit three volumes as a gift from the Edinburgh
Ladies' Emancipation Society, together with letters from women in
London, Bath, and Liverpool conveying their affection and respect
and assuring Crandall that "you are not alone," and that "the spirit
of liberty" which she was championing would "triumph at last."[80]

Nor were women the only ones in England to honor Crandall.
Boston black minister Nathaniel Paul described a meeting in the city
of Norwich where three to four thousand British people, men and
women, filled St. Andrew's Hall to hear several leading citizens
denounce "the persecutions of Miss Prudence Crandall." Everywhere in England, Paul reported, meetings were adopting resolutions
bidding Crandall "God-speed in her heroic and praise-worthy
undertaking."[81]

On both sides of the Atlantic, poetry was put to use in paying tribute to Prudence Crandall. One set of verses went:

TO PRUDENCE CRANDALL

Heaven bless thee, noble lady, in thy purpose good
and high!
Give knowledge to the thirsting mind, light to the
asking eye;
Unseal the intellectual page, for those from whom
dark pride,
With tyrant and unholy hands, would fain its treasures hide.
Still bear thou up unyielding 'gainst persecution's
shock,
Gentle as a woman's self, yet firm, and moveless as a
rock;
A thousand spirits yield to thee their gushing sympathies,
The blessings of a thousand hearts around thy path-
way lies.[82]

Garrison, too, resorted to poetry to voice his admiration for Prudence Crandall and to venture a prediction that was to be completely
fulfilled:

AN ACROSTIC
ADDRESSED TO HER WHO IS THE ORNAMENT OF HER SEX

Proudly shall History upon its page
Record in living characters thy name,
Unequalled Woman in this servile age!
Dauntless, though wrapt in Persecution's flame!
E'en as a star shall thy example shine,
Nor Time's profoundest depths obscure its light;
Cheering Posterity's extended line;
Effulgent, fresh, and lovely to the sight.

Courageously pursue thy purpose high;
Reclaim from ignorance the darkened mind;
An outcast race around thee prostrate lie,
Naked and hungry, captive, sick and blind.
Dare still to be their guide—instructress—friend.

> And bright shall be the crown of thy reward;
> Let brutal men in wrath with thee contend—
> Loved—honoured *thou* shalt be, and *they* abhorred.[83]

When he ventured another prediction in prose, Garrison was less successful. After noting the "universal joy" caused by the news that Judson, Crandall's main enemy, had been defeated when he ran for the state legislature in April 1834, Garrison wrote: "Let us now cherish the hope that the *black* laws of the State will be repealed by the new Legislature. Cheers for Miss Crandall."[84]

But Garrison's hope was not to be realized. Despite the memorial and letters urging the legislature to repeal the measure, the "Black Law" was to remain on the statute books.

V

The advertisement in *The Liberator* of November 8, 1834, announced the publication of the *Report of the Arguments of Counsel in the Case of Prudence Crandall*, that it was for sale at the rates of sixteen cents each, $1.20 per dozen, or $10.00 per hundred. At the request of Samuel J. May, the publication was at the publisher's "own risk," and Garrison explained on behalf of himself and Isaac Knapp, his partner:

As to the profits that may arise from the sale of the pamphlet, we do not expect to make any: on the contrary, we shall suffer some loss, in consequence of the difficulty of disposing any publication, however interesting or valuable in itself. But a trial so important as Miss C's—involving such momentous consequences to a large portion of our countrymen—implicating so deeply the character of this great nation—ought not to go unpublished, and *shall* not while we have the necessary materials for printing it.[85]

The pamphlet published the speeches delivered by William Wolcott Ellsworth, Prudence Crandall's chief counsel before the Supreme Court of Errors of the State of Connecticut in Hartford in the proceedings of July 1834 of "Crandall *against* the State of Connecticut in Error." Garrison was correct in writing that the trial involved issues of "momentous consequences to a large portion of our countrymen," for the arguments of counsel on both sides made it clear that the issues at stake transcended a small school for a score or more pupils in Canterbury. Indeed, Andrew Judson and C. F. Cleveland, prosecuting attorneys, began their arguments with a racist interpretation of the national significance of the trial, pointing to the

> magnitude of the question, as affecting not the town of *Canterbury* alone, but every town in the state and every state in the *Union*, as the principles urged by the counsel for the plaintiff in error, if established, would, in their consequences, destroy the government itself and this *American* nation—blotting out this nation of white men, and substituting one from the *African* race—thus involving the honour of the state, the dignity of the people and the preservation of its name.[86]

What were the principles advanced by the counsel for the defense that so threatened to blot out the existing nation? The central fact in the controversy, according to William Wolcott Ellsworth (who argued most of the case for Crandall and made the defense's chief points), was that those free blacks who resided in free states were citizens and as such were guaranteed protection under Article IV, Section 2 of the Constitution of the United States. It did not matter that in certain free states they were not allowed to vote, since voting was not a valid criterion of citizenship. There were so many restrictions in the matter of voting—property holding, military service, residence, and so forth—that it was illogical to consider enfranchisement the test, since under such a system men of all colors could lose their citizen's rights or assume a status of quasi-citizenship.

What was important, said Ellsworth, was the fact that Negroes were required to demonstrate allegiance to the country and in all other ways were treated as citizens of their respective states. They paid taxes, fought in the armed forces, and were responsible for all the other duties under the laws. The principle stated by the "Black Law" was that it was a crime to allow a black person from another state to get an education in Connecticut—a privilege that should be common to all residents of Connecticut, black or white.

To bolster this case, Ellsworth cited that part of the Constitution which said, "The citizens of each state shall be entitled to all privileges and immunities of citizens in the several states." Said Ellsworth: "This statute, stripped of its appendages, makes the *place of birth* the criterion of the rights of citizens of these states; it is not a question of color, so much as state supremacy; if a state may exclude a colored citizen of another state, it may exclude a white citizen. If we may expel these colored citizens of New-York to-day, we may expel the white youth of New-York in Yale College, to-morrow." He further stated, "let it not be forgotten, that whatever these immunities and privileges are, they are solemnly *secured* and *guarantied* [*sic*] by the constitution; and let me add, it is the clear duty of this enlightened Court to see they are made so to these pupils, if citizens, as I have contended they are." He continued:

It was admitted by the Court below, that the right of education is a *fundamental right*; and will it be questioned here? The Pope of Rome and the despots of Turkey may do it, but it will not be done in Connecticut. What right so justly valued by us? What so much applauded as the peculiar honor of our state, and so liberally secured and widely extended by the very constitution itself? How do the nations of the earth set in darkness for want of it? And tyrants and despots and chieftains reign over mankind, through their ignorance and their superstition? *Education* is the first and fundamental pillar on which our free institutions rest, and it is the last privilege *we* will give up. And here let me add, that the restrictions of this law are exceedingly onerous and distressing to the parents of these pupils; shut out as these children are virtually from the schools of white persons, they have *retired* to a place by themselves, in deference to the prevailing prejudice against them—here they have sought out a virtuous and competent teacher to instruct them in the common branches of education, spelling, reading, arithmetic, geography and the like; their parents are able to do this—many of them are wealthy, and they feel, that by education their children will be happier and better fitted for usefulness among their depressed fellows, either here, or in Liberia.

He continued angrily:

And who, *who* will rise up to oppose this effort? Let our opponents act openly; let them pass a law to immure in like ignorance the colored population of our own state, and not attempt the same thing, by selecting the blacks of other states, under the pretence that educating them will fill our state with a vicious and pauper population. The moral sentiments of this community will not sanction the idea that a man of color shall not have, *like others*, the *right* to direct, according to his ability, the education of his children. Mr. Wilberforce, aided by several benevolent individuals, established a seminary for colored people at Clapham, a short distance from London. Miss Crandall need not be ashamed to imitate his example.[87]

Ellsworth then stressed that the white people of the United States owed it to the black population to foster and support all efforts and institutions to educate them:

The people of this country forced the ancestors of our colored population from Africa; they have since kept their descendants in bonds and darkness, and now talk of right, founded in the color and degradation of the negro, as a justification for continued wrong, and the deprivation, this day attempted, on principle and morality.

Need I tell this honorable Court, that we owe a debt to the colored population of this country, which we can never pay,—no, never, never, unless we can call back oceans of tears, and all the groans and agonies of the middle passage, and the thousands and millions of human beings, whom we have sent, and are sending, ignorant, debased and undone, to eternity.[88]

Ellsworth closed the arguments for the defense with an attack on the bigotry of the slavocracy. Lashing out passionately against the laws passed in the South for the purpose of preventing the education of blacks, he said: "These laws are all of a kindred character; they call for universal denunciation, and well may we fear that a righteous Lord will not let them pass unheeded or unrevenged." How, he asked, "can excitement be kept down in the North, while such bloody and cruel laws are enforced against human beings like ourselves, of the same feelings, destiny, and hopes?" As for the "Black Law" of Connecticut, said Ellsworth:

This law . . . is denied . . . for its constitutionality. . . . It is a most wanton and uncalled for attack upon our colored population; it opens wounds not easily healed; it exasperates to madness many who live among us; it strengthens the unreasonable prejudice already pervading the community against blacks; and, in short, it rivets the chains of grinding bondage, and makes our state an ally in the unholy cause of slavery itself.

Then, prophetically, he concluded:

Deep, deep, are the feelings this moment pervading the slave states. . . . Slavery is a volcano, the fires of which cannot be quenched, nor its ravages controlled. We already feel its convulsions; and if we sit idly gazing upon its flames, as they rise higher and higher, our unhappy Republic will be buried in ruin beneath its overwhelming energies.[89]

Although Judson appeared to argue the case for the prosecution on a purely constitutional basis, with a seeming disregard for personal issues involved, it became clear that he could not conceal his contempt for black Americans. Thus, the crux of his argument dealt with the question of the Negro being the equal of the white man, and he asked:

Can it be entertained for the moment, that those who framed the constitution should hold one portion of *race of men* in bondage, while the other portion were made *citizens*? This would be strange inconsistency. Go back to the time when the constitution was made, and enquire after the condition of the country, and take into consideration all its circumstances, and all difficulties will be out of the way. *Then* it was not immoral to hold slaves. The *best men* bought and sold negroes, without a scruple. This impulse is of modern date; and however creditable to the heart, cannot alter the *constitution*. The immortal *Washington*, who presided at the convention, and who subscribed the instrument, under the laws of *Virginia*, held more than one hundred slaves, as his property, on that day; and he was not thus inconsistent. He never intended to have you say, that the portion of the human race which were held in bondage were slaves, and the residue of that same colour were *citizens*. . . .

The distinction of colour so far from being novel, is marked in numerous ways, in our political system.[90]

All that was missing to make this read like the notorious opinion by Chief Justice Roger B. Taney in the *Dred Scott* decision of 1857 was the argument that blacks, both slave and free, had no rights that white people were bound to respect.[91]

After hearing the lengthy arguments over whether Negroes were or were not citizens and whether the "Black Law" of Connecticut was or was not constitutional, the Supreme Court of Errors simply evaded these issues. As Judge Thomas Williams, the associate justice who rendered the decision, noted in his opinion, he had refrained from doing anything "to agitate the subject unnecessarily." Instead, on July 22, 1844, the court reversed the decision of the superior court that had found Prudence Crandall guilty on the sole ground of "insufficiency of the information," which omitted to allege that her school was opened without a necessary license, an omission the Court called "a fatal defect":

This information charges Prudence Crandall with harboring and boarding certain colored persons, not inhabitants of any town in this State, for the purpose of attending and being taught and instructed in a school, set up and established in said town of Canterbury, for the instruction and education of certain colored persons, not inhabitants of this State.

She is not charged with setting up a school contrary to law, nor with teaching in school contrary to law; but with harboring and boarding colored persons, not inhabitants of this state, without license, for the purpose of being instructed in such school.

It is, however, not here allowed that the school was set up without license, or that the scholars were instructed by those who had no license.

If it is an offence within the statute to *harbor* or *board* such persons without license, under all circumstances, then this information is correct. But if the act, in the description of the defense itself, shows, that under some circumstances, it is no offence, then this information is defective. . . .

This information charges, that this school was set up in Canterbury, for the purpose of educating these persons of color, not inhabitants of this State, that they might be instructed and educated; but omits to state that it was not licensed. This omission is a fatal defect; as an information on a penal statute, the prosecutor must set forth every fact that it is necessary to bring the case within the statute; and every exception within the enacting clause of the act, descriptive of the offence, must be negated.[92]

The other two judges, Samuel Church and Chief Justice David Daggett, concurred in the decision throwing out the conviction of Prudence Crandall, although Daggett (who had presided over the second trial that found her guilty) believed that the objection came too late and should not have been considered by the court. The decision to reverse was thus unanimous.[93]

The legal victory reversing the conviction of Prudence Crandall was followed by another involving one of her main supporters— William Lloyd Garrison. Early in April 1833, when he was visiting the Bensons in Brooklyn, Connecticut, his presence near Canterbury became known to Judson and several of his colleagues. They immediately issued five summonses against Garrison, complaining that he had libelled them in his paper. A sheriff was dispatched to the Benson house to serve the writs but he found that Garrison had left half an hour before. The sheriff pursued Garrison in vain for several miles, but finally had to give up the chase. After the writs were finally served, the trial was set for December 1833 at the Windham

County Court in Connecticut, but was continued until the March 1834 term. That date was to be postponed again until the January 1835 term. Before that time, however, the suit was dropped on condition that "neither party shall receive cost of the other."[94]

Prudence Crandall's opponents had now been defeated twice. But they were soon to gain the major victory—the closing of her school.

VI

Whatever joy Prudence Crandall's abolitionist friends derived from the victory, limited though it was to the State Supreme Court of Errors, was dimmed by their concern that she was considering marriage to the Reverend Calvin Philleo from Ithaca, New York, a Baptist minister of questionable character. Helen E. Benson sounded the alarm after Philleo's visit to her Brooklyn home. She found him to be an ill-tempered person and upon inquiry heard "so many informations of his ill behavior," that she feared Crandall would know little happiness as his wife.[95] Evidently she tried to dissuade Prudence from marrying the minister, a course that Garrison at first approved. The latter wrote to his future wife:

I am troubled in spirit lest our dear friend Prudence marry ill. The step which she is about to take will seal her earthly destiny, either for good or evil. Let her seriously weigh the consequences. Is not the thought of being indissolubly allied to a worthless person insupportable? To marry, or not to marry, is a most serious question for a man or woman to consider, and ought not to be settled hastily.[96]

But Prudence would not be dissuaded. Helen Benson found her to be so "blind in her love" that Philleo could persuade her "*black* was *white* if he chose."[97] At this point, however, Garrison refused to interfere. He had received a letter from Prudence, he informed George W. Benson, that expressed her joy at Philleo's arrival in Canterbury and bestowed "a very high eulogy upon his character." Perhaps, as Helen Benson lamented, "Love is Blind." "However, I will not condemn Mr. Phillip [sic], for I have never heard any special and vital allegations brought against him." Furthermore, "Prudence tells me he is for continuing the school in Canterbury, and increasing the number of its scholars, if possible to one hundred."

Then followed an interesting piece of advice: "In my opinion, how-ever, she had better take advantage of her marriage, and move off with flying colors; especially as the Legislature of Connecticut—to its everlasting disgrace—has adjourned without repealing the odious law against her school."[98]

And so Prudence Crandall and Reverend Calvin Philleo were mar-ried in September 1834, but Garrison's fear that the worst might still befall the bride and her school proved to be justified. The bigots of Canterbury did not rest with simply blocking repeal of the "Black Law." They killed a cat, cut its throat, and hung it by the neck to the school's gate, thereby adding, Garrison punned in anger, "to the long *cat*—alogue of your offence."[99]

But there was nothing to pun about when an arsonist tried to set fire to the school by stuffing combustible materials under a corner of the house and putting a match to it. Fortunately, the flames were discovered before they got out of hand, and the fire was extinguished. "O the persecuted, the dauntless, the heroic Prudence Crandall!" Garrison wrote in horror. "What severe trials now are hers! . . . She has my sympathy, my admiration, my prayer. I trust the firing of her house will yet prove to have been accidental."[100]

It was not, but it was typical of the community in which, instead of making an effort to track down the real arsonist, the authorities quickly arrested "a respectable colored man from Norwich," James Olney, and since he had been mending a clock in the school at the time the fire was discovered, charged him with setting it. As Ellen D. Larned, Windham County historian, noted, "though the evidence against him was utterly trifling [he] was committed to trial." Black pupils from the Crandall school testified at his trial in his behalf and were so convincing in proving that he could not have been the arsonist that Olney was acquitted.[101]

The attempt to burn down the school while the teacher and pupils were inside was a severe blow to Miss Crandall and her students, but it did not shake their determination to continue. Then, at about midnight on September 9, 1834, five downstairs windows were smashed by men carrying iron bars and heavy clubs, and the two front rooms were rendered uninhabitable. Reverend May was sent for, and when he arrived, he found that for the first time Prudence Crandall was discouraged. "Never before," he recalled sadly, "had Miss Crandall seemed to quail, and some of her pupils were afraid to remain another night under her roof." Finally, the teacher decided to abandon the school and put the house up for sale.[102]

The end of Prudence Crandall's attempt to conduct a school for black girls in Canterbury, Connecticut, was marked by several notices in *The Liberator*. The first, in the issue of September 20, 1834, read:

MISS CRANDALL'S SCHOOL ABANDONED

Human endurance has its bounds, and the requirements of duty have theirs. By the following Advertisements, which we copy from the Brooklyn Unionist, it appears that another cowardly attack has been made upon Miss Crandall's (now Mrs. Phileo's) [*sic*] dwelling, by some midnight ruffians in Canterbury, and that it has been deemed advisable to abandon the school in that heathenish village, and to let ANDREW T. JUDSON and his associates, with the whole State of Connecticut, have all the infamy and guilt which attach to the violent suppression of so praiseworthy an institution. *O, tempora! O, mores!*

$50 REWARD!!—During the night of Tuesday the 9th inst. about 12 o'clock, the house of the subscriber in Canterbury was assaulted by a number of lawless persons with heavy clubs or iron bars; five window sashes were destroyed, and more than ninety panes of glass were dashed to pieces, and the family greatly alarmed.

The above named reward is hereby offered to any one, who will give information that will lead to the detection of the perpetrators of the outrage, or any one of them.

CALVIN PHILEO.[*sic*]

Canterbury, Sept. 11, 1834.

FOR SALE. The house in Canterbury occupied by the late Prudence Crandall, now the wife of the subscriber. The impunity with which repeated assaults have been made upon these premises, has awakened the apprehension that the property, and perhaps the lives of those connected with the school are insecure. I have therefore thought it proper, and do hereby advertise the house and appurtenances thereof for sale.

For further particulars inquire of the subscriber, or of

PARDON CRANDALL of *Canterbury*, or

SAMUEL J. MAY of *Brooklyn*.

CALVIN PHILEO.[*sic*]

Canterbury, Sept. 11, 1834.

Another notice appeared a week later. It was a short essay "by one of Miss Crandall's Juvenile pupils, in reference to the abandonment of her interesting school," and read in part:

THE SEPARATION

It was one of the pleasant sunny mornings of September, when I took leave of my teacher and school-mates. Never, no, never, while memory retains a seat in my breast, shall I forget that trying hour. On the night preceding my departure, while all within was silent as the chamber of death, we were suddenly aroused by a tremendous noise; when, to our surprise, we found that a band of cruel men had rendered our dwelling almost untenable. The next morning we were informed by our teacher, that the school would be suspended for the day, that he was going to a neighboring town to see a friend of ours: he accordingly went. In the afternoon he returned accompanied by our friend, who requested that we might be called together. He, with feelings of apparent deep regret, told us we had better go to our homes. With regret I prepared to leave that pleasant, yet persecuted dwelling, and also my dear school-mates, in whose society I had spent so many hours; thankful to my heavenly Parent, that our lot was no worse; yet not without many tears did I return to my distant solitary home. . . .

My teacher was ever kind: with him I saw religion, not merely adopted as an empty form, but a living, all-pervading principle of action. He lived like those who seek a better country; nor was his family devotion a cold pile of hypocrisy on which the fire of God never descends.[103]

The teacher was William H. Burleigh, the friend of Reverend May. In *The Liberator* May recorded the end of the school in angry and moving terms:

Twenty harmless girls, whose only offence against the peace of the community is that they have come together there to obtain useful knowledge, were to be told that they had better go away, because forsooth the house in which they dwell is not protected by the conservators of the peace, the officers of justice, in the community in which it is situated. The words almost blistered my lips. My heart glowed with indignation. I felt ashamed of Canterbury, ashamed of Connecticut, ashamed of my country.[104]

Misfortune continued to pursue the Crandall family after the school was abandoned and the house sold. Dr. Reuben Crandall, a younger brother of Prudence, had gone to Washington, D.C., to teach botany.

He was arrested on August 11, 1835, charged with circulating incendiary publications—some of his botanical specimens were found wrapped in old antislavery newspapers—and imprisoned. Crandall was kept in prison for eight months before being brought to trial. Although acquitted, he died in 1838 as a result of tuberculosis contracted while in prison.[105]

As for Prudence Crandall, it appears that Helen Benson's suspicions of Calvin Philleo's character were confirmed, and that he proved to be impecunious, inconsiderate, and dishonest.[106]

Still, the former teacher did have the pleasure of learning that several of her black students became themselves teachers and active abolitionists, including Sarah Harris (Mrs. S. H. Fayerweather), the first of her black pupils, and Mrs. May Harris Williams. The latter was to teach black children for many years in Louisiana.[107]

In 1858 the Connecticut legislature repealed the obnoxious "Black Law," and Prudence Crandall had the added pleasure of learning that several of the legislators who had voted for the measure in 1833 publicly apologized for their action at that time.[108]

It took twenty-eight years and a Civil War for the next step in the drama to unfold. In 1866, a year after the war ended, Windham County voted not only for black education without limitation, but for black suffrage as well. At this news Samuel J. May wrote to Prudence Crandall noting that while she had not succeeded in teaching "many colored girls," she "succeeded in educating the people of Windham County."[109]

Calvin Philleo died in 1874. Prudence then moved to Elk Falls, Kansas, to spend her remaining years with her brother Hezekiah. There a regiment of black soldiers discovered that Prudence Crandall of Canterbury fame was living in poverty, and they raised a fund among themselves to present to the woman who had sacrificed so much to educate young women of their race.[110]

Final honors came to Prudence Crandall in 1886, just three years before her death. Instigated by Mark Twain, a resident of Hartford,[111] a petition that acquired 112 signatures was circulated. It read:

To the Honorable, the Senate and House of Representatives, in General Assembly Convened;

We, the Undersigned, Citizens of the State, and of the Town of Canterbury, mindful of the dark blot that rests upon our fair fame and name, for the cruel outrages inflicted upon a former citizen of our Commonwealth, a noble Christian woman (Miss Prudence Crandall, now Mrs. Philleo) at present in straightened circumstances, and far advanced in years, respectfully pray your Honorable Body to make such late reparation for the wrong done her, as your united wisdom, your love of justice, and an honorable pride in the good name of our noble State, shall dictate.

It will be remembered that she stands in the Records of the Court as a convicted criminal for the offence of teaching colored girls to read, and suffered unnumbered outrages in person and property, for a benevolent work, that now to its great honor, the General Government itself is engaged in.

We respectfully suggest that you make a fair appropriation in her behalf, which shall at once relieve her from any anxiety for the future, and from the official stigma that rests upon her name, and purge our own record from its last remaining stain, in connection with the colored race.

And your petitioners will ever pray.[112]

The State Legislature granted the petition, and voted Prudence Crandall an annuity of $400. Prudence, then eighty-two, accepted the annuity, Edmund Fuller notes, "not as charity," "but as the settlement of a 'just debt' for the destruction of her 'hopes and prospects.'" More important than the money, however, was the knowledge of "the change that has been wrought in the feelings of the mass of the people."[113]

At the height of the Crandall affair, surely one of the most shameful and heroic episodes in American history, black abolitionist Reverend Nathaniel Paul made a comment that sums it up in all its aspects. He was in London at the time, and he sarcastically assured the British public:

Yes, sir, Britons shall know that there are men in America, and whole towns of them, too, who are not so destitute of true heroism but that they can assail a helpless woman, surround her house by night, break her windows, and drag her to prison, for the treasonable act of teaching colored females to read.[114]

NOTES

1. Samuel Joseph May (1797–1871) was a Unitarian minister and one of Garrison's most devoted friends. He participated in the founding of the

New England Anti-Slavery Society and of the American Anti-Slavery Society; served as general agent and secretary of the Massachusetts Anti-Slavery
Society in 1835 and 1836 and used his home as a station for Negroes attempting to reach Canada on the Underground Railroad. He shared with
Garrison a concern for woman's rights, and his interest in reform also extended to education, peace, and temperance.

2. Samuel J. May, "The Canterbury School," *National Anti-Slavery
Standard*, July 15, 1852.

3. William Lloyd Garrison to Helen Benson, April 5, 1834, in Walter
Merrill, ed., *The Letters of William Lloyd Garrison*, vol. I, *1822–1835* (Cam-
bridge, Mass.: Harvard University Press, 1971), No. 136. The portrait of
Prudence Crandall hangs today in the library of Cornell University.

4. Edmund Fuller, *Prudence Crandall: An Incident of Racism in Nineteenth-Century Connecticut* (Middletown, Conn.: Wesleyan University Press,
1971), p. 44.

5. Ibid., pp. 13–14.

6. Philip S. Foner, *History of Black Americans, Vol. I: From Africa to
the Emergence of the Cotton Kingdom* (Westport, Conn.: Greenwood Press,
1975), pp. 412–25; Edwin and Miriam R. Small, "Prudence Crandall, Champion of Negro Education," *New England Quarterly* 17 (1944): 513.

7. *The Liberator*, January 1, 1831.

8. Letter of Prudence Crandall, dated May 7, 1833, *The Liberator*, May
25, 1833; Small, "Prudence Crandall, Champion of Negro Education," p.
508.

9. Letter, dated May 15, 1869, written by Prudence Crandall in Elk
Falls, Kansas, to Miss E. D. Larned, historian of Windham County, Con-
necticut, quoted in Wendell Phillips Garrison, "Connecticut in the Middle
Ages," *Century Magazine* 30 (September 1885): 780, and reprinted in Small,
"Prudence Crandall, Champion of Negro Education," p. 507.

10. *The Liberator*, May 25, 1833.

11. Ibid.

12. Samuel J. May in *National Anti-Slavery Standard*, July 15, 1852.

13. *The Liberator*, May 25, 1833. According to one account, that of Mary
Barker, who was a servant in the same household as Sarah Harris, the latter
told her that it was Prudence Crandall who invited her to enter the school,
"become a scholar with her white schollars [*sic*] and she could instruct her
so that in nine months or a year she could teach a school. She [Sarah Harris]
further added during the same conversation that she never would have
thought of going if Miss Crandall had not *proposed* it to her, and she had
concluded to go." This testimonial, in the form of a letter dated September
10, 1833, was read at Crandall's trial. (Small, "Prudence Crandall, Champion
of Negro Education," p. 509.) However, there was and is no corroborating

evidence as to the truth of this testimonial, and it is contradicted by a mass of contrary evidence.

14. Fuller, *Prudence Crandall*, p. 14.

15. *The Liberator*, May 25, 1833.

16. Ibid., May 25, 1833; Fuller, *Prudence Crandall*, p. 18.

17. Ibid., June 2, 1833.

18. Samuel J. May in *National Anti-Slavery Standard*, July 15, 1852.

19. *Helen Eliza Garrison, A Memorial* (Cambridge, Mass.: Riverside Press, 1876), pp. 16–18.

20. *The Liberator*, May 25, 1833; Fuller, *Prudence Crandall*, pp. 20–21.

21. *Minutes and Proceedings of the First Annual Convention of the People of Colour. . . .* (Philadelphia, Pa., 1831), pp. 6–9; *The Liberator*, August 20, November 26, and December 3, 1831; January 12, and July 6, 1833; Carter G. Woodson, *The Education of the Negro Prior to 1861* (New York: G. P. Putnam's Sons, 1915), pp. 288–90.

22. Prudence Crandall to Mr. Jocelyn, Canterbury, February 26, 1833, in *Journal of Negro History* 18 (January 1933): 80–81; G. Smith Wormley, "Prudence Crandall," *Journal of Negro History* 8 (January 1924): 74.

23. The advertisement also stated that for information respecting the school, reference might be made "to the following gentlemen, viz: Arthur Tappan, Esq., Rev. Peter Williams, Rev. Theodore Raymond, Rev. Theodore Wright, Rev. Samuel C. Cornish, Rev. George Bourne, Rev. Mr. Hayborn, *New-York city*;—Mr. James Forten, Mr. Joseph Cassey, *Philadelphia, Pa.;* Rev. S. J. May, *Brooklyn, Ct.*;—Rev. Mr. Beman, *Middletown, Ct.*, Rev. S. S. Jocelyn, *New-Haven, Ct.*;—Wm. Lloyd Garrison, Arnold Buffum, *Boston, Mass.*;—George Benson, *Providence, R.I.*" (*The Liberator*, March 2, 1833.) All of the men listed were abolitionists, and several, such as Williams, Wright, Cornish, Forten, and Jocelyn, were blacks.

24. *The Liberator*, May 25, 1833.

25. Archibald H. Grimké, *William Lloyd Garrison* (New York: Funk, 1892), p. 166. Some historians emphasize that the town's anger was intensified by "understandable resentment of the way Prudence had gone about her plan," meaning, that she had deceived some of the inhabitants into believing her visits to Boston and New York had nothing to do with the plan to establish a school. This, of course, ignores the fact that if she had told them the real purpose of her trips, she might never have been able to leave. Fuller, for example, who makes much of this point, ignores Crandall's repeated emphasis in her letters to Garrison of the need to keep her visit to him, as well as the plan for the school, secret.

26. *The Liberator*, May 25, 1833; Small, "Prudence Crandall, Champion of Negro Education," pp. 512–13.

27. Small, "Prudence Crandall, Champion of Negro Education," p. 514.

28. William Lloyd Garrison to G. W. Benson, March 8, 1833, Merrill, ed. *Letters*, vol. I, No. 86; Small, "Prudence Crandall, Champion of Negro Education," p. 514.

29. *The Liberator*, April 6, 1833.

30. Leo Trachtenberg, "The Canterbury Tale," *Negro History Bulletin* (March 1949): 125–26.

31. Henry E. Benson in *The Liberator*, March 16, 1833.

32. Samuel J. May, *Some Recollections of Our Anti-Slavery Conflict* (Boston: Fields, Osgood & Co., 1869), pp. 39–72; Samuel J. May, *The Right of Colored People to Education, Vindicated. Letters to Andrew T. Judson, Esq., And Others in Canterbury, Remonstrating With Them On Their Unjust and Unjustifiable Procedure Relative to Miss Crandall and Her School for Colored Females* (Brooklyn, Conn.: Advertiser Press, 1833).

33. *The Liberator*, March 16, 1833.

34. Ibid., April 27, 1833.

35. Ibid., April 6, 1833.

36. Ibid.

37. Ibid., April 27, 1833.

38. Reprinted in *The Liberator*, April 6, 1833.

39. Fuller, *Prudence Crandall*, pp. 32–33.

40. *The Liberator*, April 27, 1833.

41. Small, "Prudence Crandall, Champion of Negro Education," pp. 518–19.

42. *The Liberator*, July 20, 1833; Ellen D. Larned, *History of Windham County, Connecticut* (Worcester, Mass.: Printed by C. Hamilton, 1874-1880), II: 490–502.

43. May, *Some Recollections*, pp. 58–60; Samuel Sillen, *Women Against Slavery* (New York: International Publishers, 1952), pp. 13–14; Fuller, *Prudence Crandall*, pp. 34–35.

44. Prudence Crandall to S. J. Jocelyn, Canterbury, April 9, 1833, *Journal of Negro History* 18 (January 1933): 81, 83.

45. The report was inaccurate in its boast that the "whole population of color," born within the last century, had been emancipated. Under the system of gradual emancipation, which provided for freedom to be granted a child of a female slave upon reaching the age of twenty-one, there were still in 1833 twenty slaves in the state, and as late as 1848, there were several slaves in Connecticut. Most of them had been born before the law was passed, and were, therefore, not affected by it.

46. *Public Statute Laws of the State of Connecticut*, 1833, Revised as of 1838, Chapter IX.

47. May, *Some Recollections*, p. 66; *The Liberator*, June 22, 1833.

48. Small, "Prudence Crandall, Champion of Negro Education," p. 520; Fuller, *Prudence Crandall*, pp. 91–92.

49. *The Liberator*, July 6, 1833.

50. Trachtenberg, "The Canterbury Tale," p. 124.

51. Fuller, *Prudence Crandall*, p. 4.

52. *The Liberator*, July 6, 1833.

53. May, *Some Recollections*, pp. 59–60, 82–85.

54. Ibid., p. 61.

55. Ibid., p. 63.

56. Ibid., p. 64.

57. *The Liberator*, July 6, 13, 1833.

58. New York *Independent*, July 1865; Lewis Tappan, *Life of Arthur Tappan* (New York: Arno, 1970), pp. 121-23; Eugene P. Southey, "Arthur Tappan and the Anti-Slavery Movement," *Journal of Negro History* 15 (April 1930): 176.

59. May, *Some Recollections*, p. 61; Southey, "Arthur Tappan," p. 177.

60. Charles Calistus Burleigh (1810-1876) was born in Plainfield, Connecticut, the son of Rinaldo Burleigh, president of the first antislavery society in Windham County, Connecticut, and Lydia Bradford, a lineal descendant of Governor William Bradford of the *Mayflower*. Admitted to the bar in 1835, Burleigh did not practice. Instead, he became an antislavery agent, lecturer, and writer. He later edited the *Pennsylvania Freeman*, an antislavery paper published in Philadelphia. He was elected corresponding secretary of the American Anti-Slavery Society in 1859.

   Although Arthur Tappan relied mainly on the editors of *The Unionist*, *The Liberator*, and other antislavery papers to defend Prudence Crandall, he himself did some of it. In an article in the *Genius of Universal Emancipation*, he answered seven charges against Crandall: that she was "a mere instrument" in the hands of Garrison and his followers; that "the making of money was her inducement" in launching a school for black females; that she "violated an engagement that existed with the citizens of Canterbury in changing the character of the school"; that "ample provision" was made for the "gratuitous instruction of the blacks"; that the school was "under the patronage of Mr. Arnold Buffum," a leading abolitionist; that "Miss C. was actuated by a desire to bring herself into notice"; and that "amalgamation of the blacks and whites" was the real purpose of founding the school. His reply to the charge of starting the school to make money is typical: "For this charge there is not a shadow of evidence—she dismissed a full and flourishing school, for the uncertain alternative of getting a competent number of colored girls, knowing, as she says, the fearful prejudice she must contend with." (Reprinted in *The Liberator*, September 14, 1833.)

61. Only single copies of two issues of *The Unionist*, that of August 8, 1833 (in the library of the New-York Historical Society) and September 5, 1833 (in the library of the American Antiquarian Society, Worcester, Mas-

sachusetts) are known to exist, although some editorials were reprinted in *The Liberator*.

62. Reprinted in *The Liberator*, April 5, 1834.

63. Reprinted in *The Liberator*, June 21, 1834. William H. Burleigh (1812-1871) was converted to the antislavery movement as early as 1833. He later edited the *Christian Witness*, organ of the western branch of the Pennsylvania State Anti-Slavery Society; the *Christian Freeman* of Hartford, Connecticut; and the *Charter Oak*, a Connecticut abolitionist organ. In later years he devoted himself to the temperance movement.

64. See *Dictionary of American Biography*, 20 vols. (New York: Charles Scribner's Sons, 1980).

65. *The Liberator*, September 12, 1833.

66. Ibid., September 19, 1833.

67. Ibid., August 31, 1833.

68. Ibid., August 22, 1833.

69. Ibid., August 31, 1833.

70. Fuller, *Prudence Crandall*, pp. 81–84; *The Liberator*, August 31, 1833; *Connecticut Courant*, August 26, 1833; Fuller, *Prudence Crandall*, pp. 79–80.

71. *The Liberator*, December 21, 1833.

72. Reprinted in ibid., August 3, 1833.

73. Reprinted in ibid., January 4, 1834.

74. Garrison to Helen E. Benson, April 1, 1834, Merrill, ed., *Letters*, vol. I, No. 135; *The Liberator*, April 5, 12, 1834.

75. *The Liberator*, June 21, 1834.

76. Ibid., April 5, November 1, 1834.

77. Reprinted in *The Liberator*, August 17, 1833.

78. See memorials in clippings in Larned collection, Connecticut State Library, Hartford, Connecticut.

79. Quoted in Elizabeth Yates, *Prudence Crandall: Woman of Courage* (New York: Dutton, 1955), p. 209.

80. *The Liberator*, September 13, 1834. For the mob action against George Thompson while he was in the United States, see Philip S. Foner, *History of Black Americans*, 3 vols. (Westport, Conn.: Greenwood Press, 1983), II: 422–26.

81. *The Liberator*, April 12, 1834.

82. "Genius of Universal Emancipation" reprinted in *The Liberator*, March 1, 1834. See also "Address to Prudence Crandall," by F.H.W., *The Liberator*, August 10, 1833.

83. *The Liberator*, March 12, 1834.

84. Ibid., April 19, 1834; William Lloyd Garrison to Helen E. Benson, April 12, 1834, Merrill, ed., *Letters*, vol. I, No. 138. Garrison used the

plural "laws" when he meant the law that had been passed after the establishment of Prudence Crandall's school for black females.

85. William Lloyd Garrison to Samuel J. May, July 28, 1834, Merrill, ed., *Letters*, vol. I, No. 165.

86. State Supreme Court, 10 Conn., 339, "Crandall *against* The State of Connecticut in Error."

87. Ibid.; *The Liberator*, September 27, 1834. This issue contains the entire text of Ellsworth's address to the Court. The reference to "the Pope" by Ellsworth indicates that even this enlightened man was not free of the anti-Catholic prejudice so prevalent in New England during this period.

William Wilberforce was the famous British abolitionist who fought to abolish the African slave trade. Wilberforce College, established as a black institution in Ohio in 1855, was named after him.

88. *The Liberator*, September 27, 1834. The "middle passage" was the name given to the part of the voyage of slave ships from Africa to the New World, the first part being the voyage from Europe or New England to Africa, and the final part being the voyage from the West Indies to North America or Europe. Most of the fatalities in the African slave trade occurred during the long "Middle Passage."

89. *The Liberator*, September 27, 1834.

90. *State Supreme Court*, 10 Conn., 339, "Crandall against the State of Connecticut in Error."

91. For a discussion of the *Dred Scott* decision, see Philip S. Foner, *History of Black Americans*, vol. 3 *From the Compromise of 1850 to the End of the Civil War* (Westport, Conn.: Greenwood Press, 1983), pp. 212–16.

92. State Supreme Court, 10 Conn., 339, "Crandall against the State of Connecticut in Error."

93. Ibid.

94. Prudence Crandall to S. J. Jocelyn, April 9, 1833, *Journal of Negro History* 18 (January 1933): 81–82; William Lloyd Garrison to Dear K, April 17, 1833, Merrill, ed., *Letters*, vol. I, No. 94; *The Liberator*, October 10, 1834. For Garrison's attacks on Judson's role in the Crandall case, see *The Liberator*, March 16, July 20, November 2, 1833.

95. Helen E. Benson to William Lloyd Garrison, June 9, 1834, Anti-Slavery Letters to Garrison, William Lloyd Garrison Papers, Boston Public Library, Rare Book Room.

96. William Lloyd Garrison to Helen E. Benson, June 14, 1834, Merrill, ed., *Letters*, vol. I, No. 155.

97. Helen E. Benson to William Lloyd Garrison, June 12, 1834, Anti-Slavery Letters to Garrison, William Lloyd Garrison Papers, Boston Public Library, Rare Book Room.

98. William Lloyd Garrison to George W. Benson, June 6, 1834, Merrill, ed., *Letters*, vol. I, No. 157.

99. William Lloyd Garrison to George W. Benson, July 10, 1834, ibid., No. 161.

100. William Lloyd Garrison to Helen E. Benson, August 18, 1834, ibid., No. 182.

101. Larned, *History of Windham County*, II: 578–80. There was only one house at which the black witnesses could stay in Brooklyn, Connecticut, where the trial took place, and that was at the home of George W. Benson.

102. *The Liberator*, September 27, 1834.

103. Ibid.

104. Ibid.

105. The account of the trial was published under the following title: *The Trial of Reuben Crandall, M.D., Charged with Publishing Seditious Libels, by Circulating the Publications of the American Anti-Slavery Society, Before the Circuit Court for the District of Columbia, Held in Washington, in April, 1836, Occupying the Court for the Period of Ten Days* (New York, 1836). See also *The Liberator*, April 30, May 7, 1836; March 16, 1838.

Interesting is the fact that Andrew T. Judson, Prudence Crandall's most bitter opponent, testified as a character witness in Dr. Reuben Crandall's trial in his behalf. But it seems that he did so on the ground that (as he said) Reuben Crandall had once told him that he disagreed with his sister on the matter of the school and had promised Judson that "he was going to break up the school." (Fuller, *Prudence Crandall*, pp. 97–98.)

Judson died in March 1855, at which time he had been a Judge of the United States District Court for several years. In its obituary, the *New York Herald*, a leading pro-Southern paper, praised him for his "prominence" in having brought about the closing of Prudence Crandall's school and hailed him as the man who "drove the black scholars out of the state." For once the *National Anti-Slavery Standard* agreed with the *Herald*, observing that in its "Eulogy" of Judson, "justice is done. His one claim to notice is just this—that he used all the power that social position, the law, and popular principles could give him to debar the coloured children of Connecticut from acquiring the first elements of education." ("Death of Judge Judson," *National Anti-Slavery Standard*, March 14, 1855.)

106. See letters and affidavits from Crandall's relatives in the Papers of William Lloyd Garrison, Boston Public Library, Rare Book Room, and note 111 below.

107. Yates, *Prudence Crandall*, pp. 240–41.

108. *The Liberator*, March 23, 1838.

109. Yates, *Prudence Crandall*, p. 240.

110. New York *Freeman*, June 12, 1883.

111. According to George B. Thayer, Mark Twain also wrote to Prudence Crandall promising her a set of his books, but appears never to have sent

the volumes. (George B. Thayer, *Pedal and Path: Across the Continent Awheel and Afoot* [Hartford, Conn.: Hartford Evening Post Association, 1887], pp. 122–26.)

Thayer met and interviewed Prudence Crandall in her old age in Elk Falls, Kansas, during a bicycle trip across the country in 1886. (His letters about his trip for the Hartford *Evening Post* formed the book *Pedal and Path*.) In one of her statements, which he quotes, Prudence Crandall said: "My whole life has been one of opposition. I never could find anyone near me to agree with me. Even my husband opposed me, more than any one. He would not let me read the books that he himself read, but I did read them. I read all sides, and searched for the truth whether it was in science, religion, or humanity. I sometimes think I would like to live somewhere else. Here, in Elk Falls, there is nothing for my soul to feed upon. Nothing, unless it comes from abroad in the shape of books, newspapers, and so on. There is no public library, and there are but one or two persons in the place that I can converse with profitably for any length of time. No one visits me, and I begin to think they are afraid of me. I think the ministers are afraid I shall upset their religious beliefs, and advise the members of their congregation not to call on me, but I don't care. I speak on spiritualism sometimes, but more on temperance, and am a self-appointed member of the International Arbitration League. I don't want to die yet. I want to live long enough to see some of these reforms consummated." (Thayer, *Pedal and Path*, pp. 209–15.)

112. House Petition No. 48, January Session, 1886, State Library of Connecticut, Hartford, Connecticut.

113. Fuller, *Prudence Crandall*, p. 104; letters and clippings in Larned collection, Connecticut State Library, Hartford, Connecticut.

114. Quoted in Samuel Sillen, *Women Against Slavery*, p. 16.

2

MARGARET
DOUGLASS

JOSEPHINE F. PACHECO

I

On the first day of June 1852, Margaret Douglass opened a school in Norfolk, Virginia, for free black children. By so doing she broke the laws of the state, which forbade the instruction of any blacks, free or slave. The city of Norfolk prosecuted her, a jury found her guilty in spite of her plea of ignorance of the law, and she went to jail for teaching free black children to read.

Born in the District of Columbia, Douglass moved to Charleston, South Carolina, when she was quite young. There she grew up, married, and gave birth to two children. There is no record of her life in Charleston except that she claimed to have owned slaves. On the death of her only son, she found Charleston too full of painful memories and took her nine-year-old daughter, Rosa, and moved to Norfolk in 1845. Records also fail to reveal whether her husband died or was separated from her; but when Margaret Douglass arrived in Norfolk, she was the sole means of support for herself and her daughter. She rented a small four-room house in a poor neighborhood and lived there quietly with Rosa.

Like so many women of her day, when forced to earn a living, Douglass became a seamstress and specialized in making vests, those elegant adornments of nineteenth-century men. Since she was competent in both sewing and managing her affairs, she soon earned enough to keep herself and Rosa in modest comfort and was even able to hire one young servant to help with domestic chores. Rosa, as she grew older, took on some of the sewing.

The Douglasses lived a quiet, busy life. Mrs. Douglass worked long hours but did not find them a burden, for she rejoiced in her skill with the needle and her ability to provide for her small family. The family had few social contacts because of her heavy work schedule and because she would not associate with her neighbors, whom she regarded as her inferiors. Mrs. Douglass and Rosa worshipped at Christ Episcopal Church with many of the leaders of the city, but they did not make friends with any of the parishioners.

Christ Church had a Sunday school in its assembly room where black children received instruction in Christian principles. The church also provided lessons in reading, gave the children primers or spelling books, and encouraged them to study during the week. The teachers in this Sunday school were the wives and daughters of the leading citizens of Norfolk, and therefore Douglass assumed that free black children could legally attend reading classes.

One day when she had business in Robinson's Barber Shop, owned by a free black, she saw the owner's two sons studying a spelling book. Inquiring about their school, she learned from their father that "there was no one who took interest enough in little colored children to keep a day school for them."[1] When she asked why he did not send his boys to the Sunday school at Christ Church, the father replied that although that was indeed where they received instruction, they also needed daily attention and someone to direct their lessons on a regular basis. Occasionally a customer in the shop helped them, but the boys made slow progress. Robinson, himself illiterate, longed for an education for his two sons and three daughters. Douglass volunteered the services of her daughter Rosa as teacher and proposed that Robinson immediately send his children to her home. Accepting her offer with gratitude, the barber agreed to send his sons whenever he could spare them from the shop.

On hearing of her new assignment, Rosa was delighted. But the boys did not appear. Some time later, when Douglass had almost forgotten the arrangement, Robinson came to her home with two of his daughters, "who were neatly dressed, and very respectful, and appeared unusually intelligent."[2] The father said to Douglass: "I have told my little girls of your kind offer to instruct their brothers, and they are also very anxious to learn, and I wish to know if you would not prefer to have these two eldest, thinking that the boys might give your daughter much trouble."[3] Douglass assured Robinson that Rosa would be delighted to teach all of his children every day, and they would both do all they could "for their religious and moral instruction." If the children would bring the books they had received at Christ Church Sunday school, lessons could begin the next day. Before agreeing to instruct the Robinson children, Douglass made sure that all members of the family were free, "as I knew that the laws of the Southern states did not permit the slaves to be educated."[4]

On the following day the two older Robinson girls appeared at the Douglass home and explained that the brothers had to help their father in the shop. Rosa found the children willing pupils; they attended faithfully every day, did their lessons, and learned rapidly. Indeed, Rosa and her mother became very attached to them, for they were "well behaved and obedient."[5] This happy situation continued for a month, when Rosa expressed concern about the amount of time she spent teaching, time that could have been more profitably spent. The faster the children learned, she discovered, the more attention they required.

Douglass then asked her daughter if she would like to establish a school for free black children. The school fees would compensate for Rosa's loss of time from sewing, for the Douglasses remained very poor. Rosa responded to the suggestion with enthusiasm, and they decided to open a school for free blacks on the first day of June 1852, with the tuition set at three dollars per quarter. Through the Robinson family the Douglasses made contact with other free blacks of Norfolk and invited them to send their children to the school. Immediately the Douglasses received more applications than they could handle: Robinson was not alone in his longing for literacy for his children.

To find space for a school in a four-room house could not have been easy, since Douglass had to reserve one room for her sewing. Nevertheless, they converted the back room on the second floor into a classroom. We know nothing of the furnishings except that Rosa, as teacher, sat at a "humble pine table."[6]

The school opened with an enrollment of twenty-five boys and girls, "punctual in their attendance, and under good discipline." The Douglasses found their pupils "obedient and well behaved, as well as anxious to be taught," and as the months passed, they accepted other children seeking admission. Before long both women were deeply attached to the children, and though Rosa had the major responsibility for teaching, Douglass assisted her in attending to "their moral and religious instruction."[7] They visited their pupils when they were sick and cared for one seriously ill student until her death.

Early on the morning of May 9, 1853, eleven months after the opening of the school, Constable James Cherry, a police officer of the city, knocked at the Douglasses' front door and inquired who lived upstairs. When Douglass explained that she alone occupied the house, he asked if a Mrs. Douglass lived there. When she identified herself, the following conversation took place:

"You keep a school."
"Yes, sir."
"A school for colored children?"
"Yes."
"I must see those children."[8]

Douglass inquired what business he had with the children or with anything in her house. He had come, he answered, at the order of the mayor. "Very good, sir, . . . walk in, and you shall see them," she replied, and together they climbed the stairs to the schoolroom, where the pupils were gathered around their teacher. Douglass later wrote:

Never will I forget the frightened state of those children, and the countenance of their young teacher. My daughter sat paralyzed, covering her face with her hands; and it was some time before I could restore order in the room. Some were crying, some exclaiming "Oh my! oh my!" and some clinging around me in their terror.[9]

After she had calmed her daughter and the pupils, Douglass demanded to know what he wanted of them. As it turned out, Constable Cherry had orders to take the children to the mayor's office, and to do this he called in another policeman who had been stationed at the back door. "For the moment," Douglass later wrote, "I thought that my house was surrounded with officers, who perhaps fancied that they had found a nest of thieves."[10]

Cherry and his associate took down the names of the children and their parents, while Douglass protested that they were free children, born of free parents, and that nearly all of them attended Christ Church Sunday school. "It makes no difference, madam," he replied, "it is a violation of the law to teach any person of color to read or write, slave or free, and an act punishable by imprisonment in the penitentiary." Douglass replied, "Very well, . . . if they send me to the penitentiary, it will be in a good cause, and not a disgraceful one."[11]

Douglass and Rosa insisted on accompanying the terrified children to the mayor's office, so the constables waited while the women put on their street clothes. They all set off together, with the children walking two by two, one officer in front and one behind, "each with a great club in his hands," and the Douglasses "walking at a little distance in the rear." It reminded Douglass "of a flock of little lambs going to the slaughter."[12]

A considerable crowd had gathered in the mayor's office to watch the proceedings. If the action against the school had taken Douglass by surprise, others had been better informed. Douglass had previously had dealings with Mayor Simon S. Stubbs and felt a high regard for his charity and integrity. He had, in fact, visited her home to thank her for her kindness in caring for the unfortunate wife and child of "a drunken and worthless husband."[13] Thus, he greeted Douglass in a friendly manner and remarked on the large size of her family. She agreed, adding that they were all very good children. "But, are you aware," he inquired, "that it is a violation of the law of this State to instruct colored children to read?"[14] She replied that she had not known about the law until that morning, but she had been careful to ascertain that the pupils were all free children who attended Christ Church Sunday school, where they had received their primers and other books. Therefore, if she had broken the law, the people at Christ Church, who had infringed the law for years, were equally guilty. The mayor denied knowledge of the Sunday school and vowed that if he had learned of its presence he would have done his duty. A spectator corroborated Douglass's account of the Sunday school for black children, adding that violations of the law should be treated consistently.

Mayor Stubbs, ignoring the spectator's remark, read from the statutes of Virginia the law forbidding instruction of people of color, either slave or free, and providing a maximum penalty of a hundred-dollar fine and a six-month prison term. In spite of his obvious sympathy for the Douglasses, the mayor insisted that he must uphold the law. The case would be continued to the Circuit Court of Norfolk. In response to Douglass's query, he said the children would not be punished, and when he told them they could leave, they fled the room "like so many little birds let loose from a cage."[15] The children's parents would also escape prosecution, and Douglass requested that her daughter, still a minor, not be held responsible. The mayor wondered if Douglass had friends to guarantee her appearance in court. "Friends!" I replied, "I am my own best friend, and my daughter's only one."[16] She would not ask favors "at the hands of any man," and if the mayor thought it necessary to jail her, then he must do his duty. The mayor finally decided that he could trust her not to repeat her offence and "being perfectly satisfied with my good intentions, frank acknowledgment, and ignorance of the law, dismissed the matter."[17] So she wrote later. But Douglass must have known that the matter was far from dismissed, that the case was to be sent forward from the mayor to the grand jury for presentment to the city's circuit court. While he allowed her to remain free without bond, she could not have been so naive as to believe that the case had been settled.

On leaving the building, Douglass was surprised to find a crowd of black men, women, and children standing on the steps of the mayor's office. Parents and relatives of the Douglass pupils, they had hurried to the scene to find out the results of the inquiry and, poor though they were, to offer money to pay fines or court costs. Douglass thanked them for their "kindness and sympathy" and assured them that she did not need their money. Collecting the pupils, she and Rosa took them back home and returned their books and slates. They said goodbye to each child "with wounded hearts," feeling that those bright and eager children "must henceforth grow up in darkness and ignorance."[18] The children's parents and friends frequently came to visit the Douglasses, lamenting the closing of the school, and praying for the welfare of their benefactors. The children brought flowers, and during the whole summer, wrote Douglass, "it was seldom that my table did not contain bouquets from their hands."[19]

In accordance with long-standing plans, Rosa left to spend the summer with friends in New York. Douglass believed the problem of the school had been resolved, without danger of prosecution to herself, once she had dismissed the children. Her life settled into a routine of work, with few visitors apart from her former pupils and few visits except to those same pupils whenever they were sick.

In July she received a summons to appear at the November term of the Circuit Court of Norfolk to answer the charge, made by the grand jury, that she and Rosa "did . . . unlawfully assemble with diverse negroes, for the purpose of instructing them to read and to write, and did instruct them to read and to write, contrary to the Act of the General Assembly, . . . and against the peace and dignity of the Commonwealth of Virginia."[20] The arrival of the summons shocked Margaret Douglass and alarmed her because she had no financial resources or friends to advise her. As she sat sewing—and she never stopped working, as it was her only source of income—, she deliberated on her best course of action. Finally she decided that she would not discuss the case or seek assistance from anyone. She expected that "in that city of churches," someone from "the religious part of the community," would come forward with sympathy or advice, but "not one solitary individual . . . manifested the least interest in the matter."[21] Lacking money to pay a lawyer and feeling "little affection" for lawyers, she resolved to plead her own cause and rely on her own conviction of innocence. Later she wrote that she had come to that decision because she feared a lawyer would implicate the women of Christ Church Sunday school and bring to an end an educational project that she approved. When the case came to trial, however, she herself introduced the Christ Church school as a precedent for her actions.

During the summer and fall of 1853, Douglass continued to hope that if she remained quiet, the entire affair would blow over. "I could not believe that men who boasted of their talents and benevolence could be so blinded by their attachment to their peculiar institution as to farther irritate a matter that would, from beginning to end, prove disgraceful to them and to their State."[22] She believed that the newspapers kept the case alive but resolved not to reply to the "mortifying" appearances of her name in the papers.

Rosa remained in New York, unaware that she and her mother had been charged to appear in court in November. She had planned to return to Norfolk in September, but Douglass, determined that Rosa should not undergo the humiliation of a trial, arranged for her daughter to stay indefinitely with their friends in New York. Douglass would fight their battle alone.

On November 15, the first day of the fall term of the Circuit Court of Norfolk,[23] Douglass went to the office of James R. Hubard,[24] the commonwealth's attorney, to ask him to bring forward her case as soon as possible, for her mind was "heavily taxed." Hubard agreed, and when he requested her lawyer's name, learned that she planned to act as her own counsel. The attorney was taken aback; having to "plead against a lady" was not a pleasant prospect. However, Douglass urged him to fulfill his obligations in this matter, as she intended to do herself.

Hubard, in fact, confessed that the whole affair of the school had entirely slipped his memory and "that he had not before thought seriously about it."[25] Is it possible, then, that he had intended to ignore the Douglass case and that the leaders of the city had meant no further action once they were assured that the school was closed? Perhaps Douglass, in her haste to conclude the affair, forced the hand of a reluctant commonwealth's attorney, though it remains difficult to explain the summons sent by the clerk of the circuit court, ordering the Douglasses to appear.

When the day of the trial arrived, Douglass set out for the court in a "neat and becoming dress" and a plain straw bonnet, carrying in her gloved hands the summons and a small red Bible belonging to Rosa. Although she had given much thought to what she would say, she had not prepared a written statement. She waited alone in the jury room for her case to be called and entered the courtroom "with a firm step" when her turn came. As she took her seat at the counsellor's table, she caused some confusion in the court, though she herself felt "perfectly calm and collected." Judge Richard H. Baker presided.

After the jury had been sworn, the commonwealth's attorney called his witnesses. Constable Cherry and his assistant testified concerning their visit to Douglass's home, and Mayor Stubbs recounted the events in his office. C. C. Melson, a carpenter[26] and agent for Douglass's landlord, testified that he knew Douglass and had rented her the house where she lived, but had no knowledge of the school held on the premises. The prosecution had no other witnesses, and Douglass did not bother to question the evidence of the four men.

Instead she rose to her feet and spoke to the court, explaining Rosa's whereabouts and declaring that she accepted full responsibility for what had occurred, since her daughter was a minor and brought up "in strict obedience" to her mother in all things. Hubard, thinking she was beginning her argument before presenting her witnesses, interrupted her. Upset at this, she sat down. After regaining her composure, she called three witnesses: Walter Taylor, John Williams, and William W. Sharp;[27] all were members of Christ Church.

"The excitement in the Court room, when the names of my three witnesses were called, was most intense,"[28] Douglass later reported. The spectators understood that by calling those men to testify, she intended to challenge the power structure of the city. John Williams was clerk of the corporation court[29] and of the circuit court where the Douglass case was being heard; indeed, the Douglass summons bore Williams's signature. He was president of Norfolk's common council and a member of the Board of Trustees of the Norfolk Academy.[30] Walter H. Taylor owned a wholesale and retail grocery business, was an importer of brandies and wines, and was president of the City Gas Light Company.[31] William W. Sharp was president of the Exchange Bank and of the Board of Trustees of the Norfolk Academy.[32] Nevertheless, a mere woman had the audacity to question three men who represented "the aristocracy of that town."

Once the courtroom had grown quiet, Taylor took the stand and responded to Douglass's questions:

Question. Was [sic] you a teacher in the Christ Church Sunday-school?

Answer. For the white children I was, and the school was held in the church.

Question. Did you never visit the lecture room?

Answer. I had nothing to do with the school that was kept there.

Question. Did you never distribute books to the negro children of that school?

Answer. I attended the library of the school for white children.

Question. Did you not instruct colored children to read from those books?

Answer. I did not.[33]

The commonwealth's attorney did not question Taylor, and so he was excused.

When she called John Williams, clerk of the court, to the stand, he came, "with a pallid countenance, and quivering lip, evidently troubled by the position in which he found himself."[34] Douglass felt so sorry for him that she asked only a few questions and then excused him. She also remembered that his daughter Eliza, active in the

Christ Church Sunday school, had been teaching on Sundays the very children that Rosa Douglass had instructed during the week. Out of compassion for "amiable" Eliza, Douglass felt that she could not humiliate the girl's father. She was a good deal less gentle, however, with William Sharp:

Question.   Were you a teacher in the school for colored children, held in Christ's Church Lecture room?

Answer.   No, madam.

Question.   Did you not attend the Sabbath-school held there for the instruction of negro children?

Answer.   I went there, occasionally, and lectured to them.

Question.   Did you not distribute books among them?

Answer.   *The ladies had all to do with that!*

Question.   When you visited that school, did you not instruct them yourself?[35]

Sharp replied "that they did not teach them to read and write, and that he did not know that the law prohibited religious and moral instruction to negroes." Douglass had made her point well. She retorted: "If you, sir, who are engaged in the practice of law, did not know it, how could it be expected that I should?"[36]

Sharp either could not understand her question, or was too stunned to reply. However, when she had repeated it, he turned to the judge and asked leave to address the jury directly. On receiving permission, he is reported to have informed the jury

that certain negroes applied to Rev. Mr. Cummings, the Pastor of Christ's Church, for religious instruction, and were allowed to meet for that purpose in the lecture room of the church. He [Sharp] occasionally visited the school and lectured to them. *He found that some of them could read very well*, but that when they came to the hard words, *he allowed them to skip over them!*[37]

Douglass had successfully gotten her point across: A lawyer admitted that he knew the black children at Christ Church could read, for he had listened to them. He added the kind of corroborative detail that certainly gave verisimilitude: he had let them skip the hard words. The books from which they read were the identical ones used in the

Douglass school. Douglass, acting as her own counsel, had been able to prove that in her school she had simply followed the example of another Norfolk school's long-standing practice of teaching free black children. If she was guilty of violating the law, she had "abundant precedents among the aristocracy of the city."

Having made her case, she then addressed the jury. She refused to plead guilty, for in her eyes "to be a violator of any law or laws, the individual must know that they are such." A Southerner "by birth, education, and feeling," she had been a slaveholder herself and felt "deeply interested in the welfare of Virginia, and of the whole united Southern slave States." She was, she told the jury, neither abolitionist nor fanatic, and she opposed as strongly as anyone "the interference of Northern anti-slavery men with our institutions." But she added that she believed in the religious foundation of the abolitionists' principles, an attitude most Southerners would have rejected. She was convinced—and this lay at the heart of her dilemma—that every Southerner had the duty "morally and religiously, to instruct his slaves, that they may know their duties to their masters, and to their common God. Let the masters first do their duty to them, for they are still our slaves and servants, whether bond or free, and can be nothing else in our community."[38] Indeed, she was "a strong advocate for the religious and moral instruction of the whole human family." She had always taught religious principles to her own slaves and would continue to do so, though not in such a fashion as to violate the law.

She reminded the jury that her pupils had been members of Christ Church Sunday school, which her own servant had attended for two years prior to the opening of her school. She added, "In my opinion, whatever the religious portion of the community is engaged in doing, whether in city, town, or country, is generally considered as lawful and proper."[39]

So far so good, for she had made a reasonable statement, establishing her credentials as a loyal Southerner. But at that point her speech became bitter, as she lashed out at the people of Norfolk. She had taken care of her black pupils, visiting them when they were sick, and in so doing she had seen how blacks—both slave and free—lived. They received less care than animals; "dumb brutes" were blessed with more attention. "Think you, gentlemen, that there is not misery and distress among these people? Yes, indeed, misery enough, and frequently starvation." Free blacks endured heavy taxation, but possessed few of the taxpayer's privileges.

And when they are sick, or in want, on whom does the duty devolve to seek them out and administer to their necessities? Does it fall upon you, gentlemen? Oh no, it is not expected that gentlemen will take the trouble to seek out a negro hut for the purpose of alleviating the wretchedness he may find within it. Why then persecute your benevolent ladies for doing that which you yourselves have so long neglected?[40]

Douglass could not expect to win the sympathy of the jury by such a tirade. But she proceeded to ruin her cause completely by breaking the strongest taboo in Southern slave society, speaking openly about miscegenation, and even blaming white men for its existence:

In my opinion, we have nothing to fear from the true blooded negro. It is the half-breed, or those with more or less white blood in their veins, whom I have always found presumptuous, treacherous and vengeful. And do you blame them for this? How can you? Ask yourselves the cause. Ask how that white blood got beneath those tawny skins, and let nature herself account for the exhibition of these instincts. Blame the authors of this devilish mischief, but not the innocent victims of it.[41]

Recovering herself and returning to the matter at hand, Douglass then told the court that she would continue her good works, not by breaking the law, but "by endeavoring to teach the colored race humility and a prayerful spirit, how to bear their sufferings as our Saviour bore his for us all." She would show them "their duty to their superiors, how to live, and how to die." She asked the jury to remember her ignorance of the law, her good intentions, and "the abundant examples set before me by your most worthy and pious citizens." Surely the jury must realize that she had no designs against "the peace and dignity of our Commonwealth." She concluded her speech dramatically, with the declaration that if found guilty and sent to "that cold and gloomy prison," she would be as happy there as in her "little home," and with "the resources of a well-stored mind," she would not be lonely. If she went to jail, she would go secure in the knowledge of her innocence. She had disobeyed none of God's laws but only "one of the most inhuman and unjust laws that ever disgraced the statute book of a civilized community."[42]

Having completed her remarks to the jury, she turned to the spectators and said that if any lawyer would speak in her behalf, she would be grateful. No one moved to help her. As she left the courtroom to await the verdict, a number of men stopped her to offer congratulations. She felt that she had spoken clearly and effectively, and though she was exhausted, she was "by no means unnerved."[43] The jury, obviously troubled, did not reach a verdict until the third day. It found her guilty, but set the fine at one dollar and recommended that the judge omit the prison sentence. Douglass found the jury's decision a fair one; she also believed the community approved. Sentencing by Judge Baker was set for January 1854.

It was now the end of November 1853, and Rosa had been in New York since early in the summer. Having decided to bring her daughter back to Norfolk, Douglass received permission from the court to leave the state for a short period. She visited in New York for two weeks, and then, to the surprise of everybody in Norfolk, returned with Rosa to await her sentence. Surely the leaders of the city had hoped they had seen the last of Margaret Douglass. Had she stayed in New York, they could have disparaged her as a fugitive from justice. According to the newspapers, it was indeed, "the hope and wish of every one that she would leave the city." *The Daily Southern Argus*, published in Norfolk, charged that she returned because she longed for martyrdom,[44] but Douglass countered that she refused to be labelled a coward and a fugitive. Furthermore, she believed that the case was closed, that her sentencing would be a mere formality.

On January 10, 1854, Douglass appeared before Judge Baker, who delivered a lengthy opinion before sentencing her to a month in the city jail. The judge pointed out that his responsibility was not to vindicate the law in question but only to enforce it as long as it remained on the statute books. Baker then went on to discuss the propriety of education for slaves, completely ignoring the fact that the children Douglass had taught were free. He asserted that if there were people in Norfolk opposed to the law in question, and Douglass knew that this included members of his own family who had been teaching at Christ Church Sunday school, their opposition stemmed from their belief that "universal intellectual culture is necessary to religious instruction and education, and that such culture is suitable to a state of slavery." Baker had no doubt where Douglass stood on the question of education for slaves, for she had spoken of her "regard for the colored race" with "indiscreet freedom." Such opinions he regarded as "manifestly mischievous." Slaves could be taught "religious and moral duty" without being able to read or write, for though "intellectual and religious instruction" often went hand in hand, this was not obligatory. He cited the great number of white illiterates in Virginia—up to one-fourth of the population—who respected the law and conducted themselves in a moral and religious manner.[45]

Judge Baker discussed at some length the great blessings that Christianity had brought to the "negro race." The slave population of the South was "peculiarly susceptible of good religious influences." He added: "Their mere residence among a Christian people has wrought a great and happy change in their condition: they have been raised from the night of heathenism to the light of Christianity, and thousands of them have been brought to a saving knowledge of the Gospel."

Continuing to disregard the fact that Douglass had never engaged in the instruction of slaves, the judge said, "Of the one hundred millions of the negro race, there cannot be found another so large a body as the three millions of slaves in the United States, at once so intelligent, so inclined to the Gospel, and so blessed by the elevating influence of civilization and Christianity." Even Judge Baker admitted that "occasional instances of cruelty and oppression" did occur, but these were no worse than whites inflicted on each other.

While the negroes of our town and State are known to be surrounded by most of the substantial comforts of life, and invited both by precept and example to participate in proper, moral and religious duties, it argues, it seems to me, a sickly sensibility towards them to say their persons, and feelings, and interests are not sufficiently respected by our laws."[46]

Baker traced the origin of the law under which Douglass was found guilty, blaming it on the "incendiary documents" of the abolitionists. He regretted that the first offender he had been forced to punish under the law was "a female, apparently of fair and respectable standing in the community." But so far as he could tell, her sex was the only mitigating circumstance, and had a man been convicted, he would have ordered the full six months of imprisonment required by the law. Douglass should have realized the wisdom of retaining a lawyer, who might have presented her case more favorably. "The opinions you advanced, and the pertinacity and zeal you manifested in behalf of the negroes, while they indicated perfect candor and sincerity on your part, satisfied the Court, and must have satisfied all who heard you, that the act complained of was the settled and deliberate purpose of your mind, regardless of consequences, however dangerous to the peace." In other words, Douglass had been her own worst enemy. The judge believed that a nominal sentence, such as a day in prison, would be perceived by "true advocates of justice and law" as a mockery, an invitation to "still bolder incendiary movements." Therefore, as an example to others and "in vindication of the policy and justness of our laws," he sentenced Douglass to a month in jail.[47]

The sentence stunned Douglass. In spite of the fact that Norfolk newspapers had predicted that she would receive the full six months required by the law,[48] she believed that the judge would accept the jury's recommendation for mercy. In any case, she went to jail at once and served the entire month, even though she was sick for one week of her sentence. Jailer George H. Miller[49] and his wife treated her with sympathy and kindness, and she even stayed with them for a day or two after serving her sentence. Records do not reveal where Rosa stayed while her mother was in prison. In February 1854 Douglass collected her few possessions and with Rosa moved to Philadelphia, where she might live "happy in the consciousness that it is here no crime to teach a poor little child, of any color, to read the Word of God."[50]

II

Margaret Douglass was an unlikely martyr to the cause of black education. A Southerner born and bred and a former slaveholder, she expressed no distaste for the institution of slavery. Indeed, she said that if the occasion were to arise, she could own slaves again with no misgivings. How did she come to accept imprisonment in the cause of education for blacks? What sort of woman was she?

Above all, Margaret Douglass was a lady, a gentlewoman; so she perceived herself and so she acted. Though she had to endure poverty, that did not make her any less a lady. Although penury might force her to live among her social inferiors, she would never associate with them. After moving into her small house in Norfolk at 1 Barraud Court,[51] an unpaved, unlighted street, she realized that her neighbors in the tenements around her "were not of the most refined class." Consequently, she decided that she and Rosa could have no dealings with them, except in time of need. She later explained, "I endeavored to be kind and obliging to all who stood in need of my sympathies, and made it my business, if any of them were sick or in trouble, to administer to their wants by sending nourishment, or, if necessary, by calling to see them in person." Under no circumstances, however, would she entertain any of her neighbors in her home, for they were "a class of people with little or no education, and, of course, refinement they knew nothing of."[52] The neighbors understandably resented such an attitude and showed no appreciation for "character and habits"; indeed, Douglass felt that they persecuted her. It is possible that the neighbors, angry at the Douglasses' condescension and resentful of the warm welcome black children received in a house they themselves could not enter, informed the mayor of the existence of Rosa's school. At any rate, the neighbors undoubtedly understood that in Douglass's eyes, they were nothing more than what Virginians called poor white trash.

The ease of Mrs. Douglass's dealings with blacks formed an important aspect of her class perception. Perhaps the oldest myth in the South is the belief, still frequently expressed, that one can recognize a lady by her kindness toward black people. Accordingly, the aristocratic ladies of Norfolk regarded their school for black children at Christ Church as a logical extension of their place in society. Douglass subscribed to the identical attitude when she established a school in her home. Her relations with blacks had a freedom, an ease, that could not extend to her white neighbors who, believing in their social equality, might take advantage of her poverty to diminish her social status. Douglass's poverty made it absolutely essential that her position as a gentlewoman be obvious to everyone she encountered. No one in Norfolk would believe that she was less a lady for having friendly relations with blacks, and even Judge Baker agreed that she had a "fair and respectable standing in the community."[53] She repeatedly claimed that, in teaching blacks to read, she was imitating the ladies of Christ Church. In her mind such a statement not only excused her violation of the law but also identified her with those whom she called the aristocrats of the city.

A ladylike appearance was equally important to one's social standing. When Constable Cherry descended on the Douglass home to carry off Rosa's pupils to the mayor's office, Douglass insisted on accompanying them. But the policemen had to wait while she changed her clothes and prepared herself for the street. Similarly, as she made ready in November for her ordeal in court, she gave serious thought to her appearance and prepared "a neat and becoming dress" of black velvet, with "rich flowing lace sleeves." She wore "a plain straw bonnet, neatly trimmed with white," and white kid gloves; in her gloved hands she carried a small red Bible.[54] Though she was acting in an unladylike fashion in going to court, she was sure of her genteel appearance. She would act in the same way, never overstepping the "rules of courtesy" and always observing "the respect due from a lady to every true gentleman." She felt certain that, as a consequence of her refinement, all the men in the courtroom would respect her and treat her as her station demanded.

Yet if poverty did not make one any less a lady, it certainly impeded the spectator's perception of gentility, which explained Douglass's particular care in dress and deportment and her meticulous choice of associates for herself and her daughter. She would not accept charity, for that would be demeaning. On the other hand, she had to choose her occupation carefully, for most ways of making a living were not considered ladylike. Since sewing was an acceptable occupation for a gentlewoman, she was fortunate in being skilled with the needle. Fine, elegant needlework, such as that required in the making of embroidered vests, was the skill most admired in a lady. Thus, Douglass could remain a gentlewoman while supporting her daughter and herself. In this she took great pride, calling herself a "workwoman."

Her good education gave further assurance of social status. Certainly many gentlewomen suffered appalling ignorance, but in the antebellum South, where lawmakers regarded public education as unimportant, illiteracy among the poor was taken for granted. Judge Baker observed that "in many parts of our own Commonwealth, as in other parts of the country . . . among the whites one-fourth or more are entirely without a knowledge of letters." Margaret Douglass

enjoyed considerable learning, as demonstrated by the ease with
which she invoked the "shades of Henry Clay, of Thomas Jefferson,
of John Randolph, and of all the dead worthies of Virginia," when
she received her court summons in July 1853. In her statement to
the court, she asserted that in prison she could remain as happy as
at home, for "in the pursuit of knowledge, and with the resources
of a well-stored mind, I shall be . . . a sufficient companion for
myself."[55] She had been able to communicate her love of books to
her daughter so that they jointly took pleasure in the teaching profession, which ranked with needlework as an acceptably genteel occupation. Douglass never doubted her daughter's ability to teach
any more than she questioned her own ability to defend herself in
court. She knew that she spoke well, otherwise she would not have
dared to act as her own counsel.

Margaret Douglass saw herself not merely as a gentlewoman but
a Christian gentlewoman. Her beliefs about her Christian duty filled
her life and affected her dealings with her daughter, her slaves and
servants, and her neighbors. Religion for her had two main functions:
the teaching of morality to family, servants, and pupils, and the
practice of charity toward those in need. The two principles merged
in Rosa's school, for the Douglasses helped the poor while at the
same time inculcating moral and religious ideas. Thus the school for
black children fulfilled an important need in the Douglasses' lives,
providing them with an opportunity for a clear manifestation of their
Christianity. Douglass had chosen not to be a member of the altar
guilds and missionary societies with which Christian women usually
demonstrated their piety, and by avoiding active participation in the
life of Christ Church, she undoubtedly lost the sense of community
that comes through the joint endeavors of like-minded women. The
school, therefore, became an admirable replacement for an aspect of
Christian life from which she was excluded because of her poverty
and her long hours of work.

According to Douglass, all blacks, whether slave or free, should
receive religious and moral instruction. When she owned slaves, she
had always taught them the Christian principles of duty to God and
their masters. She had never gone so far as to teach them to read
the Bible, because she would not break the law prohibiting such
instruction, but her faith in Bible reading did not falter. In the
Protestant tradition, so strong in America, a Christian could best

find communion with God through reading the Sacred Scriptures and absorbing their message. Hence Douglass's outrage at a Virginia law forbidding the teaching of free blacks, for whom the school at Christ Christ and her own school provided the best means of obtaining religious learning. To allow blacks to grow up without reading the word of God placed a terrible burden on black men's souls, but to deny them the solace of Bible study was nothing less than sin. Knowledge of the Bible would not lead to rebellion but would rather teach blacks to accept their fate as Christ had accepted his. In going to court with a Bible in her hand, and especially with the Bible that Rosa had used with her pupils, Douglass demonstrated her confidence that, in opening her school, she had been doing the will of God.

Although Douglass rejoiced in her own self-sufficiency, she regarded charity toward the unfortunate as the heart of her religious beliefs. Neighbors whom she scorned as associates she would willingly help in time of trouble. For example, she once assisted the wife and children of a drunken bully, giving them money to buy food, sheltering them in her home, and nursing one of the children back to health. Her kindness in this instance brought the thanks of Mayor Stubbs. Douglass and Rosa visited their pupils whenever they were sick and thus had ample opportunity to witness the terrible poverty of the free blacks of Norfolk and their desperate need for help in times of crisis.

When one of Rosa's pupils became ill with tuberculosis—consumption in the nineteenth century—they assumed full responsibility for her nursing. The fourteen-year-old girl had been so diligent in her studies that Douglass had feared that "her close application to her books would injure her health." The Douglasses grieved to see her ill, and when she finally grew too sick to come to school, they went to her home, "a tottering negro hovel, . . . a miserable apology for a human habitation," and found the girl lying on "a wretched bed, supported by some boards and broken chairs." The mother, also suffering from tuberculosis, could not earn money even for food. As there was no one else to help the family, the Douglasses sat by the girl's bed night after night. On the night that she died, the girl whispered, "I thank you, Mrs. Douglass and Miss Rosa, for all you have done for me: you have taught me to pray and to read my Bible, and I shall never read it again; you must pray for me before you go." They prayed together, said Douglass, "and we left her in a quiet slumber, from which she awoke only, as we trust, in heaven." The Douglasses provided clothes for her burial and made all the funeral arrangements. Six of her schoolmates, dressed in white, served as pallbearers, the other students followed the coffin to the cemetery, and Douglass, "in a close carriage," brought up the rear. Assuming that her presence at the black girl's funeral transgressed acceptable Southern behavior and scandalized "the good people of Norfolk," Margaret Douglass claimed that her persecution at the hands of her neighbors dated from that incident.[56]

The religious leaders of the city showed no interest in the plight of free blacks living in poverty, and Douglass expressed contempt for so-called Christians who made no effort to assist the ill and destitute. Private charity became essential when government help for the poor did not exist, but where then were the Christians who should be following Jesus's precepts of ministering to the poor? The school at Christ Church was the only indication of religious concern for free blacks, and when members of the church, on the witness stand, denied the school's existence, Douglass could no longer restrain her wrath and demanded to know why free blacks were treated as outcasts, as "dumb brutes."[57]

It was in her refusal to remain silent that Douglass departed from the Southern conception of the role of a lady in society. Although she had long been aware of the plight of blacks in the South, and especially free blacks, she had pursued the path customary to Southern gentility and had given private assistance rather than speaking out on public issues. But under attack, she fought back valiantly, proclaiming her innocence and refusing to retreat, even though she protested, "I did not desire to step out of the natural sphere of my sex."[58] Was she herself surprised at her audacity and at the ease with which she abandoned the role she had played for so many years? Perhaps, during those solitary years, as she sat sewing in her little house, largely cut off from human companionship, she had built up a reserve of strength and resentment that made it impossible for her to maintain silence any longer. Thus she assumed a new role that took her far beyond the bounds of Southern ladylike conduct. While she continued to emphasize her good breeding, the judge, in sentencing her to jail, saw her as a revolutionary whose dangerous statements in court made punishment imperative.

If, in her statement to the court, she did not go so far as to condemn slavery, she nevertheless dared to attack the Southern treatment of blacks in general and free blacks in particular. The South, especially defensive about slavery in the decade of the 1850s, could not tolerate Margaret Douglass's plain speaking. When the judge criticized her clear pronouncement of her feelings about blacks, he was indicating the extent of her infringement of Southern propriety.

Although she detested the notoriety of having her name in the newspapers and knew that her decision to act as her own counsel and to speak frankly would attract publicity, she was unable to remain silent.

She could not afford to retain a lawyer, but she anticipated an offer of assistance from one of the many lawyers who were members of Christ Church: "I thought that in that city of churches, some one, at least among the religious part of the community, would come forward and offer me sympathy and advice without being solicited therefor; but will my readers believe me when I say, that not one solitary individual thus manifested the least interest in the matter."[59] To expect aid from a community to which she had never really belonged was perhaps unreasonable. Nonetheless, the indifference of her neighbors wounded her pride and undoubtedly made her afraid for the future. Yet, once again, her isolation served to increase her resolution. She determined to prove to the entire city that she could endure the worst. She would not be a weak, helpless female in the court action. Neither would she show fear while defending herself in court, any more than she had when, arriving in Norfolk, she was faced with the necessity of supporting herself and her daughter. As both workwoman and gentlewoman, she resolved to demonstrate to the city her strength and self-sufficiency.

Her recognition of men's weaknesses was one of the sources of her strength. The summons to appear in court stated that Douglass and Rosa had acted "against the peace and dignity of the Common-wealth of Virginia." How could "a poor weak woman," she mocked, threaten the state: "Were not the subject too serious, one might venture to laugh at the idea of the fearful perils to which that dignified and aristocratic State was subjected, by the fact that a few little negro boys and girls had learned that famous sentence 'In Adam's fall we sinned all.'" For some time she was confident that she would not be prosecuted: "I could not believe that men who boasted of their

talents and benevolence could be so blinded by their attachment to
their peculiar institution as to farther irritate a matter that would
...prove disgraceful to them and to their State."[60]

Shortsighted or not, the officials of Norfolk pursued the case,
prosecuting Douglass in spite of her sex. She in turn felt no respect
for the men she called to the witness stand. She ridiculed John
Williams, clerk of the court, noting that he "took the stand with a
pallid countenance, and quivering lip." Her comments about William W. Sharp were even harsher: "Oh, brave Mr. Sharp! You will
henceforth be remembered in Norfolk as having crept under the
ladies' aprons in order to shelter yourself from the eye of the insulted
law." As she looked back on her ordeal in Norfolk, she lamented:
"Alas! for the boasted honor and honesty of the old Virginia
nobility."[61]

She reserved her sharpest anger, however, for the Southern men
whom she saw as responsible for miscegenation. During her trial
she spoke of this problem with extraordinary frankness and later
wrote about it at length. Although all Southerners were aware of
white-black sexual relations, the subject was rarely discussed in public, especially by Southern women. But Margaret Douglass was the
exception, speaking of miscegenation with the passion of a personal
crusade. Accordingly, she first described the pupils in Rosa's school
as "little sable scholars," but then added:

Sable, did I say? No, not all; for in many cases the difference could scarcely
be perceived between them and white children. Yes, Mrs. Douglass "con-
descended" to teach free black men's children, and free white men's children—some of the latter being, very probably, among her real persecutors![62]

She refuted the Southern belief in black ingratitude, adding, "What
gratitude does that child owe to his own father, who coldly sells him
as his slave?"

Douglass was convinced that the laws prohibiting the instruction
of blacks had their origin in miscegenation and the consequent desire
to prevent black awareness of the extent of what she termed "amalgamation": "Nature herself often rebels against what instinct teaches
even the most degraded negro to be inhuman and devilish, and if to
this were added the light of intelligence afforded by even the com-
monest instruction, wo [sic] to the darling system of this offspring

of the institution of slavery." She saw miscegenation as "the one great evil hanging over the Southern slave States," the cause of "the vast extent of ignorance, degradation, and crime that lies like a black cloud over the whole South."[63] According to Douglass, the custom affected every level of society, destroying the domestic happiness of white mothers and daughters, as well as the morals of black women. Her bitterness on this subject had no bounds:

Is it to be supposed that the ordinary teachings of nature do not tell the sable sons and daughters of the South that this custom is inhuman and ungodly? Is not chastity a natural instinct, even among the worst savage nations of the earth? . . . The female slave . . . knows that she is a slave, and as such, powerless beneath the whims or fancies of her master.

The slave woman's sense of degradation extended in turn to all members of her family, developing "roots of bitterness which are destined to grow into trees whose branches will sooner or later over-shadow the whole land." "Southern Sultans" was the way Mrs. Douglass described slaveholders who tried to keep blacks in "utter ignorance and degradation," in order to hide their own depravity. For if the blacks read the Bible and worshipped God, they would feel "a deeper horror of this great wickedness," and if they learned to read and write, such "mental and moral improvement" might increase their distaste for "this gross system of sensuality and licentiousness."[64]

If, on the other hand, blacks learned true Christianity through study and through the example of sincerely Christian masters, Margaret Douglass was convinced that there would be no danger of rebellion and that "the South would become the very garden of the Lord." "But when a man, black though he be, knows that, at any moment, he is compelled to hand over his wife, his sister, or his daughter, to the loathsome embraces of the man whose chains he wears, how can it be expected that he will submit without the feelings of hatred and revenge taking possession of his heart?"[65]

Douglass's prescription for the South, then, was not an end to slavery, but an end to white sexual license and the development of an educated, profoundly Christian group of Southern blacks. She did not seek equality for blacks, "socially, politically, or even morally," for she believed in white superiority: "To the sinew, the nerve, the strong arms, the moral and physical courage, and the genius of the Anglo-Saxon race, is the world indebted for the grand spectacle we now present as a great, happy and prosperous people." Because Caucasians were the "most godlike" of people, she would not consider educating blacks "as rivals or competitors of my brothers and sisters of a superior race." In her view, whites were "the authors of all in the arts and sciences that contributes most to man's more refined tastes, pleasures, and ambition," and her exercise in Christian charity in teaching blacks to read was simply an effective way of assuring that blacks accepted their status without complaint, as God willed.[66] What the South needed was more Christian charity and more sexual self-control.

Margaret Douglass, then, transcended the customary perception of a Southern gentlewoman. While, intellectually, she shared Southern prejudices against blacks, from a sentimental point of view she was able to overcome those attitudes because of her desire to enlighten black children's minds with the principles of Christianity. She was strong, proud, pious, sarcastic, and bitter. When her reputation was threatened, she fought to preserve it, and when her pride was wounded, she responded with courage and competence. In 1865 the *Philadelphia City Directory* listed a Margaret Douglass, giving her occupation as "gentlewoman."[67] If this was the heroine of Norfolk, then she had achieved one of her dreams.

III

An examination of the milieu in which Douglass's school existed demonstrates the insuperable obstacles she faced. On moving from Charleston to Norfolk, Margaret Douglass exchanged one Southern port city for another. Norfolk, because of its location at the mouth of the Chesapeake Bay, had a long history of commerce, but it could boast neither the culture nor the fame of Charleston. In the year that Douglass arrived, Norfolk, by act of the state legislature, proudly became a city.[68] As in all port towns, the people of Norfolk complained of the danger of plagues, such as cholera, being brought into the area by sailors. But, as in all Southern ports, the plague that most worried the population was the escape by ship of fugitive slaves, with sailors' connivance.

Nevertheless, Norfolk's survival depended on trade, and the local newspapers carried detailed information on the arrival and departure of ships from all over the world. Yet, in the decades before the Civil War, the building of railroads into the city, rather than ocean shipping, had primarily obsessed the merchants of Norfolk. At that time the state of Virginia extended to the Ohio River, and Norfolk anticipated that, with the proper railroad connections, it might become the trade center of the entire state, an eventuality that did not, in fact, materialize.

Long before the advent of the railroad, Virginia had established trade patterns that hindered Norfolk's growth. The navigability of Virginia's rivers had led to the establishment of towns at the fall line: Petersburg on the Appomattox River, Richmond on the James, Fredericksburg on the Rappahannock, and Alexandria on the Potomac. Oceangoing vessels loaded on goods brought by wagon or barge to the fall line towns, to Norfolk's economic loss. In the early part of the nineteenth century, Virginia invested heavily in canal construction, designed to bypass the falls in the rivers and to maintain the existing commercial supremacy. With the development of the railroad, Norfolk had high hopes that its time had finally come, but the railroads also terminated at Richmond, Petersburg, Fredericksburg, or Alexandria, so that the old trade patterns persisted. Furthermore, the construction of the Baltimore and Ohio Railroad funneled much of the traffic of western Virginia to Baltimore, causing that city to grow by leaps and bounds. In the decade of the 1850s, Norfolk's railroad connection with North Carolina at last became a reality, and at the time that Margaret Douglass went to prison, the merchants of the city were planning for greatly increased trade.[69] The Civil War began before the long-anticipated prosperity could be realized, so that though Norfolk prided itself on being a city, it remained small and unimpressive. In 1850 Norfolk had 14,326 inhabitants, whereas the population of Charleston was 42,985 and that of Baltimore, 169,054.[70]

Visitors to Norfolk at this time found it an ugly, dirty city, periodically suffering from epidemics of yellow fever and cholera, and with notably foul slums. It appeared to be a city totally lacking in civic pride, but in the years of Margaret Douglass's residence there, Norfolk's citizens began serious efforts to improve its appearance, with especial regard to the paving and lighting of streets. The Norfolk Gas Light Company gave its first exhibition of gas lighting in October

1849,[71] and by 1851 the *Norfolk Directory* reported gas lighting for twelve streets, the City Hall, some churches and hotels, and many private buildings.[72] At the same time the city paved a number of streets in the center of town,[73] although streets in general remained muddy or dusty. When Margaret Douglass looked for an inexpensive place to live, she stood no chance of finding housing on a paved street.

Norfolk citizens supported the construction of imposing public buildings in attempts to beautify their city. In 1847 work began on a new city hall, with offices for the mayor and the sheriff, council chambers, and courtrooms. Judge Baker presided over the first sessions of the court held in the new building.[74] Mechanics' Hall opened the same year, and for the first time Norfolk had a large room for exhibitions, concerts, fairs, and lectures.[75] Two years later the city council took a major step toward cleaning up the streets by adopting a "cow law," requiring that cows be kept in enclosures or driven outside the city limits. The ordinance, however, passed only with considerable opposition.[76]

In 1840 the Norfolk Academy began the construction of elegant new quarters, described as "one of the finest school buildings in the country."[77] The academy, which had been organized in 1787 as a classical school for boys, had been unsuccessful in attracting either good teachers or sufficient pupils. With the new building, however, interest revived, and some of the leading citizens of Norfolk served as trustees of the academy, reflecting the town's growing concern with education. In 1849 the Norfolk Female Institute was established.[78] Like other schools in Virginia, these Norfolk institutions accepted only white, fee-paying students. Black children, even if they had been able to pay the fees, would not have gained admission to any school in Norfolk. Christ Church Sunday school, with its limited program, was the sole exception. Although African churches in the South often taught reading and writing as well as religion,[79] none of the four black churches in Norfolk offered any instruction.

Because religion played an important role in the life of the people of Norfolk, the beautification of the city began with the construction of ornamental churches with steeples and spires. By the middle of the nineteenth century, all the major denominations had built churches: Episcopal, Methodist, Baptist, Presbyterian, and Roman Catholic; and on Sundays fourteen churches were open to attract the faithful.[80] Blacks had three Baptist churches and one Methodist church,[81] but their buildings were surely not elaborate and were probably not included in the total of fourteen. The Sunday school movement had become a crucial aspect of religious life in the city. Norfolk celebrated Independence Day in 1847 with a "large Sabbath-school procession, numbering about one thousand children, besides the teachers." Three of the town's leading citizens, including Walter H. Taylor, one of Margaret Douglass's witnesses, organized the parade.[82]

Taylor's leadership of the Sunday school movement indicates a close involvement of Christ Church with the religious life of Norfolk. Many members of the ruling class of the city attended Christ Church, where pew rental or ownership was very expensive. In 1847 pews rented for $20 to $40, and the following year, at auction, sold for $175 to $400.[83] The willingness of such a church to allow the instruction of blacks in its Sunday school clearly demonstrates that members of the upper class in the South could enjoy a moral leeway unavailable to ordinary mortals. As long as the leaders of the city quietly engaged in their charitable activities in the Sunday school, not a word was said, and the eyes of the city remained closed to the existence of black instruction. But an outsider's demand for the rights accorded the city's elite did not meet with the same degree of tolerance.

Margaret Douglass never really understood the difference between her venture and that of the Christ Church Sunday school. However, the city's leaders most certainly did, and their inconsistency seems to have made some of them acutely uncomfortable. Eight lawyers at once requested from Judge Baker a copy of his decision on the Douglass case: "The undersigned, members of the Norfolk Bar, earnestly ask at your hands a copy of the judgment this day pronounced in the case of Commonwealth vs. Douglass, for publication."[84]

Heading the list was Tazewell Taylor, one of the most important men in Norfolk. He was president of the Norfolk Savings Bank, a member of the state constitutional convention of 1850-51, vice president of the Colonization Society of Virginia, a member of the board of trustees of the Norfolk Academy, and the owner of the most expensive pew in Christ Church.[85] Martha Taylor taught in the Christ Church Sunday school and was one of the lady managers of the Female Orphan Society.[86] Among the other signers of the letter,

Mordecai Cooke was a colonel in the local militia; William T. Hendren was clerk of the United States District Court; Simon Stubbs was mayor of Norfolk at the time of Douglass's arrest; and Hunter Woodis, a director of the Farmer's Bank and a captain in the militia, had been elected mayor in June 1853.[87] Surely these leading citizens sought to reassure themselves and the people of Norfolk that the sentence upon Douglass was just. Judge Baker's decision appeared in full in the Norfolk newspapers at the time that Douglass's prison term was coming to an end.[88] The lawyers' concern did not keep her out of jail, but their letter reveals an unease in that Southern city about the Douglass case.

Margaret Douglass broke the law prohibiting the instruction of free blacks at a time when Norfolk and the neighboring towns of Portsmouth and Newport News were becoming increasingly alarmed about black indiscipline and especially about the growing number of slaves escaping to the North. Slave owners believed that free blacks, by exerting an evil influence over their slaves, encouraged them to flout authority and finally to run away. This view resulted in a public outcry for the expulsion of free blacks from the state, directed at the Virginia legislature. Norfolk county citizens, at a meeting on November 2, 1852, described free blacks as "that bane of society" and a "serious evil" of mounting significance. According to popular opinion, free Negroes caused "great injury to our slaves, whose daily avocations bring them more or less under the degrading influence of this miserable species of our inhabitants." The citizens endorsed a resolution urging the legislature to "adopt some speedy and salutary redress whereby we may get rid of our free negro population."[89] Similar meetings in other parts of the state produced similar resolutions,[90] and a bill for the removal of all free blacks from the state was introduced into the Virginia legislature in January 1853.[91] Though the bill never became law, its introduction demonstrates the intense concern within the state about the status of the free black population.

In Norfolk the tax structure also showed clearly the popular opposition to free blacks. Whereas the tax on each free white male over the age of twenty-one and on every slave, male or female, over the age of sixteen, was two dollars, every free black male over the age of sixteen had to pay three dollars in tax. White females were not taxed, but "every female free negro over the age of sixteen years" was forced to pay a tax of two dollars.[92] The city council wanted to make life as hard as possible for free blacks, and when one considers their terrible poverty, such a charge was plainly punitive.

Norfolk citizens worried a great deal about what they saw as black insubordination and indiscipline, perpetually failing to differentiate between free blacks and slaves. When a young slave was arrested for carrying "powder, ball and caps," *The American Beacon* reminded its readers that blacks often carried, with impunity, "pistols, dirks and knives."[93] In the mayoral campaign of 1853, the lack of discipline became a campaign issue, the opponents of Mayor Stubbs citing "a spirit of insubordination, until latterly unknown, . . . among our colored population." The crisis required "decided and stringent measures to be taken for the enforcement of our police regulations," rather than "sentimentality or sickly sympathy."[94] In a letter to the editor of *The American Beacon* in August 1852, a writer who signed himself "Discipline" lamented the lack of restraint among the blacks of Norfolk. He directed his wrath at slaves for the most part, charging that they dressed in "Silks or Satins, broadcloth or bonnets," and walked three or four abreast, thus forcing whites off the sidewalks. "Discipline" went on to say that if blacks were to be allowed on sidewalks at all, then they should be forced to walk single file. Furthermore, they should not be permitted to wear "bonnets, or silks, or to wear canes or umbrellas, or to smoke pipes or segars [*sic*] in the streets." The writer then insisted that white men should be forbidden to "stand" for free blacks, demonstrating that his distrust of blacks encompassed both slave and free.[95]

A still greater source of dismay for the white population lay in the development of secret societies among the blacks of Norfolk, which "Discipline" believed were the real cause of racial trouble:

Who supported these secret societies that are banded together as associations for "Nursing the sick and burying the dead?" Is it known to you that these members of these societies (of which I believe there are no less than four) have secret signs and pass words? Is this lawful? Is it not contrary to the spirit, if not the letter of the statute? Is it not to the last degree imprudent to permit these large assemblages of men and women? with[*sic*] or without signs and pass words? When is it to end? look [*sic*]to it, if you would avoid a bloody issue.[96]

The existence in Norfolk of a "colored Lodge of Masons" was revealed when a black man consulted a white man about possible legal action against the lodge's treasurer, who had robbed the members of all their funds, amounting to $37. Because the lodge was illegal, the Masons did not dare to bring the matter to the attention of the mayor, who probably would have acted against the lodge, rather than the thief. The *Beacon* reported the story and used the occasion to emphasize to its readers that the various black secret societies met regularly and had adopted "secret signs and tokens." In a time of "impudence and insubordination among this class of our population," the blacks' societies appeared a considerable threat to the white establishment, which naturally advocated their dissolution.[97]

In another edition, the editor of the *Beacon* reflected upon the nature of the secret societies and their purpose in raising funds. He concluded that all black societies should be subjected to investigation, and if allowed to continue, "should be compelled to have a white person or persons among their managers." If close scrutiny revealed their intentions to be respectable, then there were "a number of benevolent white persons in the city who would willingly superintend their affairs for them."[98] Although the newspaper stories did not clarify the legal status of the membership of these organizations, they implied that both slave and free blacks belonged to the secret societies. This mixed membership seemed to increase the threat, and as the number of escaping slaves grew, so did the pressure for extreme measures against the entire black population.

Slaves constantly escaped from Norfolk and the neighboring towns of Portsmouth and Newport News. On November 4, 1853, a newspaper reported that two slaves from Norfolk and two from Portsmouth had successfully escaped, supposedly "in some vessel going North," while on March 28, 1854, a newspaper recounted that eight Portsmouth slaves had run away from their masters. Three slaves working at the National Hotel in Norfolk succeeded in escaping in March 1854. Five fled in April 1854, followed by three more, until the *Beacon* called slave escapes "a daily occurrence." In fact, at the end of March 1854, the *Beacon* claimed that the Norfolk area had lost more than $30,000 in slave property within the past twelve months. "It is time," wrote the *Beacon*, "that the South should take some action. Forbearance has ceased to be a virtue."[99]

It was the general opinion in Norfolk that the regular flight of slaves to the North stemmed from the presence in the city of agents determined to entice them away. The *Beacon* warned that the citizens of Norfolk must use "vigilance and action . . . to detect them," for the "abolition thieves" were in the very heart of the city.[100] The people of Portsmouth held a public meeting "to devise way[s] and means, by which the frequent escape of slaves from this port to northern states might be prevented," and after some discussion a committee was selected to draw up a plan to implement the group's recommendations, an action the *Beacon* applauded.[101]

"A Slaveholder," in a letter to the *Beacon*, urged that Norfolk imitate Portsmouth in seeking out the "abolition thieves, who no doubt are carrying on their nefarious designs in our very midst." He believed that slaves were escaping, not daily but hourly, because of an elaborate scheme of "the great Underground Railroad" to smuggle slaves onto oceangoing vessels from oyster boats that moved freely through coastal waters. While a state law requiring the examination of all small boats would help to frustrate this plot, the people of Norfolk could jointly take effective action:

There are no doubt many persons among us who are secretly conniving at and aiding our servants in escaping to the North, and we would say to every slaveholder, have your eye on all suspected persons—mark their movements well, and woe be to the emissary who is caught tampering with our slaves! No penitentiary will secure him from the wrath of an outraged populace. The penalty in his case will be fearful, swift and sure! We need a terrible example to serve as a warning to others. . . . The hanging of a few abolition fanatics might prove of . . . importance to our slaveholding community.[102]

"A Citizen," writing to the same newspaper on April 25, 1854, lamented the weakness of the federal government, whose agents would not or dared not enforce the law regarding the return of fugitive slaves. The author asserted that the situation had reached crisis proportions and required either the liberation of all slaves or the invocation by the state of Virginia of the "higher law" of self-preservation: "to pass inspection laws to guard its citizens from fraud, robbery or violence." "A Citizen" knew of the existence in Norfolk of "abolition agents," white as well as Negro, who took advantage of the constant arrival of ships bound for Northern ports.

They functioned through the black churches and secret societies, "the sources of all this mischief," which "should at once be broken up." Every black preacher should be required to have a certificate of good character from the mayor. "A Citizen" suggested many additional regulations for all blacks. "No negro, slave or free, should be permitted to pass after ten o'clock, without special permission in writing for that night only, and the object for the permit stated on the pass." Any Negro belonging to any organization other than a church should be whipped, "and all debates in negro churches strictly prohibited." Negro-manned oyster boats should not leave the harbor after dark, and all boats sailing at night should be thoroughly searched. The city ought to deny residence to any free black coming to Norfolk; black sailors arriving on Northern vessels should be lodged in jail; and a free black coming from the North, not attached to a ship, should be liable to be sold "by a summary process." The city needed to organize a secret police force, and the state should authorize a patrol of all the rivers and harbors in Virginia, with authority to search every vessel bound for a Northern state. In "Citizen's" opinion, only these extreme measures would prevent the loss of half a million dollars a year if the successful escape of slaves continued at the current alarming rate.[103]

In such an atmosphere, when slaveholders felt threatened by secret enemies who consistently eluded their grasp, how could Margaret Douglass dare to voice the wrongs suffered by the black population! Wrongs, indeed! The wrongs, in the eyes of the people of Norfolk, were all being done to the slaveholders, who were increasingly in a panic about secret enemies. Abolitionists were everywhere, and they were not easily identified. It is a wonder that Douglass did not receive a more severe sentence, when angry slaveholders were calling for lynching parties to deal with antislavery troublemakers.

Consequently, the Norfolk newspapers agreed with the justice of her jail sentence. The *Daily Southern Argus* admitted that "it was revolting to the citizens to have a woman imprisoned in our jail." But when Douglass used such expressions as "'to glory in works of benevolence and charity to a race down-trodden,'" then "sympathy departed, and in the breast of every one rose a righteous indignation towards a person who would throw contempt in the face of our laws, and brave the imprisonment for 'the cause of humanity.'" The decision of Judge Baker was "cogent and pungent":

We have in this town suffered much from the aggression of Northern foes, and a strong cordon must encircle our domestic institutions. We must preserve from discord and angry passions our firesides and homesteads. We must preserve inviolate the majesty of laws necessary for the protection of our rights.[104]

It was necessary, declared the *Argus*, to "put a check to such mischievous views as fell from her lips . . . sentiments unworthy a resident of the State, and in direct rebellion against our Constitution."[105] The *Beacon* thought so well of its rival's editorial on the Douglass case that it reprinted it word for word,[106] illustrating the united front that the press presented in the face of any perceived threat to established black-white relations.

Northern newspapers had also followed the Douglass case with great interest. The *New-York Daily Times** published a lengthy editorial attacking the law under which Douglass was found guilty and reprinted a story from the *Norfolk News* reporting her efforts to defend herself in court.[107] The *Times* observed that it would be difficult to persuade anybody except a politician that teaching children to read was "an offense against morality or the public good." The law against black instruction should have been "utterly abhorrent to the chivalry of the Old Dominion," for to argue that such a law was necessary for the maintenance of slavery "would be the most formidable attack that could be made upon the institution itself." While Southerners had insisted that the antiliteracy laws "were universally a dead letter," the action against Douglass had proved otherwise. The *Times* believed that slavery was a local institution, against which neither Congress nor the Northern states could take any action. It was up to the Southern states, therefore, to indicate that they were "inclined to take any steps toward discharging" their duties to ameliorate slavery. Then the North would be equally willing to halt "the violent movements in their midst" that so alarmed the South. "But such incidents as the recent trial at Norfolk," the editor stressed, "are formidable stumbling-blocks in the way of those who desire to promote rational and harmonizing views upon this sub-

---

*The *New-York Daily Times* later became the *New York Times*.

ject."[108] For the *Times*, then, the Douglass case had profound significance for future North-South relations.

The *Daily Express* of Petersburg, Virginia, could not allow the comments of the *Times* to stand uncontested. In a long article, reprinted by the *Times*, the Petersburg paper lamented the inability of the New York paper to take "a just or impartial view of the question of Slavery." The *Times* should realize that "the schemes of northern incendiaries" forced Virginia to adopt antiliteracy laws "as an act of necessity in self-defence." If there had been "no attempts on the part of our kind and affectionate brethren of New England, to induce the negroes to cut our throats," then there would have been no basis for such laws. The flood of abolitionist literature had aroused the literate slaves to insubordination and even murder. The South could not be blamed for taking measures to protect itself.[109]

The *National Anti-Slavery Standard* reprinted much of Judge Baker's decision and commented on the case:

It is a practical illustration of the popular religion (we will not call it Christianity) of this country, and also of the prevailing Democracy, which boasts of bearing the brand of the Old Dominion. Let it go forth to the world as an irrefragable proof that the Abolitionists, in all that they have said of the inconsistency and the shame of their country, have fallen short of the truth. Let it be published far and wide to awaken the astonishment and indignation of the civilized world![110]

In its Independence Day issue in 1857, the *Standard* printed a satirical piece, signed "L," based on the Douglass case, which showed Douglass being tried by Judge Scalawag and prosecuted by Victor Vagabond. The indictment read:

The Grand Jurors empannelled and sworn to inquire of offences committed in the body of said County on their oath present, that Margaret Douglass, being an evil-disposed person, not having the fear of God before her eyes, but moved and instigated by the Devil, wickedly, maliciously, and feloniously, . . . did teach a certain black girl named Kate to read in the Bible, to the great displeasure of Almighty God, to the pernicious example of others in like case offending, contrary to the form of the statute in such case made and provided, and against the peace and dignity of the Commonwealth of Virginia.

In "L's" account of the trial, Douglass was "arraigned as a necessary matter of form, tried, found guilty of course." Judge Scalawag admonished her that in teaching a slave girl to read the Bible, she was "guilty of one of the vilest crimes that ever disgraced society." Scalawag declared, "No enlightened society can exist where such offences go unpunished," and he sent her to jail without "one solitary ray of sympathy." The *Standard*'s correspondent commented that, on such a happy outcome, "the Doctors of Divinity preached each a sermon on the necessity of obeying the laws," while some Northern newspapers rejoiced. He added, "Let us do nothing to offend our Southern brethren."[111]

In the meantime, *The Liberator* reported that while Margaret Douglass was serving her sentence, a Quaker woman preached a sermon in Norfolk in which "She condemned slavery very pointedly":

A devoted pious woman in jail . . . did not deter this Quaker woman from declaring her testimony against slavery, right in the face of the slaveholding jailors of Mrs. Douglas [*sic*]. The women are a great trouble to our Norfolk neighbors. If they want peace, they must expel all Christian women . . . from the city.[112]

In the public argument over her case, Douglass's justification, that she had never taught slaves to read and had no intention of doing so, became completely obscure. Douglass accepted the reality of slavery and even the laws against slave instruction; her concern was solely with free blacks. By the decade of the 1850s, however, neither North nor South could accept such distinctions. The argument was over slavery, and Douglass became a factor in that great sectional controversy, her case providing yet further ammunition in the Northern attack on slavery and the Southern defense of the institution. Northern outrage at Douglass's conviction and imprisonment helped to prove the popular Norfolk view that the region and the city were under constant threat from abolitionists. Even as they busied themselves with making their city a commercial center, the people of Norfolk saw no conflict between their dream of future prosperity and their willingness to imprison black sailors, to enslave free blacks coming from the North, or to imprison a Southern woman for teaching black children to read. The South had to defend itself at whatever cost.

NOTES

1. Margaret Douglass, *Educational Laws of Virginia. The Personal Narrative of Mrs. Margaret Douglass, A Southern Woman Who Was Imprisoned for One Month in the Common Jail of Norfolk, Under the Laws of Virginia, for the Crime of Teaching Free Colored Children to Read* (Boston: John P. Jewett and Co., 1854), p. 7.

2. Ibid., p. 8.

3. Ibid.

4. Ibid., p. 9.

5. Ibid., p. 10.

6. Ibid., p. 14.

7. Ibid., p. 11.

8. Ibid., p. 14.

9. Ibid.

10. Ibid., p. 15.

11. Ibid.

12. Ibid., p. 16.

13. Ibid.

14. Ibid., p. 18.

15. Ibid.

16. Ibid., p. 19.

17. Ibid.

18. Ibid., p. 20.

19. Ibid., p. 21.

20. Ibid., pp. 21–22.

21. Ibid., p. 25.

22. Ibid., p. 23.

23. William S. Forrest, *The Norfolk Directory, for 1851-1852: Containing the Names, Professions, Places of Business, and Residences of the Merchants, Traders, Manufacturers, Mechanics, Heads of Families, Etc.* (Norfolk: n.p., 1851), p. 87.

24. Ibid., p. 85.

25. Douglass, *Educational Laws of Virginia*, p. 26.

26. Forrest, *Norfolk Directory*, p. 67.

27. Douglass did not specify Sharp's first names, and *The Norfolk Directory* lists two Sharps. According to "Christ Church, Norfolk City, Vestry Minutes, 1828-1905," Virginia State Library, Richmond, Virginia, p. 108, William W. Sharp was a member of Christ Church.

28. Douglass, *Educational Laws of Virginia*, p. 30.

29. Forrest, *Norfolk Directory*, p. 85.

30. Ibid., pp. 85, 91.

31. Ibid., p. 95.

32. Ibid., pp. 90, 91.

33. Douglass, *Educational Laws of Virginia*, p. 30.

34. Ibid., pp. 30–31.

35. Ibid., p. 31.

36. Ibid.

37. Ibid., pp. 31–32.

38. Ibid., p. 33.

39. Ibid., p. 34.

40. Ibid., p. 35.

41. Ibid.

42. Ibid., p. 36.

43. Ibid., p. 37.

44. *The Daily Southern Argus*, Norfolk, Virginia, February 9, 1854.

45. Douglass, *Educational Laws of Virginia*, pp. 45–46.

46. Ibid., pp. 46–47.

47. Ibid., p. 49.

48. *The American Beacon*, Norfolk, Virginia, November 26, 1853.

49. Forrest, *Norfolk Directory*, p. 85.

50. Douglass, *Educational Laws of Virginia*, p. 51.

51. Forrest, *Norfolk Directory*, p. 53.

52. Douglass, *Educational Laws of Virginia*, pp. 9–10.

53. Ibid., p. 48.

54. Ibid., p. 26.

55. Ibid., pp. 22, 36, 45.

56. Ibid., pp. 12–13.

57. Ibid., p. 35.

58. Ibid., p. 26.

59. Ibid., p. 25.

60. Ibid., pp. 22, 23.

61. Ibid., pp. 30, 32, 52.

62. Ibid., p. 14.

63. Ibid., pp. 20, 62–63.

64. Ibid., pp. 64–65.

65. Ibid., p. 65.

66. Ibid., pp. 52–53.

67. A. McElroy, *McElroy's Philadelphia City Directory for 1865* (Philadelphia: Sherman and Co., 1865), p. 196.

68. William S. Forrest, *Historical and Descriptive Sketches of Norfolk and Vicinity, Including Portsmouth and the Adjacent Counties, During a Period of Two Hundred Years* (Philadelphia: Lindsay and Blakiston, 1853), pp. 220–24.

69. Thomas J. Wertenbaker, *Norfolk: Historic Southern Port*, 2d ed. (Durham: Duke University Press, 1962), pp. 166–84.

70. *The Seventh Census of the United States: 1850* (Washington, D.C.: Robert Armstrong, 1853), pp. 221, 258, 339.

71. Wertenbaker, *Norfolk*, p. 133; Forrest, *Historical and Descriptive Sketches*, p. 245.

72. Forrest, *Norfolk Directory*, p. 13.

73. Ibid.

74. Wertenbaker, *Norfolk*, p. 132; Forrest, *Historical and Descriptive Sketches*, pp. 254–56. The 1847 City Hall now houses a museum in honor of General Douglas MacArthur. George Holbert Tucker, *Norfolk Highlights 1584-1881* (Norfolk: The Norfolk Historical Society, 1972), pp. 70–71.

75. Forrest, *Historical and Descriptive Sketches*, pp. 251–52.

76. Ibid., pp. 284–85.

77. Wertenbaker, *Norfolk*, p. 139.

78. Forrest, *Historical and Descriptive Sketches*, p. 245.

79. "Every African church had a Sunday school, and most supported day schools where black children attended classes free or at a minimal charge." Ira Berlin, *Slaves Without Masters: The Free Negro in the Antebellum South*, 2d ed. (New York: Vintage Books, Random House, 1976), p. 304.

80. Forrest, *Historical and Descriptive Sketches*, p. 340.

81. Forrest, *Norfolk Directory*, p. 37.

82. Forrest, *Historical and Descriptive Sketches*, p. 234.

83. "Christ Church, Norfolk City, Vestry Minutes 1828-1905," pp. 86, 92.

84. *Daily Southern Argus*, Norfolk, Virginia, February 9, 1854.

85. Forrest, *Norfolk Directory*, pp. 86, 91, 117; *Journal, Acts and Proceedings of a General Convention of the State of Virginia, Assembled at Richmond, on Monday, the Fourteenth Day of October, Eighteen Hundred and Fifty* (Richmond: W. Culley Printer, 1850), p. 1.

86. Douglass, *Educational Laws of Virginia*, p. 29; Forrest, *Norfolk Directory*, p. 92.

87. Forrest, *Norfolk Directory*, pp. 86, 90, 93; *The American Beacon*, Norfolk, Virginia, June 18, 1853.

88. *Daily Southern Argus*, February 9, 1854; *The American Beacon*, February 11, 1854.

89. *Richmond Enquirer*, Richmond, Virginia, November 19, 1852.

90. Ibid., February 1, 1853, reports meeting in Goochland County, west of Richmond.

91. Ibid., January 14, 1853.

92. *The American Beacon*, April 29, 1852.

93. Ibid., September 21, 1852.

94. Ibid., June 16, 1853.

95. Ibid., August 10, 1852.

96. Ibid.

97. Ibid., September 1, 1852.

98. Ibid., September 21, 1852.

99. *Daily South-Side Democrat*, Petersburg, Virginia, November 4, 1853; March 21, 1854; March 28, 1854; *The American Beacon*, April 19, 1854; March 31, 1854.

100. *The American Beacon*, April 21, 1854.

101. Ibid.

102. Ibid., April 22, 1854.

103. Ibid., April 25, 1854.

104. *Daily Southern Argus*, February 9, 1854.

105. Ibid.

106. *The American Beacon*, February 11, 1854.

107. *New-York Daily Times*, November 29, 1853; December 6, 1853.

108. Ibid., November 29, 1853.

109. *Daily Express*, Petersburg, Virginia, reprinted in *New-York Daily Times*, December 6, 1853.

110. *National Anti-Slavery Standard*, February 8, 1854.

111. Ibid., July 4, 1857.

112. *The Liberator*, March 7, 1854.

3

MYRTILLA MINER

JOSEPHINE F. PACHECO

I

In 1851 Myrtilla Miner arrived in Washington, D.C., to open a school for free black girls. Entirely unfamiliar with the nation's capital, almost without financial resources or influential friends, she had only her fixed resolution to guide her, and yet she succeeded in establishing a school that eventually became a college for the training of black teachers in that city. Although in time she received effective support from many members of the antislavery movement in the United States, her story is essentially one of great tenacity and the determination to overcome adversity. Miner arrived in the nation's capital with only one hundred dollars, given to her by a member of the Society of Friends. With such meager financial resources, she had to find a place to live in a strange city, locate a schoolroom, and recruit pupils for the school. She determined to proceed in her undertaking despite a lack of encouragement from the people she had approached for guidance and support. Yet there is little in the record of her life before 1850 to indicate that she would dedicate herself to the education of black children.

Myrtilla was born on March 4, 1815, in the community of North Brookfield, in Madison County, upstate New York, one of a large family of ten or twelve children. Her parents, Seth and Eleanor Smith Miner, who came from deeply religious New England farming families, were involved in the establishment and maintenance of the First Day Baptist Church in Brookfield. Seth Miner farmed his hilly acres, depending on his hops harvest for a primary crop.[1]

Although Miner bore the unusual name of Myrtilla, she signed herself Myrtle throughout her life and was so called by her friends.

As a child she was frail and was not expected to grow to maturity—
she once described herself as "puny." Her physical frailty persisted
in adulthood; in her twenties, she suffered from a serious back ail-
ment. Her childhood infirmities resulted in the special attentions of
a grandmother who lived with the family and made the delicate little
girl her "pet," entertaining her with stories of Connecticut and of
her life there when she was a girl. Myrtilla rejoiced in her grandmother's care and attributed her own strong sense of independence
to her inspiration. "Little did my . . . father think . . . that those
. . . days & nights when she [his daughter] seemed to be learning
nothing, she was imbibing the principles of independent action, that
were to take her from her home & friends & make her a wanderer
through life."[2]

Her early years reveal the determination and independent spirit
that characterized her adult life. In spite of bad health, she longed
for an education. For a while her father's sister, Ann Miner, kept a
school in the Miner home and was, said Myrtilla, *my first teacher*.[3]
After her aunt left, Miner attended the district school, which was
the sole educational facility that North Brookfield provided. Getting
to school was a strenuous, even hazardous undertaking, for although
the school lay only half a mile from the town, the road was poorly
constructed and lay over steep, semimountainous hills where, according to her recollection, she almost always slipped and fell. The
Miner home housed the town library, such as it was, so that Miner
was able to benefit from reading beyond school texts.[4] Her physical
handicaps did not prevent her from working in the field picking hops
with the other young people of the area,[5] and she probably began
to teach in the neighborhood when she was only fifteen or sixteen
years old.[6]

It is not clear how long Miner continued to teach in North Brookfield, but she had certainly decided to seek further education and
eventually to leave the family home. Her decision represented a
considerable break from her family and upbringing. Ellen O'Connor,
who knew members of the Miner family, wrote that Myrtilla's father
was "a man of uncommon natural ability, but, from his narrow
training, regarded mental culture, beyond a certain limit, as super-
fluous and unnecessary."[7] Furthermore, he assuredly could not afford to finance education beyond the district school level for his
numerous progeny.

In 1839 Myrtilla Miner applied for admission to the Young Ladies Domestic Seminary in Clinton, New York, asking that she have her tuition deferred until she could earn enough to pay the fees. She was at least twenty-four at the time, which indicates that she had spent a number of years either teaching or working at home.[8] The seminary had been established in 1821 by the Reverend Hiram H. Kellogg as a work-study school, with the emphasis on cooperative, manual labor. The school's course of study included reading, writing, spelling, composition, calisthenics, history, and geography. Each girl was expected to work, thus earning a small sum of money that was deducted from her school expenses. Tuition in 1841 was $120 for a full year of schooling. The Clinton Seminary is important in the history of education, for it may have provided the model for the work-study programs of such famous colleges as Mount Holyoke and Oberlin.[9] It also pioneered the admission of black girls to the student body. "I chose to regard and treat them as *pupils*, not as *colored pupils* . . . and allow me here to say, that my confidence was not misplaced," stated the principal and founder.[10] The seminary may have afforded Miner her first contact with blacks.

Ill health continued to plague Miner. She was very sick after she arrived at the school, and her back gave her serious trouble. At some time prior to her arrival at the school, a seton (a kind of drainage device) had been inserted into her back. The resulting lesion had to be dressed and cared for. She had "an awful issue" from the seton, which caused her to hope that her condition would improve. But in fact her illness was so severe that she was unable to engage in the manual labor expected of all the students and especially crucial for the penniless Miner, who had entered the seminary on credit.[11]

Diagnosing disease after the fact and at long distance is a hazardous undertaking, but it is not unlikely that Miner had tuberculosis as a girl, that she recovered or partially recovered, and that the disease lingered into adulthood. She certainly died of tuberculosis, for she exhibited all the classic symptoms of nineteenth-century consumption. It is possible that the drainage from her back came from Pott's Disease (contracted from tubercular cows), with infection of the vertebrae, although "drainage to the skin of the back is unusual."[12] Fortunately, however, by the end of January 1840 her health had improved sufficiently for her to be able to continue her studies and earn enough to pay her expenses. She studied arithmetic, algebra, chemistry, and criticism, and recorded that she was pleased with her progress.[13]

Either at Clinton or earlier, Miner developed a charming prose style, with emphasis on the specific rather than the sentimental, which enabled her to describe a scene with considerable skill and wit. In an essay written at Clinton, she used such florid expressions as "most beautiful and sublime scenery," but she also did not hesitate to relate that her hometown "was called Nigger City on account of its peculiar locality & the queeritiveness of its inhabitants—but now they have made some improvement in many respects & would like to have it called—North Brookfield."[14] In another essay, in which she described the town of Clinton as seen from her window, she gave the most precise detail of the layout of the town and embellished it with flashes of humor: The yards were "ornamented with shrubbery & children." She added that "an old Gentleman & his young wife," who were out in the yard looking at the shrubbery, appeared "as loving as kittens, & it is said they enjoy the *sweets*, as well as *sours*, of connubial bliss." When describing Hamilton College, she wrote: "On a pleasant morning . . . you may distinguish student, & proffessor [*sic*] climbing the Hill, who (though they possess giant souls,) resemble mere mites so insignificant do they appear, when compared with the elevated poplars."[15] Though she employed many of the typical platitudes of romantic writing, she tempered them with a wry approach to life. This mixture of romantic usage and humor would characterize much of her writing throughout her life. When platitudes would serve to move her reader, she used them, but she seldom failed to hew to the realities.

By the spring of 1840, Miner was in a quandary over whether to find a teaching job or stay on at the seminary for another session. Both the director of the school and her doctor advised her not to disrupt the steady physical improvement evident in her condition after a year at the school. Her doctor considered her not yet strong enough to undertake a teaching job, although, since the installation of the seton, she had shown marked progress.[16] Miner finally decided to remain at the Clinton seminary for another term, but in 1841, with the death of her mother, she returned home to take care of the household, though she never gave up hope for further education.[17]

Her belief in the need for educational opportunities for women was so strong that she wrote to Governor William H. Seward of New

York lamenting the lack of facilities for female education.[18] The governor, answering her letter, granted that her views were just and that there was room for improvement. But he added, "I perceive with much pleasure that the state is accomplishing much more than has heretofore been anticipated."[19]

Sometime in 1842 Miner left home once again and moved to Rochester, where she was associated with Clover Street Academy. One account states that she went there as a pupil, with an understanding that she would pay her fees as soon as she had a teaching position; another account has her teaching at the academy.[20] Perhaps the two versions are not contradictory; she may have begun as a pupil and later become a teacher. Certainly by the end of 1842 she was teaching, for she wrote to Governor Seward that she had a class of "40 young Ladies—the loveliest in the land."[21]

In the fall of 1843 she taught in Rochester's District School No. 6. Records exist of payments made to her in October 1843, January 1844, June 1844, and August 1844. Amounts authorized to be paid varied from twenty dollars to seventy dollars. She was therefore the highest paid teacher in the school after the principal.[22] But she was not content. In response to her complaints, her brother wrote:

Since I have seen so much of the wickedness of this world I have felt much inclined to propose to you that we buy a snug little cot in some sheltered vale and there far retired from the noise & *bustle* & folly & sinfulness that so much pervades [*sic*] this terrestrial ball strive to attain unto perfection."[23]

That was not at all what Myrtilla had in mind. At the end of 1843 she wrote once again to Governor Seward complaining of the poverty of educational opportunities in the state. His reply was to be expected: "The present temper of the Legislature and the people is unfavorable to grants of public money even for the purposes of education." He suggested that "public spirited citizens" join together to found "an institution for a thorough system of Female Education." These citizens, he said, should erect buildings, secure a faculty, and set up a "comprehensive scheme of education." Once that had been done, wealthy benefactors would respond and give their patronage. When the foundation had been laid by "private beneficence," then the legislature, if repeatedly asked, might give some assistance. "If this is difficult, then it only shows that the public mind is yet to be enlightened and its action must be waited for." Seward closed by writing: "I sincerely hope that you may find encouragement among your patriotic and public spirited neighbors who, it seems to me, could not over estimate the importance of such an institution to themselves or the benefits it would confer on the country."[24] Ironically, the governor, so quick to suggest that poor citizens should find the money to open a school, neglected to pay the postage on his letter.

Miner made many attempts to leave Rochester, for she was deeply unhappy there. Her relations with her family were strained. Her father wrote that he had news of his daughter only "accidentally," adding that he was glad, nevertheless, that the news of her health continued good. Would she kindly write and let the family know what her prospects were? Seth Miner ended: "I hope you may come again & that we may enjoy your visit more."[25] At this time Myrtilla also suffered a disappointment in love. Her favorite brother, living in New York City, wrote lamenting her "despondency and mourning." He rubbed salt in her wounds by asking:

Is Parsons going to marry you or not? You must not get an idea in your head that you are a going to up and die just out of spite cause nobody wont cry at nothing when youre dead, for likely as not they would and then you would'nt receive any benefit from it. So you see you better not.

And then he added—small comfort: "Now dont begin to talk any more about nobody loving you. What do we care we will love one another and try to love our Savior and our God and he will love us enough to make it all right."[26]

In addition to her personal and family problems, Miner encountered difficulty in finding another teaching job that would enable her to escape from her unfortunate situation. She was desperately unhappy teaching in School No. 6 and disillusioned with Rochester altogether. It seems that she could not get on amiably with the people running the school, for her brother wrote, in an endearing mixture of advice and banter: "Avoid if possible any difficulty with your trustees[;] be as contented as possible[;] do all the good you can and live in peace and die in a pot of grease. I am awful solemn a great deal of the time and terrible wicked all of the time."[27] But her brother's inquiries about a job for Miner in New York City failed, and he wrote that she had little chance of success there: "When a vancancy [sic] occurs there are usually applicants on hand to supply the place and they would not wait for you to come as it would not be necessary. If you were here you might eventually get a place by taking your chance with the rest."[28]

In the summer of 1844 Miner was still in Rochester and still romantically involved with a "loved friend." She considered transferring to Skaneateles, New York, before a fellow teacher visited there and advised against the move.[29] Miner began to take music lessons so that she would be qualified for a teaching position in the South. There is no indication that she wanted to move to the South in order to study slavery at first hand,[30] as she later claimed. She was simply desperate to leave Rochester, and the South seemed a logical place to find a good job, in spite of a relative's warnings of the dangers of such a move:

Now banish forever your notion of going to the south—the treacherous South. She may allure you by the *promise* of a generous reward, but if she gets you within her unhalowed [sic] arms, my word for it she will abuse you; she will repudiate, don't trust yourself to her for an hour. She is deceitfull [sic] above all things and desperately wicked.[31]

A cousin in Providence, Rhode Island, spoke to his friend the school superintendent, who responded enthusiastically to the prospect of Miner's assuming a teaching position there, saying that he wanted to "introduce into this City first rate teachers from a distance that shall bring with them various attainments new and excellent."[32] Miner's cousin's intervention was successful, for in 1845 she moved to Providence.

Family disputes continued. In the winter of 1845, Miner proposed that her young sister Achsa should come to live with her and go to school. Perhaps Miner was already planning that they would undertake a joint teaching project, but if so, they had their father to reckon with. He was vehemently opposed, writing to Achsa: "As to your going to Myrtilla I tell you positively I shall never support you with her for her to have the name of educating her sister[.] I have my hands full other ways & for myself I had doubts whether it is best for you ever to undertake a high school course." She should remain with another sister, where she would learn "habits of industry." "I think there has been an error in training the younger part of the family in that they have not been kept to those habits of industry that would render them more useful & more happy."[33]

By December 1845 Myrtilla Miner had begun to teach in Providence and felt considerable pride in the self-sufficiency that had enabled her to support and care for herself when her family regarded her as an invalid.[34] And yet, although she made many friends in Providence and enjoyed staying with her relatives, Miner seems to have felt no happier there than she had in Rochester. Her persistent restlessness and discontent led her to write to William Bentley Fowle in Boston, asking him to find her another job. By writing to Fowle, Miner demonstrated that she was aware of the current trends in education, for Fowle was one of the most ardent supporters of Horace Mann's schemes for improving the instruction of children and the training of teachers. It was Fowle who helped to revolutionize teaching by introducing blackboards and map drawings into the classroom, as well as the use of scientific apparatus. Most dramatic of all was his support of the abolition of corporal punishment. He published more than fifty school textbooks and in 1842 took over from Horace Mann the publication of the *Common School Journal*. Fowle worked closely with Mann in teacher training throughout the state of Massachusetts.[35]

In June 1846, Fowle replied to Miner's letter, asking if she would be interested in a job in the South, or, as he called it, the "South West." Thus it is clear that, although Miner would later insist that she had always intended to take a job in the South, her move was in reality one of expediency. She was offered a job and she took it. According to Fowle, Miner would receive $500 a year plus board and washing, and would be expected to teach the "higher . . . branches" of English, French, and some music. Fowle thought it a very favorable position, but he had one reservation: "I have a sort of notion that you are an *abolitionist*, let me know." In spite of his own bitter opposition to slavery, Fowle obviously realized that an abolitionist would not be a welcome teacher in the deep South in 1846. Miner had to decide immediately, for the school term began July 20. Fowle assured her that she would have a pleasant voyage to New Orleans and then would travel up the Mississippi River "beyond all reach of the sickly regions."[36]

Miner must have reassured him about her views on abolition, for she accepted the teaching position in the South and made plans to begin an entirely new life. She borrowed money to buy clothes and supplies and was ready to leave for Mississippi "when word came that the school would not open." This mishap left her unemployed and in debt, but according to her biographer, "she met the exigency with her customary courage and integrity." She prevailed on the merchants to take back her purchases, so that at least she would avoid the burden of extra debt. Miner remained unemployed for a year, when she received word that the school in Mississippi had finally opened and she would be welcome there as a teacher.[37] Her friends, believing that the position would never become a reality, expressed surprise when she finally left for the South.[38]

Newton Female Institute, in Whitesville, Mississippi, was located in Wilkinson County, close to the Louisiana line on the Mississippi River south of Natchez. It had been established in 1842. The principal was David L. Phares, who claimed to be a master of arts and a doctor of medicine. His wife served as matron of the school, which ran in two sessions of twenty-two weeks each. Dr. Phares advertised the school as having "superior facilities" and a location that was "unsurpassed" for health. The state legislature would incorporate the school in 1854 as Newton College, and as schools went in the nineteenth century, it boasted considerable stability. The students paid a fairly stiff basic fee for board and candles and extra fees for fuel, furnishings, and washing. Basic tuition included vocal music, but high fees were demanded for ancient and modern languages, instrumental music, drawing and painting, knitting and crewel work, and the making of wax flowers, fruit, and shell work. In other words, Newton Female Institute was a finishing school for the daughters of the well-to-do.[39]

What a tremendous change life in the South must have made for Myrtilla Miner! To a person from upstate New York, the South was a foreign country. And to Miner, who had worked in the fields of her father's farm in spite of her frail health, who had attended school only through a work-study program or by having her bills deferred until she found a job, who had endured a life of frugality, indeed, of poverty, the affluence of her surroundings represented a profound contrast to her previous life. Her young pupils were able to pay ten dollars extra per term to learn knitting and crewel and thirty dollars extra per term for music lessons. In Mississippi Miner herself had two servants to look after her.[40] But she did not find the life appealing, especially since its luxuries derived from slave labor.

After some kind of confrontation, the precise nature of which is not known, Miner wrote a bitter letter to her principal: "Nothing in all I have seen of the 'blessings of slavery' has been able to abate my suffering on account of it one iota." Whenever she was prevented from acting humanely toward the slaves"because I want to treat them like *humans*," then, she wrote, "I wish *to fly*, & as I have often told you, I would willingly break my own neck, if by it I could do any possible good—" But, she went on, "the truth is, there is so much meanness here, the more anyone breaks their neck to do good, the more are they hated."[41]

After such an outburst, one would expect Miner to have been shipped back to the North. But she was most likely an excellent teacher, and her employer, Dr. Phares, was not a stereotypical Southerner. Quite the contrary, for Phares responded to Miner's outraged letter by giving her a copy of his personal plan for emancipation. Miner was impressed enough with Phares's manuscript to send copies to the abolitionist Gerrit Smith and to her old correspondent, former Governor Seward. It seems, then, that her teaching abilities and the open-mindedness of the school's principal contributed to a tolerable degree of contentment. Although she did not get along well with Mrs. Phares, Miner was sufficiently accepted at the school that she was given a birthday party. At this time she wrote her friends that she was comfortable and relatively happy.[42]

Her frank assessment of the moral decay of her surroundings, however, continued unabated. In her letters to friends she included graphic descriptions of the horror and evils of slavery. One of her friends replied: "Your description of the State of Slavery there—the physical, intellectual and social effects of Slavery upon both blacks and whites, males, and females, are what always has, and, inevitably, always *will* follow the existance [sic] of the unjust, unnatural, and barbarous System of chattel slavery." Her friend proposed what Miner would later claim was one of her major aims in the South: "In heavens [sic] name my dear Myrtle do all the good you can— let your light shine, and sweet peace of conscience shall be yours, with your heavenly fathers [sic] blessing. Would that you could teach the *black* children of our Lord as well as his white ones!"[43]

Miner's hatred of the oppressive power of slavery resulted from a deeply held conviction of its inherent wickedness. She wrote William H. Seward that she was "shocked with slavery," and she believed that in Mississippi it assumed "its vilest form." She could not sleep, so troubled was her spirit.[44] In the summer of 1847 she wrote to Dr. Phares, who had gone North for the summer months, to augment his list of books to buy with texts on mental arithmetic, music, chemistry, and botany, which gives some idea of the great variety of subjects that she taught. She also warned him that her health had deteriorated so badly that she might not be able to continue her teaching. She replied to Phares's assertion that it would do her good to get out and visit more with a stinging condemnation of the Southern environment. Wherever she went "horror & despair" went with her, and she said, "I do not *wish* to become any more acquainted with a people who shock me by their injustice, & place such sights & sounds of woe before me—I already know too well, that they do not clothe the naked—feed the hungry, & pity the distressed!" Nor could she find peace at home, for she felt that Phares's own children "must be contaminated, & their consciences & sensibilities perverted" by slavery. Going visiting was even worse, for then she was "doubly impressed with the fallacy" that she could do any good "where evil influences so greatly preponderate." And then she added, "The more I know the more I hate!"[45] Phares must have been very tolerant to permit such a radical woman to teach in his school. Indeed, it is not difficult to imagine what would have become of his establishment if the parents of his pupils had ever discovered his chief teacher's views on slavery. It was her health that finally induced Miner to leave Mississippi, but her principal must have felt relieved to see her go.

When Miner finally began to formulate a theory of emancipation, she used Phares's proposal for the gradual freeing of the slaves in the South as a basis for her own ideas. She was particularly inspired by the cautious approach of her employer's plan, for she deplored demands for immediate emancipation as irresponsible and foolhardy. In a letter to Seward, written at the start of 1848, Miner expressed her preference for a moderate approach to the problem of slavery. She enclosed a copy of Phares's program, to which she hoped that Seward would be receptive, as she considered him "more intelligent on the subject of American slavery than many others" because he was not an extremist "and, therefore, far more likely to be unpred-

judiced [sic] and view the vexed question in its true light." She denied
the ability of the South to accomplish emancipation, for Southerners
"love the power of oppression too well." The North, on the other
hand, "because they emphatically lack the power," could not be
expected to achieve the aims of the abolitionists. Instead of a regional
approach to the dilemma, Miner envisaged a "union of forces,"
whereby the North would use its energies on behalf of certain right-
minded individuals in the South, most especially Dr. Phares. Although Phares's program planned for the freedom of a mere 5,643
slaves over a period of thirty years, Miner enthusiastically endorsed
the scheme and the sincerity of its originator.[46]

The urgency of Miner's commitment to emancipation and the
depth of her admiration for her principal are also reflected in her
letter to antislavery leader Gerrit Smith. She acted upon her belief
in the union of Northern and Southern forces in the abolition of
slavery, enclosing Phares's plan and exhorting Smith to contribute
money to put it into practice. Miner praised Phares as "one of the
truest men—the best of Christians and the most prompt to perform
all his promises, of anyone I have ever met."[47]

Smith responded kindly to the sentiments expressed in the Phares
plan, but had serious reservations about its practical value. He rejoiced that Miner was living with a Christian family: "There are
Christians even among slaveholders, though I think they are com-
paratively few." Smith wished to meet the author of the project, but
he refused to sanction any scheme that kept people in slavery even
for one day longer. In addition, as the state of Mississippi did not
allow slaves to be taught to read, Smith considered the proposal for
the education of slaves infeasible. He preferred his own plan of
buying the freedom of slaves directly: "Within the last year I have
in this way set ten of my fellow beings free from the irons of their
slavery." He added: "Give my love to the worthy gentleman in whose
family you live. You can teach him, as well as I can, that immediate
unconditional emancipation is a more excellent way."[48]

In spite of Miner's admiration for Dr. Phares, trouble arose in
Mississippi. In April 1848 her sister Achsa wrote lamenting Myrtle's
bad luck: "The night word came from Elon [their brother] how
things were I had another crying spell, partly on my own account
and partly on yours—I thought perhaps you would have to lose all
your $300 that you had labored so hard for—"[49] A short period of

relative stability in Miner's life was over, for in the summer of 1848 she left Whitesville and, as she said, "returned to my native hills a miserable skeleton, expecting soon to be released from my frail earthly tabernacle, & lie down to rest."[50] But she survived and had, once again, to secure employment.

Miner returned from Mississippi with even frailer health than before, a firsthand knowledge of slavery, and a glowing recommendation from Dr. Phares that she used for many years:

. . . Miss Myrtilla Miner has for more than twelve months been assistant in the Newton Institute which is under my charge—that most of the time she had the whole care of the School—that she has manifested as a Teacher and a Governess the highest moral character and unusual skill in imparting knowledge, arousing thought and disciplining in the most rational manner, while her character at all times has been most unexceptionable.[51]

In 1849 she began to teach in Friendship Academy, in Allegany County, at a salary of $250 for a school year of forty-two weeks.[52] She borrowed money to send Achsa to Clover Street Seminary in Rochester, in order to carry out her plan for opening a school with her sister as her assistant. But the decision to teach at Friendship proved a disaster.[53] The membership of the board of trustees changed, and they, in turn, appointed a new principal who wanted to employ his friends as teachers. But Miner would not agree to leave. When she was then asked by the new principal to relinquish some of her privileges (their nature is not specified), she refused, and was dismissed with the payment of three weeks' salary. She declined to accept the money and appealed to the trustees, but they would give her no relief. She then approached the Regents of the State of New York, who investigated and decided in Miner's favor, but refused to intervene on her behalf, regardless of the merits of her case. Her only recourse would be to a court of law. The Regents did find, however, that the trustees of Friendship Academy had improperly delegated authority to the principal. Furthermore, they learned in the course of the investigation that the principal had allowed the academy building to be used by traveling musicians, "whose entertainments are characterized as vulgar." The Regents therefore called on the trustees to answer for their actions, withholding financial support from the academy until they were satisfied that the situation had improved. But Miner was left without compensation or a teaching contract.[54]

Once again Myrtilla found herself unemployed and virtually penniless, and at a time when she had assumed the responsibility for her sister's schooling. Miner was thirty-five years old in 1850 and had never held any position for very long. It is possible that she had a difficult temperament and so could not get along with her superiors. On the other hand, Miner's erratic career may represent a typical pattern of job insecurity for female teachers during the nineteenth century. Certainly, the lack of legal safeguards for teachers, combined with Miner's assertive, principled disposition, did not augur well for her career.

But Miner struggled on. She unsuccessfully sought teaching positions for her sister and herself in Canton, Illinois. A relative suggested that they might find openings in Peoria: "There is no female school of high order there such as is adapted to secure the patronage of those wishing to educate their daughters." He proposed that the sisters should go west in October 1850.[55] But before October came, Achsa had died, apparently of cholera morbus.[56] Miner was grief stricken. She had planned that they would work together and had supported Achsa both morally and financially in her desire to get an education.

Miner had always had a restless nature; as early as 1849 her friend Maria had urged her not to "dart off in another tangent."[57] With Achsa's death, this characteristic became more pronounced. She grew interested in spiritualism and tried to communicate with her sister through spirit rappings. She thought it significant that Achsa and the reformer and writer Margaret Fuller had died at the same time, and she attempted to reach both of them through the spirits. It probably was at this time that she wrote to the wife of a missionary in Shanghai, asking whether it would be possible for a single woman to move to China. Although the missionary's wife thought it unwise, as there were too many temptations for unattached women, she added that there was no shortage of men looking for wives.[58] Beneath an apparent lack of direction in fact lay a hardening determination to establish a school for black girls, a determination she would later say had grown out of a conversation with Dr. Phares about the education of his slaves. Miner had wanted to teach his slaves, but he reminded her that in the South education for blacks was illegal.

When he inquired if she had ever instructed blacks in the North, she had replied, "Not as a class but only as individuals in white schools." Her principal's response to this would determine the course of her life:

I have often thought that Northern philanthropists have a great field of labor among their own colored people and if they would convince us of their sincerity they should instruct and elevate *them first*. Then when ours are emancipated we may feel that they too may be improved; but at present there is no relief.

Miner said later that at that time she resolved to open a school for black children, "should life and strength and power be granted . . . from above." She could not rest until she had done whatever lay within her power.[59] In the meantime she must continue to look for a position, for she dared not rely solely upon hopes for support of her proposed school, support that she did not, at this stage, receive.

In 1850 Miner began the long process of implementing her ideas by seeking the aid and advice of prominent politicians and abolitionists. According to one account, she had secured a teaching post in the home of William R. Smith, a Quaker of Farmington, New York, near Rochester, and it was he who became her "wise and warm encourager and counsellor."[60] She also wrote once again to Seward, now senator from New York, telling him that ever since her recovery from her most recent illness, she had felt that her "mission on earth had somewhat to do with the oppressed & the afflicted—the cast out & down-trodden *colored race*." She approached Seward in the "spirit of one ready for sacrifice," proposing that she come to Washington "or vicinity" to teach "colored citizens if such will be taught," adding, "if not, white citizens." It seems, then, that she was realistic enough to accept a gradual realization of her dream. Indeed, she asked Seward whether it would be wiser for her to obtain "a situation as governess in some good family" until she had established contacts in Washington, or to begin at once her planned school for blacks. "To the colored citizens of the city of Washington would I gladly feel myself commissioned to bear messages of love, of purity & peace, as a faithful teacher—destitute of those peculiar prejudices which afflict most of my race, & too well worn in sorrow, to fear public scorn or contempt." She hoped to start the school quietly, in order not to arouse "the most timid or fearful," and she firmly believed that a woman would encounter less opposition than a man. Miner told Seward that she had chosen the capital as the location of her school, "believing, if any influence can be felt in behalf of the colored people any where—it can be most felt in the city of Washington." Seward replied that he could give her no advice, for he knew little of the "social condition" of the city. He suggested instead that she get in touch with Mrs. Gamaliel Bailey, the wife of the editor of Washington's antislavery paper, *The National Era*, as she was "a woman of talents and zeal in any good and human work."[61] Miner wrote a letter, not to Mrs. Bailey, but to Dr. Bailey, the editor, but received no reply.

In February 1850, before her sister died, Miner wrote to Gerrit Smith, asking his opinion of her plan for opening a school for black girls in Washington. She told Smith that the idea had been put to her about a year earlier by Asa Smith at the home of his son William R. Smith. Asa Smith had asked her if she would "take charge of such a school when the hoped-for time of establishing it should come." Miner had not given a definite answer, since her health was "far from being restored" after her stay in the South. But now, in 1850, she felt much stronger and "would not fear to undertake so vast a work."

Miner therefore sought the opinion of "the leading abolitionist in our country," for if Gerrit Smith supported the idea of a school for black girls, then she was willing to dedicate herself "on the altar for *teacher*."

No man can fill the station, because *men* may be attacked by men & driven from their posts, but a woman claims lenity from her weakness, & may not be harmed. Few women would willingly throw themselves into a situation where so much opposition & disgrace must be met from the populace—but this I mind not, having lived too long, to deem it injurious.

She believed that she was offering herself for martyrdom: "My hand trembles & refuses to serve me well, as I here transcribe the offering I make of *myself* upon the antislavery altar of my country; but my spirit it is strong, & I sincerely hope it may be accepted." Miner wrote Smith that she had suffered a great deal in the South, "far more than words may tell," but if he thought the plan a good one,

"I will come to you at my earliest convenience, & discuss the time, the manner, & all else involved in so great an undertaking, with that familiarity which is so desirable."[62]

Miner did not send the letter to Gerrit Smith until she had added a second letter containing a cautionary note: The past years had been for her "years of constant struggle" and "great perseverance in overcoming obstacles." Friends in Natchez and St. Louis wanted her to teach for them, and she feared that one day she might have to "accept the lucrative situations offered by Slaveocracy—I have already suffered too much to desire this, & would gladly beg the protection of the Abolitionist of our country, & a situation under their patronage."[63] But Miner received no encouragement from Smith. She said on another occasion that he was more interested in emancipating blacks than in educating them.[64]

She then went to see Frederick Douglass in Rochester, where he was busy putting out his paper *The North Star*. Douglass later wrote that when Miner first arrived with two of her friends, he did not even deign to stop his work. He soon found, however, that he "was in a presence that demanded my whole attention." Miner startled him by announcing that she was on her way to Washington to start a school. Although Douglass initially doubted her seriousness, he said "the doubt in my mind was transient."

I saw at a glance that the fire of a real enthusiasm lighted her eyes, and the true martyr spirit flamed in her soul. My feelings were those of mingled joy and sadness. Here, I thought, is another enterprise, wild, dangerous, desperate, and impracticable, destined only to bring failure and suffering. Yet I was deeply moved with admiration by the heroic purpose of the delicate and fragile person who stood, or rather moved, to and fro before me.

Douglass opposed Miner's undertaking "in all earnestness." She in turn protested that she had lived among slaveholders and had even taught slaves to read in Mississippi. She was not afraid of violence, she said. To Douglass, "the proposition was reckless, almost to the point of madness." He saw "this fragile little woman harassed by the law, insulted in the street, a victim of slave-holding malice, and possibly, beaten down by the mob." But she would not be persuaded. As Douglass put it: "My argument made no impression upon the heroic spirit before me. Her resolution was taken, and was not to be shaken or changed." When he recalled this interview years later, Douglass admitted that he had often reproached himself that he "could have said aught to quench the zeal, shake the faith, and quail the courage of [that] noble woman." But at that time Douglass offered Miner neither help nor encouragement.[65]

Many years later the Unitarian clergyman William Henry Channing remembered that Miner had come to see him in Rochester and had told him of her plan to organize a school for blacks "right under the shadow of the dome of the Capitol in Washington, in order that she might prove to our statesmen the latent capacities and powers of the enslaved Africans." According to his recollection, he encouraged her "to carry out her bold enterprise,"[66] apparently forgetting, however, that in 1850 the Capitol had no dome.

In her drive to realize her goal, Miner wrote to John F. Cook, a black clergyman who ran a school in the District of Columbia. He replied that he was pleased "that there are those who are willing to make sacrifices, with reference to the advancement of our race in *mental moral and religious improvement,* and who are willing to contribute to their qualification for usefulness in this their native country." But he had to admit that he really did not know how to advise her "as anything savouring of abolition (or that might be considered) meets with little or no favor from the inhabitants of this community." He himself, he said, had to be very careful to steer attention away from himself and his efforts as a teacher, in order not to arouse "the indignation of the inhabitants." He urged her instead to consult her white friends: "Anything of the kind would have to be done in and through them principally, as I do not think that any thing I could say or do would contribute in any way to the advancement of such an object, however much I might be in favor of it." If a school could be started, Cook would do whatever he could to help it succeed, for he considered that a "good female school" was greatly needed. But he added, "I think the less people of color . . . have to do with its establishment the better for the object itself, and for you personally." In fact, Cook was sure "colored people" exerted little influence in Washington, having "neither vote nor voice," and he therefore asked to be excused from working on behalf of her school. Nevertheless, "that you and all may be successful under God in whatever you may undertake with reference to the welfare of our race I shall ever pray." Cook assured Miner that her school would not compete with his, as there were more than enough children needing instruction. He added, however, that a site for the school would be difficult to find,[67] and in that judgment he was prophetic.

In May 1851 Miner composed a long letter to the popular novelist Mrs. E.D.E.N. Southworth, asking for help and setting forth her motives, aims, and above all, her faith in the power of education: "I propose nothing new in principle—but only a new mode of acting out an old principle—which is that no race or people can ever enjoy their right without cultivation—& one of the best methods of securing to any oppressed people their God-given—but man-prevented rights, is to elevate them." She hoped to speed the destruction of the institution of slavery by establishing "a beautiful school" for free blacks, "including a class of misses, whose parents shall pledge themselves to permit these daughters to prepare themselves for teachers, & to *teach* after they are prepared." Miner wanted to know from correspondents in Washington whether she could pursue her teaching "undisturbed and undisturbing" and whether she could find a comfortable place to live while she performed what she regarded as a "merciful mission to a degraded people, literally classed with the heathen." Miner was convinced that many blacks were "decidedly intelligent, & possessed of much talent," but she wished them to possess "scientific intelligence, refinement & influence."

Since residing at the far south some time . . . I am more than ever convinced that the colored people will never rise *alone* & without aid—after receiving only oppression & the resulting degradation for so many generations at our hands—& now when it appears to me the time has come the merciful should stretch forth the hand of sympathy and love & employ every just & lawful means to bring them up from the prison house of bondage, & what can I better do than faithfully instruct them?[68]

Southworth replied that she had spoken with several people about the proposed school, "and they think your benevolent scheme utterly impracticable." Although they sympathized with Miner's "philanthropic views," Southworth and her friends concluded that she could not possibly succeed and hoped rather "that the spirit of God may guide you into some practicable road of usefulness and happiness."[69]

Sometime after leaving Friendship because of the conflict with the principal, Miner took a teaching position at Smethport Academy in

Smethport, Pennsylvania.[70] When she left there in 1851, she wrote
back declaring her intention to open "a school for the *colored children*
of Washington." For this enterprise Miner needed no recommendation, except for the "*moral courage* I carry in my own soul." "Still,"
she added,

if they are able in Smethport to give me something *extra*, in the belief that
I did exert an uncommon, healthful influence upon their pupils, intellec-
tually, physically, and morally, I shall cherish and be proud of it, whether
I should ever find occasion to use it or not.

She asked for money so that she could operate the school, at least
for the first term, as a free school, until, she said, she could convince
Washingtonians that she was "no humbug."[71]

Miner finally received her first donation, one hundred dollars,
from Mrs. Ednah D. Thomas of Aurora, New York, a member of
the Society of Friends. Miner begged supplies from her friends:
"Give me anything you have,—paper, books, weights, measures,
etc. I will make each one an object lesson for my girls, explaining
its source, its manufacture, uses, etc."[72] According to Miner's later
accounts, she also received support from the famous preacher Henry
Ward Beecher. Although she had requested aid from only a few,
("for in my ignorance I thought a school could be established in
Washington as well as in any other city, without money"), all whom
she had approached, except for Mrs. Thomas, either refused financial
assistance or actively discouraged her. But after "wearisome days
and visits" she went to Beecher, who, said Miner, "accepted my
faith" and told her that the idea was "too good to fail for want of
means." Beecher told her, "You must go to New England and get
money and we will try to secure books and furniture here."[73] In an
account written at the request of Harriet Beecher Stowe, Miner
wrote: "But your brother H. W. Beecher comprehended my idea &
like a good christian, granted me cordial sympathy, & prompt influence in securing much that was necessary to establish the school."[74]

With Ednah Thomas's money and a promise of aid from Beecher,
Miner determined to go to Washington by the fall of 1851. In October
she received a letter from the capital saying, "I find there may be
rooms and scholars in *various parts of the City* but on all hands it is
thought best that you should *yourself in person* decide when to com-

mence."[75] Miner set out on her great adventure with a hundred dollars in hand, promises of school supplies, no friends in Washington, and nowhere to live, much less a place to establish a school. Her health was poor, and she no longer had the support and companionship of her sister. But she was an experienced teacher, who, according to Frederick Douglass, claimed to have taught blacks in Mississippi, and she was on fire with a sense of mission and a profound conviction of the redeeming properties of education. Thus equipped for the momentous task, Miner believed that she would succeed. If she failed and was martyred in Washington, so be it.

II

When Myrtilla Miner arrived in Washington to undertake the education of black girls, she found the inhabitants of the city concerned about the place of blacks in their community. As a part of what came to be called the Compromise of 1850, the slave trade in the District of Columbia had recently come to an end, though the institution of slavery remained. Southerners warned, however, that the termination of the slave trade in the nation's capital was merely a prelude to an attempt to end slavery throughout the country. Washingtonians, like the people of Norfolk, resented the presence of free blacks and feared that they would incite the slaves to rebellion. The city's laws were designed to limit the number of free blacks, and though there is some question as to how strictly they were enforced, the District required a bond of every free black over twelve years of age and the surety of one white freeholder. Every black applying for residence had to report his arrival within five days or face a fine or a term in the workhouse. "The mayor must give express permission for any public gathering of Negroes, and secret meetings were forbidden."[76] Both Virginia and Maryland had laws prohibiting the entrance of free blacks into those states, and Washington feared that the capital would become the center of black migration. (This, in fact, did not occur; rather, the number of blacks in the District actually declined during the 1850s.)[77] In addition, Washington's neighboring states imposed heavy penalties for the education of any blacks, slave or free. When Frederick Douglass warned Miner against opening a school in the District, he spoke from experience. In his autobiography he recounted the great difficulties that he, a native of

Maryland, encountered in learning to read.[78] Miner would discover that some Washingtonians regarded her school as a device for attracting many free blacks into the District.

Miner's school, however, would not be the first in Washington; facilities for the education of black children had long been present. Almost from the beginning of the new capital, efforts were under way to educate the free blacks in the city. Especially in Georgetown, an older nearby town that would eventually become part of Washington, black children—or more accurately, mulatto children—had attended school with white children. During the first half century of the capital's existence, there were many separate schools for blacks, some taught by white teachers and some by blacks, and all of them more or less successful. At the time that Miner contemplated opening her school, the largest and most important establishment in the District was run by John F. Cook, Miner's correspondent. Cook was the first black man to be ordained a minister in the Presbyterian church. His school was large, numbering from a hundred to a hundred and fifty students, with separate departments for boys and girls. He tried to turn his school into a select high school that would give advanced education to a smaller number of the most capable students, but "his old patrons would not allow him to shut off the multitude of primary scholars which were depending upon his school." He died in 1855, but his school continued under the direction of his sons.[79] What immediately set Miner's school apart from the others in the District was that she planned, from the beginning, to train black girls to become teachers of other black children. In other words, she aimed at creating a normal school.

Miner's teaching experiences coincided exactly with the growth of interest in teacher training and the establishment of normal schools in the United States. A convention in Utica, New York, in 1842 had pushed for the development of teacher-training programs.[80] Since Utica was near Miner's home, it is logical to assume that, with her deep interest in education, she had some knowledge of the meeting. In Rhode Island, she came under the direction of Henry Barnard, state superintendent of schools and probably the most dynamic figure in the drive for excellence in teacher training. Barnard planned to establish a normal school in Providence, and though it did not become a reality until after Miner had left the state, she was present when Barnard set up model schools for the instruction of the inexperienced. Barnard's *Journal of Education* was a particularly fruitful source of information about curricula, instructional materials, institutes, and associations.[81] Notwithstanding Miner's unhappiness during her employment in New York and Rhode Island, she was able to absorb the most advanced ideas on teacher training, which she would use to advantage in her school in Washington.

Miner said that she went to Washington in the fall of 1851 with no support except her faith in God. "Impelled by a sense of duty and fitness, painful as it might be, I must go, knowing it to be contrary to all human reason and judgment all together against the wishes and advice of many friends."[82] In fact she was not alone but was accompanied by Anna Inman, a teacher and a member of the Society of Friends from Southfield, Rhode Island.[83] It is not clear how Inman came to join Miner, but in the last week of November 1851 the two women had an appointment with the mayor of Washington, who approved of Miner's project.[84] In the early days, the two women may have stayed at the home of Dr. Leonard D. Gale, who was employed at the Patent Office and later became a trustee of the Miner school. Miner became a very close friend of the Gale family and was always welcomed in their home.

Locating a schoolhouse became an almost insurmountable problem. Eventually Miner was forced to begin classes in a small room, only fourteen feet square, that a black man was willing to rent to her. The room was entirely adequate for the six pupils enrolled at the beginning, but as the numbers increased to fourteen and then to forty, Miner desperately required larger quarters.[85] In addition to finding a suitable classroom, she had to collect books, papers, and equipment, since many of the children were too poor to provide their own school supplies. Two weeks after starting the school, Miner wrote to Senator Seward to let him know that she had begun her great work and to ask urgently for financial support. She had found Washington a city "of 'magnificent' *charges*, as well as 'distances,'" and she needed help in paying a debt of forty dollars, primarily for pupils' desks.[86] Evidently furniture that had been promised by Henry Ward Beecher had not materialized. Miner and Inman divided the teaching between them, and each taught a variety of subjects. If we may judge by the books that they received as gifts from A. S. Barnes and Co., they taught history, orthography, philosophy, arithmetic, mathematics, English grammar, zoology, and natural philosophy.[87]

Local opposition to Miner's enterprise made it difficult for her to find board and lodging. Eventually she had to take a room a mile away from the school, while the school itself was pushed "nearly out of town, the people having obliged us to move twice to get out of their way, and now permitting us to have no better school-room than a private dwelling affords and that very small."[88]

The hostility of the Washington population presented a persistent threat to the continuation of the school and the safety of both its teachers and pupils. In March 1852 Miner received a warning that a mob would attack the school, "but it was only a threat." At about the same time an incident occurred that typifies the local animosity toward the school. One afternoon when the girls were leaving, walking along and chatting among themselves, a neighbor who was a lawyer approached them and tried to elbow them off the sidewalk. According to Miner, he hit some of the girls and cursed them as they hurried away. Then he visited Miner's black landlady, from whom she rented the schoolrooms, and told her "to turn out that *nigger school* or be mobbed." He told her that "she might expect to see her house torn down over her head and, if she escaped, think herself well off." The terrified landlady ran to Miner and cried: "The Lord save us! O the Lord have mercy! I can't endure this. I shan't have no home that ole massa lef [*sic*] me during my lifetime. Then I'll be so desolate. What will I do?" Miner, calling the landlady "Aunty," asked what was the matter, adding, "I think the Lord will save and have mercy, too, if we trust Him." The landlady told her of the neighbor's threat and said, "I can't afford to be mobbed and turn [*sic*] out in my ole age." Trust in the Lord, said Miner, for "if they mob this down the Lord will give you a better one. There are friends who will not see you suffer for such a cause." The landlady was afraid to trust in God alone, but she permitted Miner to remain.

Soon the neighbor made another threat of mob action, against which the landlady defended herself by asserting that she needed Miner's rent money to live on. He asked her if she would turn the school out if he guaranteed her the same rent from another tenant. The landlady refused, on the grounds that she could not evict a tenant who made no trouble and always paid the rent on time. According to Miner, the troublemaker next went to an alderman, asking how he could "break up the 'nigger school.'" The alderman said, "You cannot do it, except you can prove it to be nuisance and, as you cannot do that, you have nothing to do *but let it alone.*"

Apparently the lawyer continued to harass the landlady, because Miner asked the mayor to intervene. When he would do nothing, she resolved to visit the neighbor. She "dressed with care, knowing the importance a Southerner attaches to the outer man." The lawyer found it hard to believe that such a lady kept "that nigger school." Miner proceeded to tell him that she assumed full responsibility for her pupils and wanted to know what they had done to offend him. "Well, I'll tell you, we are not going to have this *nigger school,* anyhow, . . . for they are saucy and impudent and shove white people off the walks! It is contrary to all rules to have them gathered in such companies and we shan't have it!" She replied: "I have forbidden my pupils to ever answer the *insults* of white men. What did you say to my scholars?"

Now, Miner felt, the lawyer was on the defensive, for he burst out, "We are not going to have you Northern Abolitionists coming down here to teach our niggers. We know better what to do with them than you do." And precisely what, Miner wanted to know, did he propose to do with them? Send them out of the country, he answered, for they were not wanted in Washington. But, said Miner, as that would take time, she would go forward with her plans. The lawyer expressed his opinion that the blacks had grown "more impertinent" since Miner had arrived in the District. He demanded to know who had sent her to Washington "to teach niggers," and Miner told him, "A higher power than man directed me and *man* shall not defeat me." When the lawyer asked who paid her, Miner answered that the students paid. When he threatened her with mob action, she replied,

It seems to me a new version of "Southern chivalry" that you should mob a defenseless woman who violates no law of God or man, merely because she dare earn her living in a philanthropic way and insult her pupils because they wish to acquire sufficient knowledge to earn their livelihood and be independent of the aid of those who despise and degrade them.

Miner and the lawyer argued for about an hour, with Miner feeling that in the end she had triumphed. But in reality the lawyer had won, for the landlady continued so distressed that Miner moved the school to another location within a month.[89] It was probably at that time that a German family opened its doors to the school.[90]

Many years later William Henry Channing recounted that Miner "was threatened with a horse-whip by a young Virginian, who insulted her before her assembled school, and whom she fairly cowed by her dauntless courage and cutting irony."[91] Yet all of the trouble did not come from white opponents. Miner wrote (on a blank page, without date): "How long will it take me to convince the colored people that I am sincere in the interest I profess—Well I don't know some will never see it in a life time, but will die and go to judgment without knowing it."[92]

As the success of the school gradually became assured, the need for permanent quarters increased. The Reverend Cook had warned Miner that most of the other people engaged in similar operations had provided their own buildings, and although Miner soon understood the advantage this would offer, she had no money. The tuition payments of the students were small and not really adequate to cover the cost of the school. The prime challenge, as usual, was to raise money, and Miner would devote much of the rest of her life to that never-ending task. For example, she even tried unsuccessfully to see President Millard Fillmore to ask for a donation.[93] Her most consistent and reliable support was to come from members of the Society of Friends in Philadelphia, who may have heard of her work through Anna Inman, her fellow teacher.

In December 1851 Miner began receiving letters from Samuel Rhoads, a leader among the Philadelphia Quakers, and their correspondence continued for many years. There were others that gave more money to the school, but none that gave such careful attention to its operation. Sometimes Rhoads sent several letters to Miner in one week concerning the most minute details of the school, the building, and business arrangements. Rhoad's antislavery tract, *Considerations on the Use of the Production of Slavery, Especially Addressed to the Religious Society of Friends*,[94] had led to the formation in 1845 of the Free Produce Association of Friends of Philadelphia Yearly Meeting, which Rhoads helped to manage. In 1847 George W. Taylor, the publisher of *The Non-Slaveholder*, a journal of the free produce movement that encouraged people to boycott products of slave labor, opened a free produce store in Philadelphia.[95] During the

1850s Rhoads was either publisher or editor of *Friends' Review*, an influential Quaker publication. When he became concerned with the operation of Miner's school, he drew into the circle of interested Friends such people as George W. Taylor; Jasper Cope and Israel Morris, very wealthy Philadelphians; and Thomas Williamson, an outstanding businessman and father of Passmore Williamson, who would go to prison for helping an escaped slave. From these Friends Miner received money, moral support, a place to stay when she visited Philadelphia, and encouragement to persevere in the great work she had begun.

Soon after the school opened, Rhoads sent Miner fifteen dollars, hoping that he would be able to provide her with more and assuring her that he was discussing her undertaking with his friends. About ten days later he sent another ten dollars, and early in January an additional thirteen. A few months after the school began, Rhoads wrote: "I want to see your school fairly established—and so large and prosperous as to permit Anna Inman to unite with thee in its management." He warned against publicity, fearing that "any public notice of the school might raise opposition."[96] Within a few days he sent her more money and a list of donors, the amount adding up to $47.50. He was also able to tell her that the Murray Fund in New York would give fifty dollars toward the maintenance of the school.[97]

Rhoads thought it desirable that the school should become large enough and "sufficiently remunerative" to provide a salary for both of the teachers. He hoped that the money he had sent would relieve her of the pressure of collecting money until the tuition fees began to come in. "If thou should, however, find further difficulty, I may be able to obtain some additional aid—I have been anxious to raise some money for a suffering case in Indiana—but have deferred it as I thought yours the more urgent." He encouraged Miner by writing: "I never saw money contributed more freely than by the Friends who have handed me what I have recd. for thee—all have felt a lively interest in the undertaking."[98] Rhoads asked Miner: "Do you perceive any indications of opposition to your effort? Have you reason to think from personal knowledge that there is ability, as well as disposition on the part of the colored people, to sustain your school?"[99]

Rhoads's letters were full of helpful suggestions for Miner. For example, he proposed that she call on Thaddeus Stevens: "He is a staunch frd. of the colored race & I am told is exceedingly liberal in his contributions." She might also contact James R. Chandler, congressman from Philadelphia, a former teacher and an acquaintance of Rhoads, and "an active promoter of our public schools." Rhoads gave Miner permission to use his name in approaching Chandler, "if it can be useful."[100] However, there is no record that she approached either man.

Rhoads soon became involved in a conflict between Miner and Inman. The two women, as Rhoads tactfully expressed it, "could not labor harmoniously together." An argument broke out, largely because Inman believed that, as a Quaker, she was solely responsible for the Friends' assistance to the school. Miner admitted that she "yielded to impatience," and Inman left the school, hardly four months after it had opened. Miner worried that the Friends might cease their invaluable support for the school, but Rhoads reassured her:

I am not a sectarian—it matters not to me whether those with whom I labor for the good of mankind—morally, physically or socially—are members of the Baptist, Methodist, Catholic or any other church or of no church nor whether they use *thou* or *you*. Neither do I believe that the . . . individuals who contributed aid to the "Colored School in Washington" thought for a moment of its having any connection with *Friends*.[101]

Rhoads added that if Inman had planned to open a school for black children as Miner had done, then he would willingly have supported her as well. Later, when Inman returned to Philadelphia, Rhoads spoke with her about the school and the conflict with Miner and wrote, "I believe Anna feels really anxious for the complete success of thy school and would not intentionally speak a word to injure it or thee."[102]

The Philadelphia Friends spread the word of Miner's undertaking, and letters came from as far away as England expressing "great interest and encouragement." Someone wrote from the West:

The educational movement of those noble young women among the colored inhabitants of Washington city was altogether new to me and somewhat surprising. I did not expect that such an effort would be *tolerated* by the authorities of that city—much less countenanced. The result is truly cheering and an evidence of some progress.

To that quotation Samuel Rhoads wisely added a note of caution: "The approbation of the good and wise is cheering and strengthening tho' not always a safe foundation upon which to depend in seasons of trial and difficulty."[103]

When the parents of Miner's schoolchildren began to discuss the possibility of building a schoolhouse, the Friends in Philadelphia responded with enthusiasm. Jasper Cope had a lot in Washington that he was willing to sell for that purpose. The Philadelphians suggested that "a neat, plain house" of a size to hold sixty to eighty children could be built for about one thousand dollars. "Perhaps some of the colored people could contribute materials, work &—if a joint stock company were formed to erect and hold the school-house."[104] The Friends had always believed in helping those that helped themselves.

Cope continued to offer property for the school "much below what he would charge others," and eventually made an even more generous proposal. He listed several lots in Washington and said that Miner should choose one and "have the use of it for thy school as long as thou wishes it—paying only the taxes and charges made by the city." In addition, he would guarantee that the value of any improvements made on the land would accrue to Miner, for Cope sought no profit from the school.[105] There is no evidence that Miner ever seriously considered Cope's proposition, and even her markedly proprietary attitude toward the school does not sufficiently explain the fact that nothing ever came of such an exceedingly generous offer.

By July 1852, after approximately six months of teaching, Miner was exhausted and ill. In the spring the warm weather had forced her to slow down her activities, but she continued nonetheless to write frequent letters begging money to build a schoolhouse and to make numerous visits to "people I am obliged to call on." She had grown "thin and pale" as a result of doing nearly all her visiting on foot.[106] Nevertheless, when the school closed for the summer, Miner undertook a trip to the North to seek financial support for her school and especially for her building project. She went to Philadelphia, where she stayed with George Taylor, "a thorough frd. of the colored race."[107] She probably also went to New York and New England, for it must have been about this time that she began to attract the attention of Harriet Beecher Stowe, then the most famous woman in America.

As a result of her summer's work, Miner collected $2,500 in loans—$2,000 from Catherine Morris and $500 from Jasper Cope, both Philadelphia Friends—and gifts totaling $610. She stayed with friends and acquaintances during most of her fund-raising campaign, so that her expenses were kept to a minimum. Thomas Williamson, who agreed to serve as the school's accountant, arranged to have the money put out at interest while plans went forward for the construction of an adequate building.[108]

But progress seemed so slow that Miner grew discontented and fretted that she lacked sufficient space for more pupils. Furthermore, she continued to have difficulty with living and teaching arrangements.Her friend Samuel Rhoads suggested that forty pupils were probably all she could handle: "Thy school seems to me, enough labor, enough care and responsibility for one head and one set of hands and feet—a larger establishment might bring disappointments of various kinds—from tenants—assistants—teachers &a&a." Rhoads urged Miner to feel grateful for all she had accomplished. "Was it not something to raise nearly or quite one thousand dollars by donations and 2500 by loans in two months to say nothing of the many sustaining and sympathizing friends thou found."[109]

The Friends of Philadelphia never forgot Miner and her school, giving her constant assistance in a variety of matters. George Taylor went to Washington to visit and was impressed with the pupils. He helped make financial arrangements for the money Miner had collected and wrote in great detail about the qualities she should look for in land for the schoolhouse. In addition he undertook such minor but time-consuming tasks as buying a clock for the schoolroom and taking magazines to the bindery, apologizing that he could not do more because his major energies were devoted to the Free Produce store. "When thou art comfortably settled in a snug home of thy own, remember the Free Labour store & keep the sweets extracted by the sweat of slaves from thy table." In a letter to Miner, Rhoads regretted not having written John Greenleaf Whittier to ask for copies of his works for the Miner school. Rhoads suggested instead that Miner ask a rich Bostonian to buy the works for her, as Whittier had little money and could ill afford a donation.[110]

Mindful of the danger of dealing with slaves, Miner had made it plain from the beginning that she would limit her instruction to free blacks. Nevertheless, someone presented her with "another child," whom she in turn offered to a member of the Society of Friends. It is not clear where the child came from, but apparently Miner was putting herself and her school in danger of being charged with harboring a fugitive slave. One friend wrote another, praising Miner's "noble efforts" but urging great caution. Eventually Rhoads wrote to Miner: "I trust a homily is not needed—thou cannot consent to place the existence of thy school in jeopardy by allowing thy sympathies to lead thee into dangerous enterprises." He understood "the strong claims of suffering humanity," but he felt strongly that Miner should stick to her original intention of teaching black girls and "most carefully avoid every thing that would conflict with this purpose or in any way disable thee from the accomplishment of it."[111]

The search for property continued, and by the middle of February 1853, Rhoads had come to Washington and signed a contract with a C. Alexander for a piece of real estate where the Miner school could operate.[112] However, the Philadelphia Quakers worried persistently, especially because the deed to the property had not yet been executed. But now that a settlement seemed imminent, Rhoads desired to alleviate some of Miner's burden of responsibility for the school. In a letter, he wished that she had "some *practical* friend in Washington to give attention to the repairs of the house & the fence and the arrangement for cultivating the lot." Rhoads continued: "My desire is to promote thy labor—to place thee in a position as free as possible from pecuniary liability and trouble of various kinds—so that thy mind may be unburdened by other cares than those appertaining necessarily to thy school."[113] That, unfortunately, was impossible, for the people most seriously interested in the school did not live in Washington, so that Miner was left to look after important business alone.

But as the weeks passed and the title to the property had not been established, the Philadelphia Friends grew more and more alarmed. Miner became distraught, for she had believed the problem of a school building was finally resolved, and now it seemed to have fallen through completely. Rhoads wrote her comforting words: "I am glad to know thou hast been able to bear thy disappointment like a—

woman! There is certainly no use in fretting—tho' it is difficult, I well know, to preserve equanimity of mind under the various trials which beset us in passing through this beautiful world."[114]

Miner finally retained a lawyer to search the title, an elementary precaution that should have been taken much earlier. When they realized that there was indeed no clear title to the property, Rhoads and Williamson refused to send the agreed-on sum. Miner either would not or could not understand the legal situation and charged them with "sheer neglect" in withholding the funds. Her obtuseness irritated the experienced Philadelphia businessmen, and Rhoads, after explaining why the money was not forthcoming, lectured her on the virtues of patience: "It is cause of deep regret and disappointment to me that the difficulties in respect to the title of the lot exist—but let us not add to these difficulties the estrangement of our best friends by unjust censures." And then came the sermon:

Let us preserve our patience under all these trials and not despair of final success. We all make mistakes and omissions when trying to do our best and it is comforting to have charity extended towards our false steps. I sympathise deeply with thee under thy repeated trials and disappointments and do not wonder that thou art sometimes a little disposed to attribute blame somewhere and that it is occasionally misapplied.[115]

As the months passed and the Washington lawyer could not establish a clear title, Rhoads and Williamson continued to worry. But they had met their match in Miner, who went ahead and recorded the deed, even with a cloudy title.[116] The owner, sensing the bind she was in, demanded more money before agreeing to a final settlement, so that Miner could not, after all, take possession of the property. She was at her wit's end, but got little comfort from the Philadelphians. Rhoads advised her "to take the matter on thyself— that is get Dr Bailey & some other good friend to furnish thee with the [additional] Money." The fact that he ended the letter "Tenderly sympathising in thy trials,"[117] did little to calm Miner's anxiety. Succumbing to self-pity, she saw herself alone and deserted, a martyr to the cause of black education. She sat down and wrote a letter to Philadelphia that would have proved disastrous if sent to anyone less charitable and less devoted to the cause of black improvement than Samuel Rhoads. After quoting his sentence about taking the matter on herself, Miner began her lament. How could she deal with the matter alone, she asked, conveniently disregarding the fact that she had taken it upon herself to record the deed. She owned no property and had no claim on the land bought for the school by Williamson and Rhoads. She had to account to the trustees for every penny she had collected during those exhausting trips every summer, and she had to pay travel expenses, insurance on the school furniture, and the incidentals necessary to the running of the school. Miner reminded Rhoads that she received only a pittance from the pupils, many of whom could pay nothing. Furthermore, she had a debt of one hundred dollars that she had incurred while paying for her sister Achsa's education. There was no use in her signing a note, "because I could give no more security than a *slave* who is trusted to work out her freedom."

Miner blamed all her troubles on Thomas Williamson, who, she thought, should have come to Washington to resolve her numerous difficulties. After all, she said, "*You hold the property* which is full security for all your responsibilities." Miner concluded that the Friends had been guilty of "*an excess of caution*" whereas "God would teach us to move calmly, candidly & fearlessly onward to the accomplishment of what seems best." She decided to rent a building and reopen her school, leaving the trustees to handle the matter of the property in any way they thought best. But finding scarce rental property required energy that she did not have: "My two days of long walking in the warm sun, without dinner, & returning with headache & nerves, having taught me this—& all for no good." As Miner surveyed her situation, she grew more and more embittered and sorry for herself. But finally she came to the point: She would arrange a fair price (or what she now perceived as a fair price) for the property, take possession, and open the school. "I think I can easier beg $500. more with the school in successful operation, in a permanent place—than meet other results of your cool judgment, in saying 'refund the money or give possession of the property.'"[118]

The next day, having thought it over, Miner felt that she had been too hard on the Philadelphians. She wrote a more or less penitent letter, finally asking for a clearer explanation of their recommended course of action. "Certainly, neither Thos. Williamson nor thou, can have any other object in view than the good of the school & the cause it involves—it would be as impossible to believe any thing else of thee as of myself." But, she insisted, up in Philadelphia they could not understand the urgent need to open the school; when children were waiting, time seemed more important than money. "*Our word* has gone forth, that the school shall speedily have a resting place— & what are a few dollars compared with its suspension, discomfiture & destitution?"[119]

Miner's accusations stung both men deeply. Rhoads replied that they had neither offered the seller an unfair price nor taken advantage of the seller's ignorance. "If he was ignorant of the value of the property, it was his own neglect—every man is expected to be cognisant of the value of his own property—and it is not usual to offer more than is asked." Rhoads sought to vindicate Williamson as a man "accustomed to the transaction of business in a strictly just, proper, legal, straightforward manner." He carefully explained where Miner's lawyer in Washington had been at fault and then added: "But it is useless to dwell upon errors, mistakes and misapprehensions—or to criminate and recriminate." Rhoads patiently agreed that if some definite sum could be settled on, then he and Williamson would try again to make whatever arrangements were necessary. He wrote: "As one of the Trustees I am perfectly willing to give the matter my most careful consideration and to do whatever the interests of the school require."[120]

On October 1, 1853, Miner wrote to Harriet Beecher Stowe, thanking her for a magnificent gift of one thousand dollars, "earned by Uncle Tom's death, & appropriated to our school for *his* children & children's children to the latest generation."

This is to assure thee my friend that I for one will strive to redeem its value in light & love & liberty to many in this generation, leaving a kind providence to raise up laborers who will more than fill my place, in opening the prison doors of ignorance & letting the light of truth into generations yet unborn, who shall in this "National Institute," receive blessings richer than we in these days of restriction have yet conceived.

Following this effusion, Miner admitted that they had not yet succeeded in gaining possession of their "long-wished-for, & beautiful home," but she expected that eventually the matter would be well settled, with occupancy within a month or two.[121] There was, perhaps, considerable irony in the arrival of so important a gift at the time that Miner was despairing of ever gaining possession of the property.

While Miner lamented the failings of her Philadelphia supporters, they in turn were feeling increasing alarm at the amount of time she was devoting to the affairs of a young man named Walpole Cecil. Some aspects of this matter remain obscure, but it is clear that Miner became strongly attached to a young ne'er-do-well, to both the amusement and despair of her friends and supporters. Walpole Cecil was a handsome young man, variously described as being seventeen and twenty-six years old,[122] who in 1852 came to Miner's attention when he was in danger of going to jail for theft. Miner sought to save him from imprisonment and in the process became deeply involved in his problems.

His early life was mysterious, and accounts vary as to his origins. Apparently he was born in Charleston, South Carolina, and was taken first to Alabama and then to Pennsylvania, where his father left him in the Philadelphia home of Dr. Charles Treichel, who raised him to adolescence.[123] Cecil entered the United States Naval Academy in Annapolis but was dismissed almost at once for unknown reasons. He then moved to Washington, where he found work but was caught stealing from his employer. Sympathetic friends, reluctant to believe in his guilt, arranged another post for him, but, once again, he was charged with theft. It is, apparently, at this point in his life that he attracted Miner's attention, for they lived in the same rooming house.[124] She set out to reform him and to save his immortal soul, urging him to "penitence & relinquishing all recklessness & wild thoughts."[125] She decided to write a novel about Cecil that would have even greater social significance than *Uncle Tom's Cabin*,[126] and pressed him for information about his background. She herself wrote to Wilmington, North Carolina, seeking information about his past, and for a while she believed that he belonged to an important Southern family. In the course of her investigations Miner discovered, or thought she discovered, that Cecil was legally a fugitive slave and that the woman he believed to be his nurse was actually his mother.[127] Meanwhile, people laughed at her obsession with a young man they regarded as worthless: "It became a standing joke that Miss M—— had become the dupe of her credulity."[128]

Afraid of arrest because of the charge of theft, Cecil fled from Washington to Baltimore. Miner followed him and for three days she "immolated" herself, "soul and body," while getting him to promise that he would "relinquish forever" his "destructive pride, & desperate folly & be good *always*." She longed for him to "live & die a good man—& not be evil, base & cruel."[129] She sent him off to Massachusetts, where her friend Professor E. N. Horsford promised to make arrangements for him to sail either on a New Bedford whaler or a California and China vessel.[130]

Instead of going straight on to Boston, Cecil stopped in Philadelphia and went to visit the Treichels, who had raised him. Miner was furious, either out of jealousy of the Treichels' influence or fear that they would encourage his bad habits. She wrote Dr. Treichel an angry letter, in which she vowed to disown Cecil now that he was back under Treichel's care, for she knew that the Philadelphian had denounced her as "a wild fanatical abolitionist" who had designs on Cecil's property. She did not believe that Cecil had any considerable property, having desired merely "to save him from destruction."[131]

In fact, instead of abandoning Cecil, Miner sought to interest her friends in Philadelphia in his affairs. Rhoads refused to have anything to do with him. Indeed, he said he would not have him in his home, and he certainly would not interfere with Dr. Treichel's care. He warned Miner against trying to get the other Philadelphia Friends involved, for people with a deep interest in her school should not be allowed to perceive that her attention was diverted from that great interest and her "strength expended in other matters—however important." Miner's high hopes for Cecil mystified Rhoads; he could not share her vision of Cecil as "a great benefactor to our country." Although it was indeed a noble aim to reclaim the young man ("and if thou hast time and strength to spare from thy special 'calling,' no one has a right to complain"),[132] Rhoads plainly thought she was wasting her time.

A particularly moving appeal to cease her involvement with Cecil came from Quaker Margaret Robinson, who warned that, although he was handsome and "elegantly dressed," he was not a "*frank* young man"; he would not look one right in the face. She begged Miner not to squander her "precious strength for one while the whole race may be the sufferers." Miner ought to remember that her "great mission" was to help "the poor women, for whom no colledges [*sic*] are built—whom no one cares for, intellectually."[133] Miner's friend Horsford wrote from Cambridge, expressing the hope that when she became free of Cecil, she would not assume another such burden, for she was "hazarding greater interests" by neglecting her school. "Your legitimate mission is sublime. Hundreds can compete with you in offices of simple humanity in Washington. Few, if any, in the great object of educating the colored race."[134]

Eventually Cecil reached Massachusetts, but since he had delayed so long, he lost the place on a ship that Horsford had secured for him. Horsford made various attempts to find him another berth, but when none of the possibilities materialized, he resolved to take Cecil into his laboratory. This decision proved a disaster. The spring and summer of 1853 abounded in letters recounting the misdeeds of Walpole Cecil, until Horsford finally decided to wash his hands of the worthless young man.[135]

In spite of Cecil's misconduct, the lengthy correspondence between Miner and the young man reveals her deep affection for him, his inability or unwillingness to conform to her high standards, and the peculiarly intense and tortured relationship between them. He sent her a lock of his hair, yet called her an old maid, adding that everyone knew that spinsters were "queer people." He told her that he loved her but despised her school. "You with your niggers," he wrote. He mocked her "undying affection," her "mothers love," and tormented her by threatening suicide.[136]

Miner got her revenge by taunting him with his racially dubious origins. She wrote: "You are a fugitive slave: Your mother is a colored woman!" She told him that his mother was alive and loved him, "but with her you can never enjoy any feeling in common, no mother's sympathy, for she is like her people, while you have been educated like us—& like us should be noble & true!" She reminded him of the Fugitive Slave Law, and recommended that he go to sea until it was safe for him to live in the United States.[137] Yet she could not easily give up her attempts to reform him, begging him to study his Bible and scolding him for "indolent idleness—& playing the fop." Finally she advised him to go to Africa, "lie down in your foppish dress under a palm tree & *die*—for of what account is your *life?*" In the face of his profitless existence, she thought that after all he might have been better off in the penitentiary. But she continued to pray for him. At the end of a long, scolding letter, she signed herself "Still in love thine own."[138] In her last surviving letter to him she wrote:

In spite of all your faults, I love you most tenderly—& because I cannot take care of you myself & make you good, I pray my Heavenly Father to take care of you, & make you *so good* that the day may come, when those who have scorned you . . . will be proud to say he is an honorable, truthful, useful man. I hold you only by *faith*, my Cecil, & firmly believe God will one day save you from your many, multiplied sins.[139]

Whatever happened to Cecil is not known, but Miner's obsession with him discloses the depth of her need for affection. Since she had lost her sister Achsa, she had not found anyone for whom she could care as she did for Cecil. She wrote a friend in Philadelphia:

How I wish I could take his hand & look into his eyes once more, for my soul has labored for his soul with a yearning which nothing but a God-power could awaken in one of stern spirit like me—& this letter goes to you with the treasure of my *tears* upon it—A harvest that has not been gathered till *now*, since my last earthly hope went away, with my sweet sister to heaven.

Even her educational aspirations could not fill the profound emptiness in her life. Indeed, she believed that God had directed her to care for the "poor boy" because her "heart was narrowed to complete concentration" on the school.[140] Although she was as involved in the school as ever, she longed for a closeness that her pupils could not satisfy.

Sometime in the fall of 1853 Miner acted on her proposal to rent property and found a place where she could reopen the school. "The scholars were all impatient and anxious, and twice . . . came out with their satchels of books," she reported. The property that she rented, the fourth location of the school, had two large, not very convenient rooms, one above the other. The pupils were delighted: "When the school did open . . . the pupils rushed in so happy in the appreciation of the blessing, so hearty in study, so neat in appearance, and so quiet in manners, that I have experienced only joy in teaching them." The old man that rented the rooms described the students: "Why I never see nicer looking scholars in my life; nobody will disturb these! and then they are the quietest set I ever see. You would not know there was a school in the house, to come into the hall unless the door was opened in the schoolroom."[141] In spite of some threats of violence, nothing happened to disturb Miner's satisfaction in beginning the new school term in reasonably adequate quarters.

Circumstances had forced Miner to continue to use a rented building, but she must have felt content in the knowledge that in less than two years she had organized a school of such high quality that the girls were eager to resume their studies. Furthermore, she had been able to begin the school year without violence and had, somehow, in spite of her impatience and ill-advised letters, retained the admiration of the Friends in Philadelphia, who held on to the money for the school and reported her accomplishments to other sympathetic people. Most importantly, skeptics notwithstanding, Miner had accomplished her goal of establishing in the nation's capital an effective school for black girls who would later assume the education of other black children.

III

In February 1854, with the signing of the final agreement and the payment of $4,300, Myrtilla Miner at last took possession of the property for which she had longed.[142] Included in the purchase were several old buildings, "a small frame dwelling of two stories, not more than twenty-five by thirty-five feet in dimensions," and three small cabins.[143] On the first of March Miner moved into the frame house, where she would live and teach; a tenant would occupy the best of the cabins. At last the school had a home of its own.

The new campus had more than three acres of land, and Miner reported that it was located "a little out of town, in a thriving neighborhood, convenient to market, etc."[144] But on actually moving in, she sounded somewhat less enthusiastic: "For a few weeks after we moved to this place, which was in a most forlorn and desolate condition, with no fence to bound its broad acres and thrifty fruit trees, no security to its old clattering houses, the locks and bolts, blinds and fastenings, seeming to have had a general rebellion and 'stepped out.' "[145] The place appeared to be very isolated. Located between Eighteenth and Twentieth Streets and N Street and New Hampshire Avenue, to the north of the White House, it is today in the heart of downtown Washington. The land had been used for market gardening, and raspberries, strawberries, rhubarb, asparagus, and fruit trees remained.[146]

Miner could not have expected to open her school without opposition, and she soon received a note, signed "Citizens of the First
Ward," that threatened, "If you are not out of that house with your
niggers by the tenth of April you and all your effects will be set in
flames." Miner claimed that she paid no attention, "thinking they
would find it difficult to set *me* in flames."[147] But her memory of
her responses to such intimidation apparently varied, for she also
recalled having to endure "rowdies . . . occasionally stoning our
house at evening, and we nightly retiring in the expectation that the
house would be fired before morning." Once, when the "stones were
falling upon the house weightily," Miner rushed out to the nearest
house and persuaded a neighbor to go for the night watch. "In about
fifteen minutes four very savage-looking men, armed with clubs,
etc., made their appearance, giving the kind assurance that they
would keep an eye to our safety."[148] When two of the "ruffians"
who had stoned their house were imprisoned for setting fires near
to the school, Miner felt assured of divine intervention. "Knowing
the great pleasure it would have afforded them to see our house in
flames, I am more than ever awed by a consciousness that His power,
alone, has stayed the hand of him that deviseth mischief and of him
that plotteth against the just."[149] But Miner evidently believed that
the Lord helps those who help themselves. For added security, she
and the young black girl then assisting her began to practice pistol
shooting. With the installation of a high picket fence and the arrival
of the tenant family with a dog, she felt more protected. The school
soon opened in the new quarters with forty-five pupils.[150]

Miner decided that in order to raise more money for the school
she would have to close it for the summer and travel to Philadelphia.
The warmth of her reception there clearly indicated her importance
to the antislavery movement in the Quaker city. Her colleagues
among the Friends arranged for her to stay with one or another of
them during her visit, and they greeted the news of her arrival with
enthusiasm, as though she brought something rare and edifying into
their homes.[151] Nevertheless, the collection of money went badly,
for there were so many other pleas for financial aid. Miner and
Rhoads agreed that because times were hard, they should not give
way to depression; but in fact they could hardly help being discouraged. Miner's chief hope for success had rested with wealthy
Stephen P. Morris of Philadelphia. Thomas Williamson had prom-

ised to *"triple his subscription"* if Morris made a large contribution, but Morris donated a mere fifty dollars.[152]

In December 1854 the notice of taxes due on the school property startled Rhoads and his associates. It seemed obvious that the demand was a "gross imposition," perhaps aimed deliberately at undermining the school. Although the money was forthcoming, Rhoads exhorted Miner to "please . . . get an acct of the assessment and amt of taxes for *last year* with the assessment of adjoining lots and any information which may explain this extraordinary assessment."[153] In addition to the tax burden and the diminishing contributions, Miner received almost no money from the cultivation of the land around the school, since the arrangement for a tenant proved unsatisfactory.

Whatever the problems Miner encountered, there is no doubt that she was making a real contribution to raising the standards of education for black children in the District. When she first opened the school, she found the quality of black education alarmingly low. "There were previously five or six private schools in the District taught by colored men, from which some of these girls [her pupils] professed to have graduated." According to Miner, "they were unable to apply the knowledge they had acquired to any practical use." Miner said that though they claimed to read well, they did not understand what they read; the same was true of their claims to knowledge of grammar and arithmetic. "These graduates were from fifteen to seventeen years of age, and unfortunately, some of them very uncultivated in mind and matters." According to Miner, these adolescent graduates of other black schools promptly withdrew from Miner's establishment when they discovered that they would have to study with much younger girls, simply in order to acquire what Miner regarded as the basic essentials of knowledge.[154]

By 1854, when the school had been in operation for about three years, standards had improved and Miner reported that her students were "earnest seekers after knowledge," who had more than lived up to the expectations of their teachers. "They cheerfully respond to every effort made on their behalf, and seem to appreciate the privileges afforded them for acquiring such an education as shall render them independent in the duties that devolve on them in future life." Miner intended for the school "to enlighten their minds, refine their tastes, cultivate proper habits, and develop all their powers for usefulness and happiness." She anticipated that many of the girls would become teachers who "by their refinement and good morals [would] exert such an influence upon their associates, as shall relieve the world of much degradation and consequent misery."

After her twenty years of teaching experience, Miner felt competent to make a declaration of racial equality: "I do unequivocally assert, that I find no differences of native talent, where similar advantages are enjoyed, between Anglo-Saxons and Africo-Americans." She felt, furthermore, that "God having so constituted us that it becomes a *duty* to seek the highest good of our better nature," it followed that the black people of America and especially of Washington were entitled to the same free education enjoyed by other Americans.

While Miner lamented the city's disinclination to institute proper schools, she could see no valid reason why the federal government should not provide them. The city, of course, granted its black population no privileges "except those of being *taxed* without representation, and *punished* for violating laws which they have no voice in enacting." But Miner asserted the right to an education of those whom she called a "faithful class of laborers." "Miss [Dorothea] Dix nobly pleads for the criminal and insane—but we plead for the *workers,* upon whom the personal comfort of all so much depends, that *they may be saved from crime or insanity* by the removal of those fearful maladies—ignorance and want." Miner called for the United States to provide for "the relief of all her poor." There always seemed to be enough money to help the poor of other nations, but the government should first remember the "sufferers at home." "These suffer for want of soul-food! for enlightenment of mind! such as a Christian nation should be careful to bestow, ere it require strict obedience to its laws!"

Miner believed that if the rights of the black population were continually denied, an uprising would inevitably result.

If left in *ignorance,* no wise counsel can stay the tide, should they rise in their might and desperation, to roll back the flood of power that deprives them of privileges, which, ignorant as they are, they know to be the "inalienable right" of every honest person who treads American soil. This *you* have taught them without schools, and now they must be enlightened and

awakened to a full consciousness of things as they are; of the difficulties to
be met, and of the best mode of disposing of them.

She also favored the conversion of blacks to Christianity and "the
principles of love and peace." Only such proper instruction could
"ward off the evils shrouded in the future."[155]

In school Miner was a conscientious teacher with very high standards. She preserved much of her pupils' work, which reveals a re-
markable level of achievement, especially in writing. A nine-year-
old girl, who had come to her unable to write legibly, produced,
after less than a year of enrollment in Miner's school, a neat and
readable letter in which she correctly spelled such words as "knowledge," "instructive," and "Institute." In spite of a few minor errors,
her progress was indeed astonishing, and one can only hope that
Lizzy Snowden was properly pleased with herself.[156] In April 1852
John F. Cook, who ran the best school for blacks in the District,
sent his daughter Mary Victoria to study with Miner, who must have
felt victorious to know that the city's leading black educator thought
she had something worthwhile to offer his daughter. Cook's action
may well have encouraged other parents to take similar action.

Unfortunately, Lizzy Snowden's spelling deteriorated, but her
concept of education broadened during her stay in Miner's school.
Mrs. Orville Dewey, the wife of a famous white clergyman, visited
the school and lectured the students on the danger of being educated
above their station or expectations. She set off a storm of indignation
among the pupils, which Lizzy Snowden stated very well (the letter
is reproduced with her spelling):

I would rather be discontened. O let me be discontened. Let me be learned
and be discontened. If Mrs Dewy had asked me if I would be better contened
without education. I would say I do not wish to be cotened with ignorant.
I would ask her if she would rather be contened and be ignorant. I would
ask her if colored girls had not as much right to learn as white girls. Let
me be discontened. I would rather be learned than to be contened and be
ignorant. I will be Learned. I must be learned! I would ask her if colored
people should not enjoy every right as white people? Colored people had
been like the Pilgrims left there homes and gone away and said we cant stay
her to be oppresed.[157]

What an eloquent and passionate statement of the meaning of education. This letter demonstrates that Miner's school provided her pupils with an opportunity to express their understanding of the profound importance of education and the fundamental right of every American to proper schooling.

Mrs. Dewey was not happy with the pupils' reactions to her talk, for she sent a letter to the school defending herself. Addressed to "My dear young friends," the letter emphasized her warm feelings for the students and reiterated that the question she had raised ("May not these girls be educated to a point beyond that which will be most happy for them?") was merely an attempt to encourage the students to "look at things as they are." Reminding the girls that they were "in absolute dependence upon God," Mrs. Dewey praised the virtue of dutifulness for each "in the lot in which he finds himself—grateful or submissive as the case may be." In all society, she asserted, there was no such thing as independence, for each is dependent on the other. "It has pleased God to permit the African race to be hardly treated—& in our apprehension by none more cruelly, than by the Africans themselves." Slavery was "a great evil," but it might have been the means for "that wise & gracious Being, who ordereth all good things . . . *to bring good out of evil.*" She hoped that her words would "induce a patient waiting, to observe the ways of Providence, & a careful doing of all that seems right." Mrs. Dewey went on to rejoice that the mind could not be enslaved and that death brought the end of all tribulation. She stressed, however, that earthly trials might be "the peaceable fruits of righteousness." "It would give me pleasure to know, that much as you like your school, yet that you are happy, when circumstances keep you at home—tending children, nursing the sick, cooking, sewing or keeping the house orderly & nice."[158]

Miner read Mrs. Dewey's letter to the school and asked the students for their opinions. Mary Brent had already learned the meaning of tact, calling the letter "kind and affectionate," and appreciating her "great interest in our present and future welfare," but adding, "I have thought though men enslave the body yet they cannot enslave the mind and prevent it from thinking."[159]

As a good nineteenth-century educator, Miner undertook to teach morals as an integral part of the curriculum. "*Character,*" she wrote, "is what the age calls for; character that dare do a noble deed; that can outlive the ebb tide of a false world's judgment; that can be true to God and man."[160] When instructing a group of children who came from what she saw as an almost hopelessly benighted community, Miner must have felt more than ever called on to inculcate morality and rectitude. A pupil leaving the school to move to Baltimore wrote to Miner expressing her sorrow at her departure and thanking her teacher for "the trouble you have had with me to make me become useful in the world." She had not only acquired "book knowledge" during her term at Miner's school, but had also learned to be "moral and lady like, that I may be useful to society."[161]

As part of her instruction, Miner encouraged the pupils to write moralizing tales. Matilda A. Jones wrote two such stories: one, called "The Two Little Girls," in praise of filial obedience; the other, entitled "The Widow & her Children," about a gentle widow who "did not storm & scold" at her children when they did wrong, but "spoke to them in gentle & mild tones fulfilling the prophesy in the Bible, 'Soft words turneth away wrath.'"[162] Another student, Nancy Waugh, composed a story to illustrate the extent and depth of human weakness, in which she demonstrated an independent-minded charity. Nancy felt that people should not condemn Eve for tasting the forbidden fruit in the Garden of Eden when, in similar circumstances, they would have proved no stronger in resisting temptation.[163]

Miner and her pupils also discussed slavery. M. A. Beckett envisaged the spiritual advantages of providing millions of slaves with the Bible, although she did not explain how they would be able to read it. She wrote: "The Bible is the protector of religion and they cannot consistently undertake to carry the Bible and religious freedom to Rome, until they make them universal at home."[164] (Miner obviously had been attacking Roman Catholicism.) Another student, Marietta T. Hill, submitted a particularly thoughtful and impassioned discussion of slavery:

I sometimes think that slavery will never be abolished, & then I nearly despair of freedom's swaying its banner over a suffering world. Sometimes a dark cloud seems to over-shadow me; and since the Nebraska bill has passed the cloud appears thicker & darker—& I say, will slavery forever exist? But a voice says, "It shall cease!" "It shall and must be abolished!" I think there will be blood shed before all can be free, and the question is, are we willing to give up *our* lives for freedom? Will we *die* for our people? We may *say* yes. But I fear our hearts would grow sick at the thought, if we knew it must be.

> Marietta cited Jesus's reluctance to face death and concluded, "I fear *we too* may be found sleeping in the fearful hour of freedom's betrayal!"[165]

By the end of the school year in 1855, some of Miner's pupils had made astounding progress. Matilda A. Jones wrote a letter of extraordinary clarity of expression to the daughter of Mrs. Dewey, their onetime lecturer. Matilda mentioned that two years earlier Mrs. Dewey had asked the students whether their educational advantages would bring them greater happiness. Matilda now felt qualified to answer, for her feelings had changed greatly while at Miner's school: "I not only needed intellectual cultivation, but partially a moral development of character, as did many others." She was delighted to report that one of her schoolmates had already left for Wilmington, Delaware, to become a teacher. "This does us all good, & shows that Miss Miner has not calculated wrongly, respecting our capacities." Matilda hoped that she and her fellow pupils would be willing to undergo hardship in order to acquire an education and impart it to others.

> We need it [an education] more than your people do, & ought to strive harder, because the greater part of our people, are yet in bondage. We that are free, are expected to be the means of bringing them out of Slavery, & how can we do it, unless we have proper educational advantages? We must get the *knowledge* & use it well. I expect the day will come, when the voice of my people, shall be heard & felt, as strong as the voice of your people.[166]

Matilda's maturity of expression was matched by the students' maturity of conduct, for she measured the school's improvement partially by the ability of the students to run the classes themselves. "Two years ago, when the teacher left the school alone for a day, we were noisy, & did not learn our lessons carefully." Now it was quite different, for "our teachers can leave for a few days, with perfect confidence in our behaving properly, & learning our lessons well."[167] Margaret Robinson of Philadelphia verified this phenomenon. Visiting the school one day and finding Miner absent, she and her friend were disappointed, thinking that they would not be able

to learn anything about the school. "What was our surprise on en-
tering, to find every pupil in her place, closely occupied with her
studies. We seated ourselves by polite invitation—soon a class read—
then one in Mental Arithmetic exercised itself, the more advanced
pupils acting as monitors; all was done without confusion." When
Miner returned, Robinson discovered that it was not unusual for the
pupils to conduct the school. "On one occasion, being obliged to
leave for several days, she [Miner] referred to the scholars the question, whether the house should be closed, or they continue their
exercises without her—they chose the latter. On her return she found
all doing well, not the least disorder having occurred."[168]

Miner undertook to give her pupils as varied an educational experience as possible. From her friends and supporters she begged
books, maps, a globe, and especially newspapers and journals. Her
emphasis on current events was surely years ahead of standard, nineteenth-century educational practice. She took her pupils to the
Smithsonian Institution to learn about science and invited a lecturer
to come and talk about the blind and their education. This lesson
so impressed one student that she wrote: "I think I could learn better
if I were blind, than I can now; because I know that all my thoughts
would be turnd [sic] inward more than they are now." The Reverend
M. D. Conway, pastor of the Unitarian church, gave a series of
lectures on the "origin & use of words." Mrs. Horace Mann came
once a week to teach grammar, and her niece instructed the students
in drawing. Miner preserved many of her pupils' sketches, and they
show that her concern was not for originality but for precision and
attention to detail. Flower drawings emphasized shading of leaves
and petals. A nicely drawn map of Mexico is still carefully sealed in
tissue paper; it must have been one of Miner's treasures. Anna Inman, the first assistant at the school, held French classes, and at
least one of the pupils spoke French "with great ease."[169]

Miner soon collected a library of about five hundred volumes,
"contributed principally by publishers in New York and Boston,
and *Friends* in Philadelphia," and she regularly received "12 weekly
and semi-weekly papers, 26 monthlies and semi-monthlies." These,
said Miner, "afford means of acquiring general information, never
previously granted to the colored people of Washington." She thought
that the papers helped a great deal "in awakening intelligent thoughts
in the minds of the pupils." As textbooks provided by friends were

never sufficient, money had to be raised to buy more books for classroom use.[170]

During the first four months of 1853 more than a hundred people visited the school, and Miner hoped that they would spread news of the school throughout the country.[171] Certainly the testimonials printed were uniformly enthusiastic about the seriousness of the pupils and their application to their studies. The Reverend Orville Dewey wrote about the school: "It is really an attractive spectacle—bright faces—and appearance of as much intelligence as I see in any other Schools—as quick and ready answers to questions—as much neatness, order and good behavior." The Reverend W. H. Channing commented on the students' "proofs of intelligence, good feeling and earnest desire to learn," and the Reverend G. W. Sampson praised the aspirations of the parents for the improvement of their daughters and their "deep interest" in the school.[172] Professor Horsford wrote from Cambridge about his visit to the school:

The exercises were in spelling, reading, geography, penmanship, composition, analysis of authors, moral philosophy and translations from the French. The degree of attainment some had made, the manifest interest of all, and the prevailing healthful moral and religious tone were such, as to show that the School had been eminently successful.

Horsford found that the pupils varied in age from eight to sixteen and that "they consisted of mulattoes and quadroons for the most part, though some were obviously of pure African blood, and others could with difficulty be distinguished from whites."[173] Miner herself said that some of her pupils were very dark and others fairer than herself. "Some have red hair & blue eyes & slightly tinged complexions—They learn very fast & some of them are so smart, it seems quite wonderful indeed." In another letter she mentioned "a little white slave girl with blue eyes and yellow hair,"[174] who could not have been one of her pupils, as she refused to accept slave children as students in order to avoid the possible charge of harboring a fugitive.

Throughout her years as head of the school, Miner was beset with parents' requests to teach their children to read. While many parents sought Miner's help principally because it would enable their children to read the Bible aloud to them, they all sincerely desired that their children achieve a literacy level that they themselves lacked. But, despite the parents' pleas for rudimentary schooling before their children were forced to begin work, Miner often had to refuse because of a shortage of space. Miner told the story of one father who brought her his nine-year-old child, "fairer than many who claim pure Anglo-Saxon origin." The father asked that Miner teach the child, for "I have so many children," he said, "I can hardly feed and clothe them, much less give them learning, but I want this one taught, and if you will educate her you may have her." Miner answered that she would agree to teach her, "if you will not prevent her from being a teacher or a missionary." The constant presence of such children, unable to pay the fifteen-dollars-a-year tuition, made it impossible for the school to operate without outside assistance.[175]

By the spring of 1855, Miner's health had deteriorated to such a degree that she was rarely in the classroom; her students had to carry on without her. In the fall she entered a health resort in Elmira, New York, her fees paid by Harriet Beecher Stowe. As the days passed, it became obvious that Miner was much too ill to return to Washington. Horace Mann's sister, Lydia B. Mann, who always signed herself Lucy, took leave from her post as superintendent of the Colored Female Orphan Asylum in Providence to reopen Miner's school that year.[176] Harriet Beecher Stowe also provided the money for Lucy Mann's salary.

Throughout the fall and winter of 1855, Mann carried on the many duties that running the school entailed: collecting fees, keeping in touch with sick pupils, making pickles and preserves from the produce of the garden and orchard, whitewashing the schoolrooms, supervising the installation of a new stove, ordering coal, and laying carpets. All this was in addition to teaching pupils of various ages and degrees of accomplishment, and keeping Miner informed of the school's progress.[177] Mann constantly anticipated Miner's return, but as the weeks passed, Miner faced the possibility that she would never be well enough to take up the burdens of running her school. Since Mann was anxious to leave Washington, both Miner and Stowe undertook to find a replacement. It was not easy. On learning what the position entailed, the women Miner approached shrank from the awesome responsibilities involved.[178]

When Miner finally realized that a replacement for Lucy Mann could not be found, she returned to Washington early in 1856 to carry on the duties of teacher and administrator until the end of the school year. Before long it became evident that she had taken up the burden too soon, and she found herself seriously ill. Consequently, when she could arrange to close the school, she hurried back to Elmira for further treatments. By the fall of 1856 she had improved considerably: "The pain in my head which has been incessant for two years, is but just gone, & now I feel strange & bewildered, like one waking from a terrible dream." She described herself as a "worn craft, lying on dock for repairs."[179] Once again she sought a substitute teacher to assume the duties that she felt too weak to fulfill, but when none appeared, she decided that the school would have to remain closed during the year 1856-57.

Miner, increasingly desperate for a replacement, finally found a teacher as dedicated as herself, but fortunately blessed with firmer health. Her name was Emily Howland, and she kept the school functioning after Miner had given up the struggle. A young Quaker from western New York, Howland had been inspired by hearing Miner speak about the school and in 1856 volunteered to assist in its operation.[180] Although she lacked experience, she took a course in painting and then engaged in practice teaching. She had found her vocation, she said, and felt certain that she was destined to work "with the poorest most despised of earth."[181] Miner, unwilling to return to Washington, hoped that Howland would assume full responsibility for the school. But Howland was afraid; after all, she had had no experience and feared she could not manage without Miner, who reassured her: "God will take care of and deliver you. He will shut the lions' mouths that they cannot harm you." The path would be illuminated for Howland as it had been for Miner.

When I consider the way in which I was led, with no light which human eyes could discern, beaming on my path, nothing but the Divine Illumination—which was unrevealed to all others—and to me only on this particular subject, I being in all else as weak and erring as ever and as mortal as any woman could be, I am filled with astonishment and wonder, awed with fear and trembling as was Moses when he had seen God."[182]

In April 1857 the faithful Samuel Rhoads sent Miner ten dollars toward settling Emily Howland and a companion in Washington.[183]

But Howland stood firm: She would not open the school without the help of its founder. Consequently, Miner and Howland began the fall term together, the *National Anti-Slavery Standard* carrying a notice: "Miss Miner has reopened her school in Washington, we are happy to learn, with great success. Her object is to educate coloured girls, and prepare them to be teachers and missionaries to their people."[184] The two women lived together, sharing the housekeeping duties and running the school. Howland reported to her friends that she was teaching six hours a day and that she and Miner did all their own housework, cooking, and marketing.[185] Howland's friends, in turn, worried about her ability to endure Miner's pace and urged the new teacher to take time for recreation. "Miss M.," wrote one of her friends, "with her relentless activity will work thee—not to death perhaps—but into a state of nervous derangement which I hate to anticipate, if thee will permit it."[186]

By the beginning of 1858, as soon as Howland had grown accustomed to the routine of the school, Miner departed once again, this time on an intensive fund-raising campaign. Early in February she stayed in Boston with a member of the Stowe family. From there she went to Albany but fell ill again and so had little success in collecting money. Back in Brooklyn, New York, by April, and using her brother's home as a base, she visited Henry Ward Beecher at his famous Brooklyn church and conferred with Harriet Beecher Stowe, who was visiting there. Beecher and other friendly clergymen provided her with lists of parishioners, and she set out on a series of begging visits. She also planned to take some "galvanic baths" that she believed would improve her health.[187]

During Miner's absence, Howland ran the school with the assistance of former pupil Emma V. Brown. Years later Howland boasted of her courage in managing with only a black helper, and indeed the school prospered under their care.[188] By June, however, Howland was in need of "rest and quiet" and went home to see her family. "Not being accustomed to teaching it soon wore her down," her assistant reported. "For some weeks before her departure, she lost her appetite and grew rather nervous."[189] Miner diagnosed the trouble as "my impatient mania," the same malady from which she herself had long suffered.[190] Like Lucy Mann before her, Howland discovered that administering the Miner school entailed a great deal more than teaching. She mixed paint and with the help of the tenant painted the house inside and out. "When you are away down the common, you can see the little cottage gleaming out like a 'city that is set on a hill,'" wrote Emma Brown. Howland supervised hedge trimming, window washing, and yard cleaning. She discovered that the taxes had not been paid, and that the tenant, whose responsibility they were, claimed he had no money. Although everyone seemed to think that Howland would take care of them, she refused.[191]

During the summer of 1858 Miner and Howland came to an agreement that, beginning in the fall, Howland would have total control of the school. Miner wrote: "Having given the school over to you, I shall in no way interfere with any plans you see fit to propose or execute, until such time as I am able to resume my duties there." The two women could try living together on Miner's return to Washington, but if the arrangement did not work, both would go their separate ways. In the meantime, the older woman promised to leave the running of the school entirely in Howland's hands.[192]

Miner spent the fall fund raising in New England, going from town to town, and staying with supporters of her project who introduced her to possible contributors. Although her friends noted that Miner was an eloquent pleader and made a profound impression on her listeners, donations merely trickled in. Miner was hampered by a wracking cough that would not "abate its fury." Nevertheless, she declared, "I . . . *will* have a new house next year, if it be built with only the three thousand we have in hand now."[193]

When Howland reopened the school in the fall of 1858, she had the assistance of Anna Searing,[194] her good friend and "a most faithful teacher & coworker." Searing intended to stay only during the fall term, and Howland was anxious to leave at the same time, but she agreed to remain the entire year if there was no one else to manage the school's affairs.[195] Dedicated to serving the oppressed, she could not bear to see the school closed down. The pupils crowded in, fifty-eight of them, and it is not surprising that they became unruly in such close quarters. But if Howland was inexperienced, she was also tenacious and a good Quaker. She refused to use physical punishment, though she thought that was what the students wanted. "I would not rule a brute by fear . . . much more will I not rule you by it." She appealed to their consciences: "When I walk the street and see the poverty, ignorance, and crime I see there is no time to waste, no time to be frivolous." She reminded her pupils that every one of them had a responsibility to try to overcome the misery of their people: "We must all feel that our duty is never done until we have done something toward showing some poor soul the better way of right and truth."[196]

Howland held the school together, even presiding over its expansion. She and Lucy Mann furthered Miner's plans and helped to make her school a significant part of the life of Washington blacks. Without their dedication to keeping the school alive, Miner's struggles and acquisition of a schoolhouse would have amounted to nothing. It was Miner's dream, but it needed the assistance and devotion of other people to make that dream a reality.

IV

When Myrtilla Miner opened her school in the District of Columbia, she knew that she could count on the opposition of Southerners and pro-Southern Washingtonians, for Washington was a Southern town. Accordingly, she was not surprised when white Washingtonians threatened the school with violence. She had not anticipated, however, that she would become involved in a controversy over the American Colonization Society, an organization devoted to the removal of blacks from America to Africa, which was opposed by antislavery groups. Nor was she prepared for the blunders of a well-meaning supporter who unwittingly threatened her school's existence. But on occasion Miner became her own worst enemy. She was petulant, impatient, and too hasty in writing reproachful, angry letters.

Miner and her supporters faced a dilemma in opening the school. In order to gain the necessary financial assistance, they had to spread word of the school's establishment to sympathizers. But in doing so, they would also attract the attention of people hostile either to any assistance to blacks or to the use of money for anything other than direct attacks on slavery.

Harriet Beecher Stowe unwittingly contributed to the controversy that engulfed Miner's school. In 1853 Stowe traveled to Great Britain, where she basked in the admiration of thousands of Britons who applauded her attack on slavery. The *National Anti-Slavery Standard* reported that at Liverpool she would receive an address of welcome signed by half a million British women and a large donation of money from grateful readers of *Uncle Tom's Cabin*.[197] American antislavery circles buzzed with speculation as to how Stowe would use the money. Samuel Rhoads hoped that Miner's school would benefit from British generosity. Stowe could raise a great deal of money, he said, "if she feels prepared when she arrives in England to announce to her friends an intention of establishing a National School," which had already acquired "a fine lot in a high, healthy and commanding situation in Washington." He, of course, intended her to describe Miner's school and thereby stimulate British assistance, which could end the school's financial worries. Rhoads wrote to Miner: "What a glorious consummation we might hope for, from thy beginning in faith and tribulation!"[198]

Although Frederick Douglass shared Rhoads's hope that the gift to Stowe would be channeled into education, he favored an industrial school rather than Miner's normal school concept. The *National Anti-Slavery Standard*, on the other hand, published a communication from the *London Anti-Slavery Advocate* that opposed using money donated in the spirit of antislavery for the education of freedmen: "Notwithstanding all their disadvantages, there is still spirit and enterprise enough left among multitudes of the free coloured people to maintain their own churches and pay their own ministers; and we do not see why they cannot support their own schools, with whatever assistance they can get from their white friends." The English writer was glad to see free blacks helped, but not with funds raised to assist slaves in gaining their freedom. Stowe should understand that anti-slavery money could be used only to free slaves. "The slave feels more overflowing gratitude to the man who pays down the money for liberation than for all the Abolitionists who are labouring to uproot the system that makes chattels of him and of millions of his race."[199]

Douglass believed that what Stowe did with the money remained her own affair, though he had not hesitated to advise her. "No person, either in England or America has any more right to inquire into the particular mode, in which this money has been or is to be appropriated, than they have to inquire into the disposal of her private fortune." Nonetheless, by the spring of 1854 Douglass was able to inform his readers of some of Stowe's beneficiaries: "That she has given a large sum to Miss Miner's school in Washington; assisted the Reform Tract and Book Society; helped in the support of Anti-slavery papers; and in the assistance of Fugitives, we have occasion to know."[200] The *National Anti-Slavery Standard* named the amount of the gift—$1,000—to Miner's school, adding that since she had had "some difficulties to contend with," the donation would prove "very timely."[201]

In the summer of 1854, when Miner undertook her annual fund-raising trip through the North, two of her pupils accompanied her as proof of the success of the school. Douglass reported that when Miner called on him in Rochester, she was "accompanied by two of her darling little scholars—the latter so nearly white as to make it impossible for the unpracticed eye to identify them with the African race." Douglass found the children smart "and remarkably free and easy in their manner, considering the latitude from which they come."[202] This report infuriated George Thomas Downing, a prominent black businessman, triggering a virulent attack on the Miner school and the Stowe donation.

Downing was the owner of a hotel in Newport, Rhode Island, the manager of the House of Representatives dining room in Washington, an active supporter of John Brown of Kansas fame, and, like many blacks, a vehement opponent of the American Colonization Society.[203] Having spoken with Miner and read the promotional pamphlets of her school, Downing became convinced that her school was "a Colonization affair," "an auxiliary to the Colonization Society," and he found that sufficient reason to oppose her. Downing claimed that "Miss Miner told me, in the presence of two individuals, whom I have lately questioned to verify the correctness of my memory, that the colored people need not hope to be elevated in this country; that it was our duty to go to Africa." Rather than give money to such a school, he declared, Stowe would have done better to leave the funds in England.

Downing questioned Miner's claim in her promotional literature that hers was the first acceptable school in the District of Columbia, denying her statement that children who had attended other schools in the District had come to her unable to read or write accurately: "Why this expose? Was it to tell the world that we must have *white teachers* for our children instead of having them 'taught by colored men?'" Did Miner seek to demonstrate that blacks were not proper guardians of children's "mind and manners"? According to Downing, Miner's low opinion of the black teachers in Washington proved

her "colonizationist tendencies." In addition, Downing distrusted
Miner because she had taught in Mississippi and had included in
her recommendations a statement from her principal that "for more
than twelve months her character at all times had been most unexceptionable." He would have felt happier about Miner if her character in Mississippi had been less exemplary. What Downing wanted
from her and did not find was a statement to the effect that her
school was principally concerned with "Justice to the Colored American at home."

However, in Downing's eyes, Miner's greatest culpability lay in
her persistent emphasis on the almost-white children in her school,
about whom Douglass had written and Miner frequently had spoken.
Why, Downing wondered, should Miner exhibit her lightest colored
pupils? Why should she imply that the children three-fourths white
were particularly deserving of an education? Downing found this
inexcusable: "Thus it is to be said that in the opinion of Miss Miner,
all that are 'three-fourths white' may thank their stars, or rather,
their licentiate slave-driving parents, who are both fathers and masters,
for being 'three-fourths white,' inasmuch as it entitles them 'particularly' to consideration and the blessings of education."[204]

Samuel Rhoads could not permit such a harmful attack, already
copied by several newspapers, to go unanswered. In his usual gentle
but persuasive way, Rhoads sought to set the record straight. Although he understood Downing's sensitivity to the question of African colonization, that did not excuse his unfounded criticism of
Miner and her school. Rhoads reasserted his own long-term opposition to colonization, inquiring how Downing could possibly believe
that he and Thomas Williamson would hold title to a school property
that was an "auxiliary to the Colonization Society." "I have ever
regarded the Colonization scheme as productive of evil—and only
evil—to the colored population of the United States," commented
Rhoads, and he challenged Downing to present any evidence to the
contrary.

What M. Miner's private sentiments are on the subject of Colonization I
have not thought necessary to inquire; but, even supposing they are such
as G. T. Downing avers, I cannot admit that they disqualify her for teaching
a school for colored girls, or that the possibility of some of these becoming

'principals of female seminaries in Liberia' is a good reason that they should not be educated.

Rhoads felt that Downing had deliberately misinterpreted Miner's sentiments. "No unprejudiced person acquainted with M. Miner, can, for a moment, believe that she would make any distinction herself, between the pure blacks and those 'three-fourths white.'" It was true that Miner took two "light-colored pupils" north with her during the last summer vacation, but that was due to the simple fact that their fathers were able to pay their traveling expenses. "I believe," stated Rhoads, "she would as willingly have had with her girls of 'pure African blood.'"

Rhoads waxed especially indignant over Downing's intimation of Miner's insincerity in her opposition to slavery because of her experience teaching in Mississippi. Rather than "adapting" to life and slavery in the South, she had been revolted by what she saw; "her nervous system, and all her bodily powers became so completely prostrated, that it was with difficulty she reached her home in the North." From that moment, declared Rhoads, even though she could easily have secured an excellent position in a seminary for white girls, "she resolved, under strong convictions of duty and the deep interest she felt in the welfare of the colored people—not only of those 'three-fourths white'—to devote her life to the education of colored females, at whatever sacrifice."[205]

Nancy Day, one of Miner's supporters and apparently one of her pupils, also replied to Downing's letter. Downing had participated in the first Colored Men's Convention in America, which had endorsed the idea of an industrial school for blacks. Day inquired what had become of the school, asking if "a liberal subscription & *prompt action*" might not prove more useful than an attack on Miner's school, which had received Stowe's subsidy precisely because the concept of the industrial school had never materialized.

It was not until great *exertions* had been made by Miss Miner to establish a school in Washington, not until it was really established, that Mrs. Stowe aided her, & I have no doubt if you would nobly contribute *yourself* & make efforts to collect funds & start the "Industrial School," Mrs. Stowe & many others would be found ready to contribute towards its permanency.

Day condemned as false the claim that the Miner school was simply a front for the American Colonization Society. If some of Miner's pupils went to Africa as teachers or missionaries, they did so of their own free will and not as a result of Miner's indoctrination. "It is no sham,' but a virtual *labor school*, in which the head, the heart, the body, all must be active & true, to rise to the standard so well sustained by the principal, & nobly aspired to by her pupils."[206]

There was, however, some basis for Downing's charge that the school was connected with colonizationists. That had certainly not been the intention of Rhoads and the other Friends supporting the school. It seems, however, that in her anxiety to secure assistance, Miner exploited every possible argument that might prove financially remunerative. A columned account sheet, found among her papers, although empty of contributions, reveals the following heading:

The undersigned, anxiously desiring the education and elevation of the African population growing up around us, warmly commend the School established by Miss Miner. . . . As many of the colored race are looking to Africa as a permanent home, it is desirable that those who go should be educated, in order that the influence of their example may have an elevating effect upon the heathenism and ignorance of that unhappy land.[207]

Although Miner may not have been a colonizationist, some of her supporters undoubtedly were. For example, her cousin Stephen Atwater of Providence, who found her a teaching position there, was an ardent advocate of colonization. He wrote Miner a very long letter with the intention, as he expressed it, of trying to impress upon her mind the advantages of a close connection between her school and the back-to-Africa movement. Atwater wanted Miner to make contact with the "champions of African civilisation" in Washington. "I hope yet to see you at the head of an Institution that will send out a score of accomplished teachers Yearly who will do great execution both in this country and in Africa in promoting the great work of elevating their Race to a high point in the scale of Christian Civilisation."[208]

Miner herself never declared her position on African colonization, no doubt because the education of black teachers, regardless of where they might undertake to serve, absorbed all her attention. She must have realized that involvement in the bitter conflict over the resettlement of American blacks in Africa could only prove harmful to her ambitions. She had enough struggles on her hands without taking on another.

As a result of Harriet Beecher Stowe's good intentions, Miner was drawn, against her will, into another conflict that seriously threatened the survival of the school. Stowe did not limit her contributions to the very generous sum of $1,000—the nucleus of the funds used to buy the school property—but gave a great deal of time and additional sums of money for the advancement of the school. As we have seen, she financed Miner's 1855 trip to the Elmira water cure and paid Lucy Mann's salary while she ran the school in Miner's absence. In the fall of 1855 Miner approached Stowe about raising money to erect a new schoolhouse to replace the inadequate buildings on the property. Either Stowe or Miner proposed employing a professional fund raiser. When Charles Beecher, Stowe's brother, refused the position, both Miner and Stowe looked around for a likely candidate.[209]

Stowe proposed the services of another of her brothers, or perhaps he volunteered. At any rate, early in the spring of 1856 William H. Beecher wrote Miner that by the first of May he would be unemployed, or, as he put it, he would "soon leave my present people." He claimed to have had considerable experience in fund raising, having "got up" a large female seminary in Putnam, Ohio, and an academy in Euclid, Ohio. Therefore, while he was aware that such a project required hard work and "much prayer," William felt confident of his ability to manage the fund raising for Miner's schoolhouse. "In the mean time," he wrote, "do not let your faith fail[;] the ever blessed Saviour loves you and your poor despised pupils— for he was himself despised & rejected & persecuted—& he sympathises with you & will raise you up helpers."[210]

Rhoads favored the arrangement, especially since Stowe, according to her brother, would be responsible for his salary: "Any agreement which H. B. Stowe may think proper to make with her brother cannot be otherwise than satisfactory to us." In addition, Rhoads looked forward to the alleviation of at least one of Miner's innumerable tasks, so that she might "go to bed without a burden on thy mind and arise in the morning without anxiety."[211] In fact, William Beecher's involvement with Miner's school proved nothing short of calamitous. Indeed one can say in retrospect that Harriet should never have endorsed William as a candidate for the position, for the entire Beecher family knew that he suffered either from extremely bad luck or utter incompetence. The biographer of the Beechers called him "William the Unlucky," for he had a long history of failure, and the family strove continually to keep him employed.[212] Although Stowe probably thought that the fund-raising venture would provide a safe and harmless berth for her ineffectual brother, he not only failed to collect any money, but he involved the school in a bitter controversy that jeopardized its very existence.

Between May and July 1856, Beecher collected a total of $1,262.31 for the school, presenting for the same period an expense account of $1,262.33, leaving the school in his debt to the tune of two cents. Beecher charged the school for invitations, circulars, postage, and all traveling expenses, and when those costs were deducted, there was nothing left of his collections.[213] If his sister paid his salary, the school was liable for everything else. Such an expense account emphasizes by contrast Miner's frugality on her fund-raising trips.

To add insult to injury, Miner learned that Beecher had taken time off from his duties to go to a water cure. Rhoads, in his usual role of arbitrator, tried to soothe her by pointing out that summer was a bad time for raising money. Clergymen had learned that there was little point in asking for donations to worthy causes when all the wealthy parishioners were traveling or taking the waters themselves. The autumn was the best time for charitable appeals. Furthermore, Rhoads felt sure that since Stowe herself had recommended her brother, "it seemed highly proper to engage his services." But he agreed that if Beecher's performance did not improve, they would have to seek a new fund raiser.[214]

Beecher continued in his post, and in December 1856 he published a "Circular," an appeal for funds that aroused great hostility. Miner and her friends had always operated under the assumption that since Washington was a Southern city, the inhabitants naturally feared a large increase in the number of free blacks. They had therefore made every effort to raise money as quietly as possible and had pursued a policy of approaching only known sympathizers in their financial appeals. They had rejected all proposals for extensive publicity as detrimental to the future of the school. Beecher's pamphlet changed all that. In his bid for $20,000 to launch a serious program of education for the half million free people of color in the United States,

he announced that 11,000 of those "suffering people" lived in the
District of Columbia and an additional 130,000 "equally destitute"
threatened to spill over from Maryland and Virginia into the District.
Beecher thus thoughtlessly fed the fears of white Washingtonians
about an influx of blacks into the capital. It is impossible to believe
that either Miner or Rhoads approved the text of Beecher's appeal.

The "Circular" went on to say that the Miner school was especially
anxious to serve the needs of the mulatto children of white masters,
who previously had been unable to free their offspring.

We would open an asylum near them where they may be brought, emancipated, educated, taught housewifery as well as science, and thus be prepared to become teachers among their own mixed race, and places of usefulness
guaranteed to them; and we doubt not many fathers will gladly avail themselves of it, so soon as it is known that our accommodations are adequate.

It was the school's design, declared Beecher, "to receive the more
intelligent daughters of this people, educate and return them to their
homes to extend, as parents and teachers, the blessings of knowledge
and religion." It appeared, then, that Beecher was encouraging whites
who had fathered children of slave mothers to deliver their offspring
to Miner's school. Furthermore, he argued that, following their education, the girls should return to their homes to spread their knowledge to their fellows: And this in Washington, when across the
Potomac River in Virginia it was illegal for a black person, whether
slave or free, to learn to read. Beecher could not have contrived an
appeal that would more effectively damage the school in the eyes of
Washingtonians.

As if that were not enough, Beecher also managed to revive the
question of Miner's association with the American Colonization Society. George Thomas Downing must have felt that his arguments
were vindicated when he read: "We call on the friends of colonization, for if we succeed, teachers and others for the colonies may
be multiplied." Nor could Downing have missed the implication of
the next sentence: "Finally, we beseech all friends of missions; for
where shall we find missionaries and teachers for the hundred millions of Africa, now opening to our view and calling for aid, unless
we educate and Christianize our free people, the Anglo-Saxon-Af-
rican race?"

The circular included an emotional appeal to people of good will: "We intreat all ministers of Christ . . . we intreat the women of our Country . . . we intreat the happy mothers of our land . . . we intreat all friends of the oppressed, for can slavery be removed while the free colored man remains degraded?"[215] In one small pamphlet Beecher had succeeded in creating an injurious portrait of Miner's school, the ramifications of which would be felt for some time to come. It is no wonder Beecher was without a church, for what congregation could have survived his ministering care?

In April 1857 *The Boston Journal* published an appeal for Miner's school based on Beecher's pamphlet. It mentioned the 11,000 free blacks in Washington and the 130,000 in Virginia and Maryland, as well as repeating Beecher's proposal that the school serve as a refuge for the children of liaisons between white planters and black slaves:

It is hoped through this means to reach a class of girls of peculiar interest, of the most beautiful and intelligent, and yet the most hopelessly wretched, and who are often objects of strong paternal affection. The slaveholder will gladly educate and save these children, but domestic peace drives them from his hearth; he cannot emancipate them to be victims of violence or lust; he cannot send them to Northern schools, where prejudice would brand them.

Miner's school was hailed as a solution to the dilemma of mulatto children. According to the article, Miner planned to build "a larger and more suitable edifice for the reception of the applicants pressing upon it from the numerous free colored blacks in the District and adjacent States." This expansion would provide space for 150 students, as well as housing for teachers and for pupils from out of town.

The *Journal* also reported that Beecher expected to raise $10,000 in Boston alone. "The pastors of several churches in New York have pledged their churches in the sum of a thousand dollars each." In addition, Beecher planned to hold a public meeting in Boston and undertake fund raising in "the principal towns of Massachusetts."[216]

The National Intelligencer, a Washington newspaper, reprinted the *Journal*'s story, along with an angry letter from Walter Lenox, a former mayor of Washington. The *Journal*'s account, taken directly from Beecher's "Circular," had obviously aggravated Washingtonians' fears of black migration into the District in response to the educational opportunities offered there. Lenox was pro-Southern in his outlook and eventually joined the Confederacy when the Civil War began,[217] but he probably reflected the mainstream of Washington opinion when he protested: "Now it is plainly manifest that the success of this school enterprise must largely increase our negro population by the inducements it offers." In Lenox's view, Miner's school would attract entire families as well as young people, "until our District is inundated with them." Lenox favored instead the prohibition of further immigration of free blacks, who already constituted a growing charge upon the community, since they lost their jobs as laborers and servants as whites took them over. The mounting scarcity of employment for blacks in the District made their augmented presence in the city a threat to the order of the community.

According to Lenox, the Miner school was a precursor of other institutions of learning in the District that would serve as centers of Republican and abolitionist agitation to end slavery, first in Washington and then throughout the country. Although he did not impute such motives to all of Miner's supporters, he was convinced, nonetheless, that abolitionists would eventually gain control of the school. "This school was started some years ago in humble guise, and in the foothold it has already gained it feels secure of its future progress. Earnest, prompt action can now arrest it peacefully; tumult and blood may stain its future history." Lenox advised the advocates of black education to establish their schools in the North and engage in philanthropy there. Washingtonians could best judge what was beneficial or harmful for the District: "We cannot tolerate an influence in our midst which will not only constantly disturb the repose and prosperity of our community and of the country, but may even rend asunder the 'Union itself.'" The city government should persuade the supporters of the school to abandon it; otherwise, "the responsibility will be with those who by their own wanton acts of aggression make resistance necessity and submission an impossibility."[218]

It fell to Gamaliel Bailey, editor of *The National Era*, to come to the defense of Miner and her school and to deplore Lenox's threat of violence. Bailey had long experience in antislavery agitation. He had lost three presses in riots against his publications before he finally came to Washington in 1847 to begin publishing *The National Era*, which was supported by the American and Foreign Anti-Slavery Society, largely through the assistance of antislavery leader Lewis

Tappan. Even in Washington Bailey endured threats of violence, but he survived and for twelve years remained an effective voice in the capital for the antislavery position.[219] Although he had welcomed and supported Miner, he had given the school little publicity because he believed (wisely, as it turned out) that it would do more harm than good. But in 1857 Bailey decided that he must speak out against Lenox's threatening letter.

The antislavery editor responded with a clever article, in which he deplored Lenox's insinuation of direct action against the school and questioned the source of his vehement opposition: "A southern man we knew him to be, but he had never given any indication of being a sectional, an illiberal, or a suspicious one." At a time when Washington was growing and developing new concepts of the capitol's role within the nation, Lenox's attempt to arouse "popular violence" seemed misplaced and extreme. During the six years the school had been in existence nothing untoward had happened. The value of real estate had not fallen, crime had not increased, and "the teaching of some score or two of colored girls reading, writing, arithmetic, geography and history, has not even shaken the foundations of the Union, or brought down the price of stocks." As a matter of fact, said Bailey, Lenox as mayor of Washington had promised protection for Miner and her school when she had been threatened with violence, and everyone in Washington knew that the school had operated with the support of the president's family: "The President's carriage not unfrequently was seen bearing Mrs. Pierce and Mrs. Means, her aunt, to the humble school of this devoted teacher."

Bailey conceded that the *Boston Journal* had been carried away in its enthusiasm: "Newspapers, as we all know, say a good many grandiloquent things, whether they are talking about great matters or small." Lenox had concluded, on seeing the article, that there was "a plot of the Abolitionists to get up a grand institution in the District of Columbia, to gather together here all the free colored people of the Union, and so put out the light of white civilization!" Bailey quoted statistics to prove that there had been no substantial migration of blacks to the District, thus discrediting Lenox's claim that the education of a few girls would "invite such an irruption [*sic*] of free colored people as shall prostrate the white population, and dissolve the Union!"

Bailey did not hesitate to present the potentially destructive consequences that the closure of Miner's school would have upon the
city's future. If, as a result of Lenox's inflammatory letter, Miner's
school ceased to operate, Bailey believed that the new Republican
party would turn the situation into a political issue. He reminded
Lenox and his readers that the Republicans would have over ninety
members in the next session of Congress, enough to halt any legislation they opposed. If the people of Washington aroused "sectional
excitement" by "open and direct antagonism against the usages,
sentiments, and institutions, of more than half of the Union," they
should not be surprised if Northern representatives saw the District
"converted into an implacable enemy." Northern enmity might result in agitation for the removal of the capital to another site or in
a refusal to appropriate money for the District. Punitive action against
Miner's school could not possibly benefit the taxpayers of the city
and might cause the project that Miner had started to become a
casualty of the rapidly growing sectional conflict. To avert such an
outcome, Bailey advised tolerance:

Can they never be induced to let well enough alone, and act upon the
assumption that Washington city is, and must be, so long as the Union shall
last, common ground, where citizens from all the states meet each other on
an equal footing, and whence all proscription and intolerance should be
forever banished.[220]

Bailey's defense was denied the exposure granted to Lenox's attack, which was reprinted in numerous journals, notably in papers
in Massachusetts, New York, New Hampshire, and Rhode Island.
The result was antagonism against the school not only in Washington
but also in the North.[221] William Beecher began to hear from prominent people in Boston opposed to the school. He admitted that
churches in his own Congregational denomination had disapproved
"from the beginning," but now "the Unitarians & business portions
were thrown off by the Mayor's letter."[222] Clearly, hostility to the
education of blacks transcended regional borders.

Miner went to the editor of the *National Intelligencer* and asked
him why he published "so infamous an article." He replied that he
was "ignorant of any incendiary tendency in the article—but was
advisory to it, inasmuch as it referred to collecting the colored people

here in *masses*—to which he was opposed for any purpose whatever—but was not opposed to educating those already here." Although Miner dismissed the editor as "a real old fogy,"[223] the uproar against her school continued and eventually cost the job of one of her most devoted supporters.

When Miner, homeless and almost penniless, arrived in Washington, she was taken into the home of Leonard D. Gale, chief examiner of patents at the United States Patent Office. He and his family supported Miner in every possible way, and when in 1856 she undertook to form a board of directors for the school, Gale agreed to serve. When Gale first read Lenox's article, he considered that silence remained the wisest policy, for surely the agitation by the school's opponents would soon die down and be forgotten.[224] But the furor over the school escalated rather than diminished, as it became an issue in the approaching city elections. Gale reluctantly decided that he had to sever his connections with the school: "The excitement which has been made here by the Democratic and slavery interest respecting the School, based on the report made in the Boston papers . . . has so reacted on my position as an Employee of the Government that I have been compelled to resign my place as member of the Board of Trustees." The only alternative was to resign his position at the Patent Office, but he could not in conscience relinquish his family's livelihood.[225] In point of fact, severing his connection with Miner's school did Gale no good, for he lost his position in the Patent Office anyway.[226]

Somehow the school survived the turmoil aroused by William Beecher's publication, but the controversy demonstrated the extraordinary degree of hostility throughout the country, not just in the South, toward the concept of education for blacks. Miner had accomplished a great deal in opening and running the school, but this incident made clear both the limited extent of her support and the tenuous nature of her establishment.

For a while, William Beecher struggled on, drawing up a "subscription paper" that he vainly hoped would bear the names of prominent people, and he appealed to the leading clergymen of New York and Boston to collect pledges from their parishioners.[227] By the end of the summer of 1857 he relinquished his duties completely, sending all the papers relating to the school to his brother-in-law Calvin Stowe. Although Beecher claimed that he had $7,000 in pledges, none of the money was in hand. "I collected no more money than was needful for expenses and salary and have nothing in my hands." He hoped that the pledges would be made good, but he had not one cent to turn over to the school as a result of his efforts. "I am very sorry," he wrote to Samuel Rhoads," for this poor result of my effort. I have worked hard & suffered more than in any year of my life." He told Rhoads that he had written letters "all over the country" and preached sermons about the school, adding, "& hope I have done some good."[228] He had, of course, done a good deal of harm.

In announcing his resignation to Rhoads, Beecher implicitly returned the responsibility for fund raising to the man who had voluntarily carried much of that burden since 1851. For many years Rhoads had been Miner's most faithful supporter as she struggled to establish the school and to acquire land for a permanent building. They parted company, however, on the question of the construction and size of the new schoolhouse. Rhoads, conservative in finances, refused to consider borrowing money for building until the debt for the land had been settled. Miner was too impatient to follow so slow a route. Once she had possession of the property she could not be satisfied with its meager housing; she was determined to have a large and elegant schoolhouse and to have it quickly. Rhoads applauded her vision but urged restraint. Unfortunately, that was not Miner's style; she turned to William Beecher with unfortunate results.

Miner also had an obsessive fear of losing the property that had been acquired with so much labor, the title of which (when finally cleared) was vested in Rhoads and Williamson, both uncommonly cautious and conscientious businessmen. Rhoads sought to reassure Miner, protesting that neither his heirs nor Williamson's would ever lay claim to the property being held in trust for the school. Both men would willingly transfer title to a board of trustees, but it was not easy to assemble such a group. In the meantime, Miner should feel confident that unless both he and Williamson died on the same day, no legal problem could arise, for the survivor would continue to hold the land in trust.[229]

Finally, in May 1856, Williamson and Rhoads executed a transfer of title—or what they assumed was a transfer—to the Washington Association for the Education of Colored Youth, which declared its aim to be "the establishment & maintainance [sic] of a High school for colored youth in the city of Washington, D.C. or elsewhere." The school would bear the name of The Washington Normal School for Colored Youth.[230] In fact, the proposed association never became a reality, and the title to the property was never transferred. By the summer of 1857 Rhoads and Williamson concluded that the school must continue, in spite of the failure of the proposed association and the failure of Miner's money-raising schemes. Rhoads was discouraged neither by the controversy over Lenox's letter to the *National Intelligencer* nor by the negative results of Beecher's schemes. He desired nothing more than to see the school in operation, and he believed this goal was in reach. Rhoads advised that Miner and Howland return quietly to Washington, clean the building on the property, and then privately notify the students and their parents when the school would reopen. Miner and Howland should behave as though there had never been any trouble, "precisely as if no movement had been made for collecting a large fund—and no angry denunciations had found their way" into the newspapers. In addition, they should "consult no ex-mayors nor anybody else."[231] (Rhoads had a sense of humor as well as good sense.)

Rhoads was right in his assessment of the situation. The school began to function again without any problems, and at the beginning of 1858, as we have seen, Miner felt secure enough to leave Washington on another fund-raising expedition.[232] Meanwhile, she continued to worry about the legal status of her school. She persuaded Sayles J. Bowen, a Washington businessman, to talk to lawyers in the District, who unanimously agreed that a school for colored girls could not legally be held in Washington. "They say that the courts of the District would, without hesitation, declare such an institution, located here, against public policy and would either indict it as a nuisance or declare it forfeited to the county or city corporation." Bowen believed that the lawyers' opinion accurately reflected the situation in the nation's capital.[233]

Bowen's appraisal must have seemed to confirm the worst of her nightmares, but Miner still refused to give up her dream of building a fine new schoolhouse on the property acquired in 1854. In 1859 she wrote to Rhoads, insolently demanding that he and Williamson sign the necessary papers to begin construction. Once again, Rhoads flatly declined to do so until the necessary funds were in hand. "I will not enter into any engagement to pay money on the strength of

any *promises* to raise funds." Rhoads rejected Miner's charge of the
"crime" of blocking construction: "Thy charges . . . have no other
ground than thy assumption that it is our duty to make ourselves
responsible for the payment of money which we have no security
will ever be paid into our hands."[234]

When Miner lost her temper, she seems to have said whatever
came into her mind. In addition to accusing Rhoads of preventing
construction, she now blamed him for the William Beecher fiasco.
Rhoads responded that he felt "no responsibility in the matter,"
which was, he reminded her, the work of Beecher's sister, "whom
thou as well as we supposed to be an ardent friend of the School."
Rhoads thought that Beecher had acted "disgracefully," and he said
"T.W. [Williamson] and I have endeavored to obtain justice from
H.B.S. [Harriet Beecher Stowe] without success."[235]

Rhoads surely had the patience of Job. His profound commitment
to the cause of blacks, both slave and free, strengthened him to
endure Miner's tirades. In his eyes the important work she had
undertaken largely excused her difficult temper. Finally, however,
in 1859, after eight years of close association with her, Rhoads had
reached the end of his tether. He and Williamson had long been
prepared to transfer the title to the property, but had been unable
to find anyone to assume the responsibility. Miner continued to
admonish him to "give up the trust to someone who will do justice,"
and her attacks at last convinced him to relinquish his hold on the
land for the school. He wrote, "Any further correspondence must
therefore be confined to this single point," closing his letter, "Hoping
thou wilt find more efficient laborers in the work."[236] Miner had lost
her firmest friend. From the beginning Rhoads had pledged his time
and attention in place of personal financial support. He had consci-
entiously kept his promise, working to secure assistance from other
Philadelphia Friends and campaigning tirelessly for the school. Sayles
J. Bowen had declared that Miner was "partially deranged—at least,
she says so."[237] Although that may be too harsh an estimate, she was
not well balanced in her judgment, as her relations with Rhoads
clearly demonstrate.

Miner now turned to Bowen, for he had encouraged her to build
a new schoolhouse. Rhoads and Williamson made it clear to Bowen
that they would not participate in any building project until money
to pay for it was in hand. They only awaited the choice of three

trustees to whom they could deliver the deed to the property.[238] In spite of his enthusiasm for the school, Bowen refused to become a trustee, declaring, "Nor am I willing to accept a position which will cause me much labor, trouble and inconvenience, without fee or reward, when to do so I must submit to have my private affairs laid open to the investigation of others."[239] Miner must have missed Rhoads. She approached Benjamin Tatham, a New York businessman, who declined to undertake a building project two hundred miles away, but was willing to help her in any reasonable way.[240]

Generally speaking, Miner's relations with Bowen were strained and unproductive. Having placed some of the school's money in his care, she infuriated him by making what he termed a "peremptory demand" for the return of the funds. He had made investments that could not be terminated without loss. Miner was in Rhode Island, not in Washington; why did she want the money, when construction was certainly not about to begin? Bowen wrote: "I regret very much the tone and temper you have manifested towards me." Miner had obviously written Bowen one of her characteristically impetuous letters, and he was less forgiving than Rhoads. Bowen's anger baffled Miner, who scribbled on his letter that she had only sent him a "hasty little note." Miner's little notes were lethal. Bowen assured her that she would have the money when the time came to commence construction, but not before.[241]

Having alienated Rhoads and Williamson, lost Bowen's services, had Gale resign as trustee, and found William Beecher unreliable, Miner turned in despair to Benjamin Tatham. He opposed starting construction in the unstable political climate of 1860, but he agreed to serve as a school trustee.[242] Miner then informed Tatham that she also wanted him to take full charge of the property, for she no longer expected to live in Washington. Tatham refused, advising Miner to sell the property to the builder and then buy it back once the school was completed.[243] But willing or not, Tatham received the deed to the property from Thomas Williamson in the summer of 1860, as well as the money that Williamson had been holding. By the end of August 1860, Tatham held $2,413.35 as the Miner School Fund. The following year Bowen sent him $776.62, which brought the building fund to something more than $3,000. Tatham had the deed recorded in March 1861.[244]

He examined the plans for the building but questioned the "propriety" of starting construction while the political situation continued unsettled. If Virginia and Maryland joined the South in secession—and Tatham expected them to do so—then Washington would surely fall to the Southern slaveholders.[245] He repeated that warning after the war had actually begun. Perhaps the conflict would end quickly, but Miner should beware of being overly hasty "to spend the money so long and difficult of collection in a place which may possibly be given up to Confederate knaves—or their friends." There was now no possibility of collecting more funds for the school, for if people were called on to donate money for a school in Washington, Tatham feared "it would make many sick at the stomach."[246]

So, after what had seemed a promising beginning, Miner found her plans frustrated by her failings and others' frailties. She had planned for a large new building when it probably was not practical, and she had misplaced her trust in at least one incompetent man. She had antagonized her warmest supporters and encountered difficulty in finding replacements for them. But she still had the school, the good will of some antislavery supporters, and a small fund for the construction of a new school building. The property was potentially a valuable asset if Washington remained in Northern hands, but as the Civil War began, it was not clear what future lay ahead for Miner's school.

V

Myrtilla Miner reflected the limitations and conflicts of many nineteenth-century women's lives. She was anxious for marriage yet longed for independence. She grew up in religious orthodoxy but could not resist the appeal of spiritualism and magnetism. She insisted on the importance of ladylike behavior while chafing at the physical restraints of female garments of the period. She believed and practiced self-help but felt bitter resentment of women's limited opportunities and rewards. As a young woman, she had longed for advanced education as a way to free herself from the narrowness of rural life. In her struggle for self-improvement, she became a crusader for women's rights, particularly their right to education and fair wages for their work. Since her interest in education and her concern for the rights of women were closely related, her decision to open a school for black girls was a logical extension of her belief that learning meant freedom. In spite of her ideals and ambition, however, poverty and ill health defined Miner's life to a major extent, limiting her achievements and often frustrating her ambitious goals.

Miner never had enough money to live in comfort. Her teacher's pay was meager, and she had difficulty collecting the little that was due her. She borrowed money for her own and her sister's education and found it nearly impossible to repay her debts.[247] The only time she experienced luxury, during her stay in Mississippi, she could not enjoy comforts that accrued from slavery. She had almost no personal possessions: An "elegant sofa-bedstead which she used during all her years" in the Washington area[248] and an Argand lamp for her table were among her few belongings of any value. Although she claimed that her sole objective in life was to open a school for blacks, she in fact sought work wherever available, even considering taking a position in China.[249] She never knew the peace of mind derived from financial reserves, and surely no one ever opened a school with less capital. In 1856, when the land for the school in Washington had been acquired and money was slowly accumulating for the construction of a schoolhouse, Miner confessed that she was completely destitute, "living upon charity & making over old clothes."[250] Her excessive resentment toward the trustees of the school no doubt resulted from her terrible poverty: The school was the only thing she had ever owned, and she would not allow anyone to take it from her.

Throughout her life she worried, probably justifiably, about her health. A frail child, she grew up with her family's resignation to the belief that she would not live to adulthood. She suffered terribly from a spinal infection, but somehow survived and went on to live an unusually energetic life. In 1845 she boasted to her father: "I can take care of myself if nothing more, & that is much more than you once expected I would do."[251] Whatever the cause of the spinal difficulty, it apparently did not result in any deformity or spinal curvature. In an age that equated plumpness with health, she was always thin and frail in appearance, but whether picking hops on her father's farm or walking miles in the hot sun of a Washington summer, she performed feats that would seem to tax the strength of the healthiest woman.

Miner was not above using her physical weakness as a weapon when she was angry, occasionally threatening the parents of her students with her death and the subsequent demise of the school. Her friends evidently subscribed to this attitude. Harriet Beecher Stowe considered Miner "as much the school as Louis XIV was the State & a good deal more. At present under God everything depends on you, therefore before everything take care of your health."[252] Stowe demonstrated her concern by paying for Miner's stay at the Elmira Water Cure.

In 1856 Miner provided a graphic description of the illness that plagued her: "I have suffered from a half-idiotic sensation, ever since the fever left my brain & passed downward into my neck, shoulders & chest—about three weeks ago—previous to which time I had not known a moment's relief from pain in my head, for more than two years."[253] Miner said that she had "barely escaped the horrors of complete insanity, after suffering for two years from a partial derangement of the brain."[254] Miner's friends regarded her illness as "distracted nerves and distressed mind," caused by overwork and constant worry. One of them wrote to her: "Poor Myrtle! . . . Your poor brain has been so overwrought, or rather I should say, your nervous system—that I think you should never, *never* again take upon yourself such cares & labors as you have borne for the last few years."[255]

Miner was susceptible to lengthy spells of depression, when she felt that she could go on no longer. Her friends sought to raise her spirits: "It is not in human nature to have such responsibilities as yours—accompanied by so many perplexing and vexatious circumstances constantly impeding your efforts & plans for the future—without some seasons of depression." They reminded her that because Providence had ordained her to establish the school she must trust that Providence would see her through.[256] When she despaired of her life, Miner concluded that she had accomplished little and that her school probably would not survive her death. In reply to a profoundly despondent letter, her friend W. H. Channing wrote, praising her "nobly disinterested perseverance." Eventually she would see that her work had not been in vain. "And however much your efforts seem to fail doubtless they *do succeed*, in a far more real way, than you can now see, even with the eye of faith."[257]

Notwithstanding her periodic depressions and constant preoccupation with her ailments, Miner did not appear a melancholy person. People enjoyed her company, and her relatives remembered her as bright and jolly, with a hearty laugh.[258] The Friends in Philadelphia clearly rejoiced in her presence and came to regard her as a personal friend. When they communicated family news to her, they were assured of her interest.[259] People in Washington missed her when she went away and gladly undertook tasks on her behalf, from collecting and forwarding mail to installing a new caretaker for the school property.

Miner showed surprisingly little interest in politics, particularly in view of the fact that she lived in the nation's capital during a period of intense political ferment and strife. She did not want her school to become a political issue because she feared that notoriety would destroy her project. But that did not deter her from asking for help from politicians, and though she was a Democrat,[260] it was usually Republican members of Congress and their families who gave her money, franked her mail, and visited the school to provide moral support. Although strongly opposed to slavery, Miner supported neither immediate abolition nor the use of force to achieve emancipation. Indeed, she had favored the emancipation scheme of her Mississippi principal for its gradual approach. Her close friendship with members of the Society of Friends probably reinforced her opposition to the use of violence in the struggle to end slavery.

Although Miner was aware of political developments, from her viewpoint the crucial improvements in American life were to come in religion, in education, and in the rights of blacks and women. She responded to almost all the currents of cultural and social change in the first half of the nineteenth century, and her life reflected both the turmoil and the enthusiasms of the age.

For example, she took great stock in the water cure, an extremely popular medical device that made great claims for the curative properties of water, even in diseases such as cholera. Water cures offered a road to health that probably helped many people, merely by encouraging cleanliness and a liberal consumption of water. Hydropathy, as it was called in the nineteenth century, led to the establishment of at least seventy health centers in the United States.[261] One of the first, the Elmira Water Cure, directed by Doctors Silas and Rachel Gleason, must have had particular appeal for Miner, for the management and medical treatment were shared equally by husband and wife, both of whom were physicians.[262] After her visit to the Gleason establishment, Miner subscribed to the *Water-Cure Jour-*

nal and became an ardent convert to the precepts of cleanliness and the frequent use of water. Although she had always been careful of appearances, she believed, following her stay at the water cure, that extensive bathing was essential: "I require every scholar to bathe all over every day, and should not like a person in my house who would neglect it."[263]

Miner was also deeply interested in phrenology, the study of the shape of the human skull as an indicator of character and personality. She subscribed to the *Phrenological Journal* and in 1860 went to Fowlers and Wells's Phrenological Cabinet in New York to have a reading. The phrenologist accurately described Miner as "very intense, wide-awake, sharp, active, sprightly, lively, and industrious; cannot keep still, nor be lazy." Although he mistakenly judged her health as vigorous, the reader correctly assessed her resolute spirit: "You have an uncommon amount of energy, spirit, resolution, and efficiency; have a great amount of will, perseverance, and determination of mind; are very much devoted to the cause which occupies your attention." The phrenologist commented on her independence and self-respect and, apart from his comments on her health, analyzed his subject quite precisely.[264]

Miner's passion for betterment extended to those around her and most particularly to her younger sister Achsa, whose life she undertook to regulate. In fact, Miner moved forward with her plans for their joint operation of a school, even though it was plain that Achsa was not designed for teaching. "It confuses my brain to teach school," Achsa complained,[265] but Myrtilla paid no attention. Her tendency to bully her younger sister is one of Miner's least attractive characteristics, for though she arranged Achsa's life with the best intentions in the world, she never once thought to consult the girl's wishes. Achsa, on the other hand, worried incessantly about her older sister's opinion, begging Myrtilla not to scold her if she made mistakes in her letters and smarting under suggestions of ingratitude: "Myrtle I think you misjudge me for I certainly do appreciate your kindness and have said repeatedly that you exerted yourself more on my account than any other person living."[266] Achsa ventured to suggest that she would be more effective teaching embroidery than reading, writing, and arithmetic. However, this scheme did not fit in with Miner's plan, and she sent her sister off first to Clover Street Seminary in Rochester and then to Providence, Rhode Island, where she was to study piano. Even though she was separated from her more dynamic sister, Achsa felt her presence strongly:

I am trying to take good care of my clothes and I will be more careful what remarks I make. The new tooth-powder you sent is nice, and I don't pick my face scarce at all. I am trying to turn my toes out, and I hope you will find me the least bit improved.[267]

Achsa worried that her sister would not love her if she did not live up to Myrtilla's standards. Myrtilla, of course, loved her younger sister very much. When she was unemployed and deeply worried about her lack of funds, she made sacrifices to send money to Achsa for shoes, gloves, laundry, and stamps.[268] At the same time, Myrtilla depended on Achsa for the understanding that she did not receive from the rest of the family. "Perhaps you remember with what earnestness I used to plead your cause if any of the family said aught against you," wrote Achsa. "If you wish to see me eloquent, let some one speak against you and I should soon become so."[269] Achsa suffered from her sister's demanding temperament and yet sensed that Myrtilla relied on her for unquestioning love: "I wish I were with you, wish I could . . . be your Guardian Angel, and greatest comfort, but it seems when I am with you I am generally your greatest trial instead."[270]

Achsa studied the piano assiduously, practicing six hours a day. She bought drawing materials to study art and considered learning to play the organ and taking voice lessons. According to Myrtilla's plan, the younger sister would become proficient in the areas in which Myrtilla did not shine, and together they would be able to open a very good school, possibly in St. Louis. In June 1850 Myrtilla and Achsa agreed to leave together for St. Louis at the end of the summer. But Achsa became ill with cholera morbus and died within a few weeks.[271] Miner's heart was broken: "Just at the hour when I thought my hopes realized in full fruition—the very week she was to come to me manifesting in herself the complete realization of all I hoped and had labored for, the news of her death reached me." She seemed to grieve more for her aborted scheme than for the loss of her sister, yet she wrote: "I half think I will return to Providence in November and stay there as long as I live and die as soon as I can and be buried under the same evergreens."[272] Family tradition held that Achsa died as a result of excessive study, especially from practicing the piano for many hours a day.[273] Myrtilla's family sympathized with neither her intellectual ambitions nor her plans for her sister.

In her distress over Achsa's death, Myrtilla turned to spiritualism for comfort. She had been raised a Baptist, quoted the Bible frequently, and instilled Christian principles into her students. Her strong Protestantism led her to attack the Roman Catholic church. However, her extensive contacts with the Society of Friends helped to relax her denominational rigidity. She also grew very close to Unitarian clergyman William Henry Channing, and it was he who conducted her funeral service. The major support for her school came from Quakers, Congregationalists, and Unitarians, and clergymen of various denominations always headed her lists of possible contributors. In her notes are pious statements about Christianity: "Before Christ came to the earth hope was presumption—but now despair is desperation!" and "Before men could realize that God was a God of pity, it was necessary for Him to assume a human form and bind his peaceful footsteps to earth to mingle with the wretched."[274] She wrote to one of her brothers: "How much I thank you for your views on *prayer*, words may not tell."[275] Yet one of Miner's closest friends criticized her indifference to churchgoing, whatever the nature of her theological views.[276]

Miner's commitment to spiritualism was the strongest force behind her changing perception of Christianity. American interest in spiritualism probably began in 1848, when the Fox sisters began their careers as mediums in Hydesville, New York, near Auburn. The following year in Rochester the sisters held a public demonstration of their powers, and by 1850 they were practicing as mediums in New York City. All over the United States people reacted to spiritualism with great enthusiasm, but western New York was afire. "During the summer of 1850, some one hundred mediums blossomed in Auburn," and in 1859 eleven mediums and lecturers were operating in the county where Miner was born and where members of her family continued to live.[277] At the time of Achsa's death, many bereaved people were seeking to communicate with their departed relatives through the assistance of mediums, and Miner quite naturally sought a potential source of comfort through contact with her sister's spirit. When Margaret Fuller died in a shipwreck in the summer of 1850, the same summer that Achsa died, Miner was convinced that this dual loss held a very special significance.[278] Although Miner had never known Margaret Fuller, she admired her writing and identified strongly with her career. She attempted to reach the spirits of both of the departed, and though she never reported any success with Fuller's spirit, she contacted Achsa through a niece called Celia, who received the message in the form of doggerel:

Lift up thy heart lift up thy eyes
  Me seeking in the uper [sic] skies.
And Myrtle tell her I'll be there
  God's joys with her to freely share.
Tell her to teach the darkened child
  Of Jesus teachings meek and mild
Then to ascend—come up—make haste
  No more on earth her time to waste.[279]

Miner naturally wanted to relate to her friends, "new and truthful things about spiritualism," but they were not always receptive. Mary Abigail Dodge, a journalist who wrote under the pen name of Gail Hamilton, reported meeting Miner in the spring of 1859. According to Dodge, Miner had long been an invalid, though she remained a "very energetic, practical woman with an indomitable will." She reported the following encounter with Miner:

She came to see me recently, when I remarked how bright her eyes were and how abundant her hair. She said she would tell me the secret of it. . . . She has a firm belief that an intelligence higher than her own has taken her in hand, and has been and is effecting a cure. For a long time her hands, without any will of her own, would beat the distressed parts of her body severely—first spine, then liver, head, throat, etc. daily for five hours. Now, it only begins when she is weary. She is sensible, not given to vagaries, and her testimony would be admissible in any court of justice.[280]

Miner went into trances and had visions.[281] By the time she moved to California in 1861 she had made a connection between spiritualism and magnetism, concluding that she would be able to cure illnesses by combining her power of spirit communication with the healing magnetic forces of her own body. Consequently, she set herself up as a physician, advertising in the papers of San Francisco that she dealt in clairvoyance, magnetism, and spiritual consciousness. She was prepared to "hold conversations in the normal or entranced condition with individuals or select parties on the Laws of Life and Health." She prescribed for diseases and was prepared to "delineate the characters of persons, directing those who are doubtful or troubled to a successful application of their time, talents, money and power." She proclaimed "vital magnetism" the "most powerful healing agent known," to be used to cure diseases or mental states. Mothers would be able to "save their children from premature death." Miner offered her services as a "sympathetic Clairvoyant, in which she temporarily feels in her own system the disease of her patient, and can prescribe the natural remedies to cure all."[282]

Miner appeared to her friends after her death. Through a medium she reenacted her deathbed scene, "& finally spoke & said she ought not to have gone yet." Through the medium she declared that "she was satisfied with what was done up there, pointing in the direction [of the school]. . . . But there was something that was not done, & *she wanted it done*," though she did not explain what it was. She appeared once again through the same medium, when she discussed her journey to California. "This lady had not the least knowledge of Myrtle at all. It was very satisfactory to me," concluded a member of Miner's family.[283]

Many Christians, including clergymen, were convinced of the truth of spiritualism. Spiritualism did not necessarily weaken one's commitment to the teachings of the Bible, but it helped to weaken denominational fervor. As was the case with Miner, spiritualism catered to the prevalent belief that there was a dimension to life that churches did not adequately consider.

In addition to the distresses of her illness and the death of her sister, Miner suffered from not being married. She liked the company of men. In 1856, when staying at the water cure, she lamented the absence of interesting men with whom to talk. She also believed that "most old maids [were] very disagreeable."[284] When she was living in Rochester, her plans for marriage fell through, and this failure may well have been one of the reasons for her unhappiness there. We have already seen the intense quality of her emotional involvement with Walpole Cecil, the feckless young man she sought to redeem. Indeed, years later one of her friends described Miner as a complete romantic:

It does seem to me that her romantic nature, her irrepressible nature, her wildly, foolishly romantic nature are some of the reasons why [she acted as she did]. She looked at me that day so long ago . . . with such a wondering pity in her face because I was so indifferent to the regard of a young man who, although many years younger than herself was yet very, very interesting to her.[285]

In response to Miner's complaints, one of her oldest friends told her that she ought not to grieve over her unmarried state, for Providence had kept her single so that she could teach black children. "Believe me my dear friend, constituted as you are you could not be as happy married as single."[286] Nevertheless, Miner continued to long for marriage, exclaiming that she wanted either to marry or to die, she did not care which. Her friend replied: "But really, Miner, I don't think you had better marry, for you cannot have your own way so entirely as you do now, & I am afraid you would not be happy without it."[287]

In Washington Miner had a "beau," a Quaker named Jonathan Dennis, who, according to Samuel Rhoads, "kindly tendered his assistance in any matter that he could be serviceable." The Friends in Philadelphia believed that Dennis could give Miner wise advice on buying land for her school.[288] In the spring of 1857 Miner apparently decided to get married, perhaps to Dennis, but her plans were to be thwarted once again. A friend wrote, in an attempt to reassure her in a moment of disappointment: "I know not what men may think of your 'unattractiveness,' but I know I think you handsome, not luxurious & voluptuous, but bearing the impress of purity, self respect, and enough of tenderness to meet the want of any nature above the sensual merely."[289]

Miner never married, but by the summer of 1858 Jonathan Dennis had married someone else. Although he maintained an interest in Miner's school, he laughed at her, especially mocking her commitment to spiritualism.[290] Nevertheless, after Miner died, it was Dennis who went through her papers, found her will, and accompanied Emily Howland to the cemetery in Georgetown to have "the body buried in a very deep brick grave & sealed up."[291]

Miner was impatient with the lesser frustrations endured by women of her day. She disliked housework and could not bear the complicated ritual of dressing in the clothes that women were condemned to wear in the nineteenth century. A member of her family recollected that she sewed all her undergarments together so that she could get them on in a hurry and embarrassed her relatives by hanging the curious combination on the clothesline.[292]

Miner resented the limited career opportunities open to the women of her day. At one time she considered studying medicine, in imitation of Elizabeth Blackwell, but one of her friends, while insisting that she was not "squeamish, over nice or a would-be-fine lady," urged Miner not to follow that profession. If Miner wanted to try something different, her friend suggested that she become a writer like Margaret Fuller or leader of an expedition to California, like Eliza Farnham.[293]

In 1849 Eliza W. Farnham engaged a packet ship to carry a hundred or more "intelligent, virtuous and efficient women" to the gold rush state, all of whom would be under the age of twenty-five, have $250 for expenses, and recommendations of good character from clergymen.[294] Miner was interested and secured a copy of the articles of agreement for the voyage, but in the end decided not to go, noting that Farnham sailed to California "accompanied by two widows & a maiden lady."[295] She may also have been influenced by the recognition that since she was well past twenty-five, she did not meet the age requirement.

Miner's interest in Farnham's expedition is an indication of the restless spirit that both amused and troubled her friends. When she accepted the teaching post in Mississippi, they wondered if the next news would tell of her joining the American army to fight in Mexico. A former colleague affectionately ascribed to Miner the quotation about one venturing to do

> what others only dreampt [sic] about
>   And say what others only thought, & *do*
> What others did but say & glory in
>   What others dared but do.[296]

When Miner read an article that chastised women for being "restless and foolish" and for saying "silly things," she wrote an angry reply to the editor, attributing female restlessness to their "dependent condition, which condition brings a proportionate degradation."

Miner correlated the condition of women with the institution of slavery. Slaves were forced to "say pretty things to appease their masters, & gratify their vanity—& the condition of women being in many respects no way superior—they must act the same part." Because men enjoy independence, said Miner, they "have no need to immolate their consciences on the unholy altar of man's vanity, where woman is bound to burn incense continually." Miner attacked the article's complacent acceptance of the double standard that allowed a good woman a role in helping a man to gain fame and fortune but denied her any share in his success. In her eyes such a man was a parasite. "This is indeed man's nature, & will continue to be so, until woman improves the right her Heavenly Father gave, the right to enjoy the honor, as well as endure the toil, & her sons inherit from her the nobility which the sons of dependent man fearing mothers never yet inherited."[297]

Since Miner spent much of her life in upstate New York, she must have been familiar with the Seneca Falls Conference of 1848 that adopted a Declaration of Independence for women. At any rate, on Independence Day 1850 Miner reflected on what the day meant to her. She concluded that unlike the Constitution, the Declaration of Independence had "a prophetic spirit, pointing to the full freedom of the future." Yet the day depressed her.

Why the full benefits of the great struggle wrought out by the war of the Revolution, were limited to *"white, male citizens,"* is very mysterious; while History records the fact, that all classes, even to the slave, were equally active in achieving the victory, & winning the liberty, which should have been as broad & boundless as the efforts that had secured it.

If men loved liberty so deeply and "thought it so glorious a boon to secure to their sons," why was it not "equally precious for their daughters," who remained as degraded as slaves, apparently deserving oppression rather than "rights and immunities"? "If so, Heaven defend the sons as well as the daughters of the next generation—for 'no power of man can save him whom the gods have abandoned,' and he who is cursed with a *weak mother* must be so abandoned!"[298] On every Fourth of July Miner wrote "a protest against the celebration of the day, for she declared that it had not proclaimed the equality and independence of woman."[299] Miner was not really so indifferent to the political process as her other writings would indicate.

When Miner submitted an article to *The Wreath*, a magazine published in New York, the editor rejected it as unsuitable on the grounds of its "slightly *controversial* character." The magazine welcomed articles on "the reciprocal duties of the sexes," but Miner had taken issue with the editor's position that woman needed "a double portion of self-denial, & self-sacrifice." The editor held that woman's truest friends were those "who would prepare her for what she will inevitably meet, rather than to encourage a vain dream of social equality which will never be realized."[300] The editor, closing her letter of rejection with the Christian platitudes of female sacrifice against which Miner had directed her article, had apparently missed Miner's point.

Miner was a close friend of Paulina Wright Davis, one of the organizers of the first woman's rights convention and the editor and proprietor of *The Una: A Paper Devoted to the Elevation of Woman*, which began publication in Providence, Rhode Island, in 1853.[301] It was Davis who gave Miner her Argand lamp, probably during one of Miner's numerous visits to her home. Davis also gave support to Miner's project by printing several accounts of the school's progress in *The Una*. Describing Miner as "earnest, energetic, enthusiastic" and "capable of entire self abnegation," Davis praised her for her mission "to teach our heathen": "Had she taken her life in hand and gone out to India or the South seas, she would have had the sympathy of all Christendom; have been spoken of with reverent affection." But here in the United States, said Davis, "she toils with few to care for or sympathize with her, but she is, nevertheless, doing a glorious work, for she is caring for the souls of those whom no one has regarded in the past."[302]

Miner of course perceived the parallels between the exploitation of women and the enslavement of blacks. By opening a school in Washington she would strike a blow for the advancement of black women. She had originally planned to establish a school for white girls in St. Louis, but that scheme had perished with the death of her sister Achsa. Although she had exceptional skill as a teacher, Miner could not expect to open her own school and attract white pupils of the highest class without Achsa's musical accomplishments. Hence she arrived at her alternative scheme. Rather than remain a compliant female and accept the fate of the underpaid, ill-used women teachers whom she knew so well, she reacted in a positive way to the uncertainties of female employment and opened a school that she could run almost single-handed. Her dramatic decision brought economic distress and emotional crisis. But it was her choice alone and one that brought considerable independence in its effective defiance of the nineteenth-century exploitation of female teachers.

Miner's first statement about equal treatment for females concerned education. As early as 1841 she had written to Governor Seward asking his support for improved facilities for the education of women, stating the position that preoccupied her on the Fourth of July in 1850. Educated women made better mothers. She wrote to Seward: "By a little observation you will discover, that indigent females find it almost impossible, to obtain means of acquiring sufficient knowledge, to render them competent to, or I might say capable of training their offspring as the necessities of our beloved country require." Why was it, she wanted to know, that there were many colleges "with all the privileges, & advantages, guaranteed to them which America can afford, & all for the male sex?" Why was there nothing for females? Miner's longing for an education is reflected in nearly every line she composed, especially in such expressions as *"the anguish* of an inexpressible thirst for science, without means to quench it."[303] A year later she wrote to the governor: "You do not tell me *why* there are no institutions for females." Was it perhaps because women, with so much learning, would become "unfitted for the society of men?"

Miner complained to Seward about the abysmally low salaries paid to women teachers. She had contracted large debts in the process of getting an education, and the salary she now earned made repayment impossible. Men, on the other hand, with the same training and the same number of pupils, earned enough to "dress genteely" and to save money as well. Miner ironically agreed that men should receive "reasonable compensation" for their greater "muscular power." But she questioned whether in teaching there was "so great a difference between the power employed by a man & a woman." Male teachers could save enough to continue their education, but women could not. Miner felt that she was an "ignoramus" because she had not had the education that men enjoyed. She asked the governor's help in rectifying the situation: "Will you Sir, oblige me by answering

this, & tell me if in your judgement I may ever hope to see any
advancement in America beyond this barbarian custom" of privileges
for men that were not available to women.[304]

Miner wanted two things: adequate public education for women
and equal pay for women teachers. Seward assured her that he did
not subscribe to the theory of the "supposed intellectual inferiority
of the Female Sex." He reminded her that he had made speeches
asserting that women excelled men in "the moral and intellectual
instruction of children and youth." Women should have access to
public instruction equal to that "in colleges and academies," and
Seward promised that he would heartily support any efforts that
Miner and her friends might make to improve the quality of female
education.[305] Not satisfied with such vague words of encouragement,
Miner wrote again to Seward and received the following answer:
"Reforms never begin with rulers, even in a Republic." He added:
"They are adopted by statesmen when the public mind is preparing
to sustain the agents who shall undertake to carry them forward."[306]
In other words, it was the responsibility of Miner and women like
her to press women's claims and win government support.

One of Miner's colleagues in Providence, while calling for "war
to the death" against men's tyranny, declared that in general men
were petty and "contemptible" rather than threatening. Furthermore, women themselves were at least partially responsible for their
position in society:

You speak of the privileges man has taken to himself. I would rather say
that woman has weakly, blindly offered them up at the shrine of idolatry
and like the poor Indian bartering his lands for a few beads she has exchanged
the reality for a dream. And in my estimation, our own sex are far more
culpable for the continued existence of these evils than their brothers, for
as far as my experience goes, I find two men for every one woman who
bestows one serious thought on the subject.[307]

Miner positively did not agree. In a speech, apparently to a teachers' association in New York, she warned that women should not
be deceived by men who claimed to care more for women's rights
than women themselves. She acknowledged that woman is often
powerless and docile, because "she is placed in a condition where
she cannot help herself." Yet Miner stressed that there were two

practical means of altering the female condition: for women to write about their grievances and to teach young girls to write and to write well so that they would grow into useful and productive women.[308]

Miner believed—and her teaching indicates that she practiced what she preached—that learning to write was the single most important thing that a woman could do. "As we would have the world know that we possess souls, noble, generous, and philanthropic, souls exalted by a cultivation of all that is good, lovely, and amiable in woman's nature and a suppression of all that is disagreeable, let us write!" Learning to write well would force women to discipline themselves and would give them an opportunity to prove their accomplishments to the world. Miner considered that, with their weak voices and excitable natures, women found it difficult to speak in public. But writing would enable them to "form a part of the intellectual and moral whole," and they had an obligation to try to "alleviate the woes of mankind."

Miner knew perfectly well that it would not be easy for women to gain writing skills, when the use of "colleges, libraries and various other literary privileges" was denied them.

On those she [a woman] may look with ardent desires for the advantages they afford; but to her they are forever forbidden, as much as was the fruit of the tree of knowledge to Eve and in the view of many, the results of partaking them would be but a renewal of the dreadful curses which descended upon her guilty head.

Nevertheless, women could gain education by determination and hard work: "Thou shalt dig thy education from the bowels of the earth!" Miner returned to the recurrent theme of the discrepancy in pay for women and men teachers:

For thy labors are so slightly rewarded, that thou canst never gain more than a mere subsistence; and when, with all the powers of earth against thee, thou hast gained the prize, thou shalt see weak men, whose qualifications are in every respect inferior to thine, teaching but the same number of pupils and perhaps with not half the success, command more than double the sum that thou canst obtain, because thou art a woman.[309]

Miner's teaching experiences had not been happy. She had moved restlessly from place to place, always feeling exploited and collecting her pittance of a salary with persistent difficulty. Nevertheless, in spite of her negative experiences, she maintained a touching faith in the power of education to solve the problems of the world. In propounding her concept of the teacher's task, she employed trite images, such as minds as "easily moulded as the clay in the hands of the potter." "From this extreme susceptibility of young minds a teacher's influence may be said to be without limit, for mind once brought to act upon mind never ceases."[310]

Because of her tremendous faith in education, Miner believed that educational opportunities for women would mark a near-victory in the battle of the inequality of the sexes. The same faith spurred her on when she decided to open a school for black children, which would strike a blow for the freedom of both blacks and women. Thus she regarded education as the great liberator. When she stressed the importance of adequate pay for women teachers, she was dealing not only with a personal problem, but with a crucial issue in the struggle for adequate teacher training. She knew very well from her own experience and that of her acquaintances that all too often people began to teach after a few months' schooling, simply in order to eke out a meager living. Miner longed for public training for teachers to be followed by decent salaries that allowed for further education. If education was to be a liberating experience, then teachers must be adequately prepared for their vocation.

Miner was acquainted with the educational theorists of nineteenth-century America. As we have seen, she corresponded with William B. Fowle and secured employment through his assistance. She knew the family of Horace Mann very well, and Mann's wife and sister helped out in Miner's school. When Miner taught in Providence, the director of public schools for Rhode Island was Henry Barnard, who was second only to Mann in his international reputation as an educator. Barnard set up a traveling model school "to give demonstration lessons in the art of teaching."[311] Miner and her friends also followed with interest the career of Catharine Beecher as she spoke and wrote on the importance of education for women.[312]

Over the years Miner developed clear ideas about the qualities required of a good teacher. Although discipline remained paramount, it should not have to be enforced by corporal punishment, for if men thought they could beat knowledge into children, women could only persuade their charges to learn.[313] Miner was a strict teacher, demanding obedience and good order in the classroom. Only in a calm and orderly setting could learning take place. Furthermore, in accordance with nineteenth-century practice, morality was an important part of the curriculum. The girls she taught must be not only wiser but also better when they left her school, for they would be the instruments to bring knowledge to thousands of ignorant blacks throughout the United States and Africa.[314] Miner constantly reminded her pupils that they were united in a great enterprise.

She and her friends had ambivalent feelings toward the blacks with whom they dealt. Although they constantly stated that the girls in the school were intelligent, competent, and highly motivated, they frequently commented on the character weaknesses of both parents and pupils. One of her closest friends urged Miner not to sacrifice her health for the sake of her students: "*Let the school go* rather than sacrifice your precious life for such a thankless generation." And later she wrote: "You must *try* . . . to let the negro subject alone for a year at least—'*Can* an Ethiop change his skin?' or can the white man's intellect change the deep sensuality and degradation of the African? If so, only by the slow process of ages."[315] Still another friend, close to the family of abolitionist Gerrit Smith, believed that the plight of blacks in the North was worsening: "To be sure there is a great deal of sympathy felt for them in the *abstract*—but personal contact with them as equals & associates seems to me removing farther & farther."[316]

Miner felt deeply the ingratitude of the blacks she was trying to help, calling them "poor miserable people, who are so degraded that even while they receive the blessing, they cavil because it is not greater or more, instead of improving by it & giving thanks as reasonable beings should." She interpreted their ingratitude as an indication of how desperately the blacks in the District required her help, as "the highest proof of the necessity of effort on their behalf." She described the blacks of Washington as "doomed to waste life, hope, health, love."[317]

But they would not be doomed if she had her way. She urged her students to prepare themselves in every way for "the great battle of freedom." "God grant you may prove yourselves good stewards of your opportunities." They should seek to better themselves in every aspect, from writing style to manners. Courtesy, said Miner, was not "servile respect such as you would readily grant some finely-

dressed nobody who would willingly trample you under her feet."
Politeness did not mean suppressing "one particle of the feeling of
. . . equal humanity," but rather was the "outgrowth of polite, gentle
minds." Miner sought to divest her pupils of "any awe of race,"
without sanctioning rudeness. "Let not this reproach which I have
often heard flung about you, that you were spoiled by being made
equal, be true of you."[318]

Miner paid great attention to her pupils' behavior, trying to instill
in them habits that would make them models for less fortunate
blacks. She constantly urged them to be prompt in arriving at school,
to avoid quarreling with their fellow students, to sit quietly and
calmly in their seats, and to be tidy in caring for their clothes. She
disliked them to crowd around the stove—a commentary on the
draftiness of the schoolroom—and she discouraged vain preoccupation with clothing. "Is it not a dreadful thought that the sun has
risen and set seven times upon our lives, moved us on just so much
nearer the grave, which ends our work here and now finds us no
whit farther toward the perfect than we were last Monday?" But
like the good teacher she was, Miner emphasized the great importance of learning:

The scholar's conscience should speak thus—There is a great deal in this
world for my mind to learn, this world is a sort of primary school where
my spirit begins to grow. In this life probably I have the only chance to
learn the lessons and the knowledge which the Creator has given me here;
if I neglect this chance it is lost forever, my mind goes starved and dwarfed
in the sublime temples of God's Universe.[319]

Miner knew exactly the kind of women she wanted her students to
become, and no matter how much she praised them in public, in
private she insisted that the students match her high standards.

Visitors to the school noted that the pupils manifested every gra-
dation of color, from very light to very dark. Miner seems not to
have distinguished among them, and to the horror of at least one of
her friends, concluded that intermarriage, or, as her friend termed
it, "amalgamation," was the solution to the problems caused by a
mixed society. "Whatever may be practicable or desirable at the
South—it is utterly repugnant to a Northern mind to contemplate
practical amalgamation." Miner's friend asserted that in intermar-

riage "the whites must be great losers—and the colored people very *questionable* gainers."[320]

It is true that Miner stressed the almost-white members of her student body, and even Mary Mann mentioned those with "good Anglo-Saxon heads."[321] But Miner probably emphasized their presence in an attempt to arouse the sympathy of potential contributors to the school. There is no indication that she showed any favoritism in her treatment of pupils regardless of their color. Her complaints about the pupils' parents were equally unrelated to color or class. For example, when Philadelphia Quaker Passmore Williamson, after assuming the guardianship of the daughter of a slave and a white doctor from Georgia, enrolled the child in Miner's school, Miner did not hesitate to complain that the child was a great burden and a terrible liar and that her father had reneged on his promises to pay for her keep.[322] It made no difference to Miner whether the pupils were pampered near-whites or poor and dark-skinned; all had to live up to her standards and obey her rules.

If Miner was often discouraged and despondent about the success of her undertaking in Washington, the thought of two of her pupils, Emma V. Brown and Matilda Jones, made her certain of the extent of her accomplishment. For she gave to those two girls an unquenchable thirst for learning that eventually took them both to college at Oberlin. Emma Brown became the assistant teacher at Miner's school and was so listed in the publicity pamphlet in 1858. From January to June 1858 Emily Howland ran the school with only Brown's assistance. When Howland went home, Brown ran the school alone until the end of the term and reopened it in the fall of 1858, before Howland's return.[323]

The young woman was deeply grateful to Miner, writing to her, "A void is left in our hearts by your absence that can *never* be supplied, for are *you* not the *founder* of our school?" Although she could never repay Miner adequately, she could help to fulfill Miner's ambitions for her pupils by becoming a teacher. "If I teach others although it may be ever so little, and they teach succeeding generations, your good work will be increased and in this way *only* I feel that I can repay you for all your kind teaching." The discovery of the joy of teaching was among the blessings that Brown had received at Miner's hands. "When I see one of the scholars eyes suddenly brighten with some intelligent idea that I have conveyed to them—

then it is that I feel *true* happiness."[324] Brown determined to study harder, to satisfy the insatiable desire for knowledge that Miner had awakened in her, "a restless craving for something higher and better that no efforts of mine can subdue."[325]

Matilda Jones, another of Miner's prize pupils, believed that the school had changed her entire life. "I no longer think or feel as I did, but instead there is an indescribable longing after something higher & higher, and sometimes I get so dissatisfied with the life I live, that I nearly turn away with disgust," she wrote Miner. Nonetheless, she rejoiced in her changed perception of life:

Miss Miner if you had never come to Washington, I'm afraid that we would not have had the aspirations and feelings, that we now have, we can scarcely be grateful enough to you, & the strengthening Power that supported you through the obstacles & trials, that you have had to surmount & endure in teaching us the only true way to escape from this galling bondage, that is to get knowledge, & use it.

And she added: "God help us to be true to the teaching!"[326]

Jones faced the difficult questions of life with considerable courage: "Why is it that the Anglo-Saxons have held these people in Slavery so long?" For her the answer was ignorance on the part of both the enslaver and the enslaved. She too believed that the blacks of the District of Columbia did not appreciate Miner's efforts in their behalf. She lamented the stupidity of "my own people," regretting that she must speak the truth, however unpleasant.

I think that the reason that these efforts are not appreciated is, because of the system under which we as a people, have lived so long—they have been deceived so many times, & been taught that they must not be educated, not even learn to read, that they have acquired a habit of distrust, even to those who would help them.

Jones asked Miner to overlook those faults. "I trust that all may soon come to a knowledge of the truth, & then we will be in a fair way to break the chains that confine us."[327]

In 1858 Miner began negotiations to secure the admission of Emma Brown and Matilda Jones to Oberlin College. Not until January 1860 did a representative of the college inform Miner that she had been able to arrange funds for the two girls, and if they were willing to do "some light work that will not involve much care & responsibility," it was probable that all the costs of the college could be met. Miner herself should not try to supply money "from your little treasury," for "the Lord will provide." A postscript added that the names of both girls had been entered on the lists for the term beginning in February.[328] The Oberlin *Alumni Register* records them as enrolled in the College of Arts and Sciences, Brown from 1860 through 1862 and Jones for the session 1860-61 and again 1865-66. Neither girl received a degree.[329]

In 1865, after having operated her own school in Georgetown, Brown became one of two teachers in the first public school for blacks in the District of Columbia. She was then made principal of Sumner School, "the focal point in our school system," according to one account. She eventually married a supervising principal in Washington, lived a long and full life, and remained a close friend of Emily Howland for as long as she lived.[330]

In 1861 Matilda Jones and a friend opened a school in the building where her father kept a feed store.[331] She reported to Miner in the fall of that year that she felt more or less optimistic about her school, though the pupils were slow in returning. In expectation of eventually returning to Oberlin, she planned to study Latin and geometry.[332] After her second stay in Ohio, Jones returned to teaching in the District and eventually married the Reverend S. W. Madden, pastor of the First Baptist Church in Alexandria, Virginia.[333]

Brown and Jones were Miner's great success stories, and through their example she demonstrated the validity of her passionate belief in education as the liberator of the oppressed, whether women or blacks. She had a profound faith in the power of education to create productive and useful human beings. By her action in creating the school in Washington, she proved, not only that a woman could achieve great things, but also that blacks could learn and aspire after knowledge and become competent, effective teachers. Miner, then, was a true pioneer in education.

VI

In 1858 Myrtilla Miner passed the control and direction of her school to Emily Howland, while she sought to regain her health and raise funds to erect the elusive but much desired new schoolhouse.

Miner had become interested in spiritualism to the extent of acting as a medium, and it appeared that she would no longer participate in the operation of the school that she had opened in 1851. Howland liked her work, enjoyed her independence in running the school without Miner, and took pride in her success as a teacher.

In February 1859 Miner suddenly appeared at the school, without notice. Howland was furious, claiming that Miner had arrived "without a note of warning," that she had "popped catlike upon us." She reminded Miner that she now had full control of the school and that Miner's return was in breach of their agreement of the previous summer. Was the older woman ill and retreating to the only place that was home for her? Had she heard of Howland's great success as a teacher and jealously returned to reclaim her school? Did Howland react too violently because she herself felt insecure about her rights over the school? Although we do not know what passed between the two women, it must have been a harsh exchange, for Howland immediately made plans to live somewhere else, refusing to remain in the same house with Miner. "I have told M. Miner that I will never live with her again, that experiment has been fully tried," Howland wrote to her family. She wanted no part of the school with Miner at its head and within a month had decided to return to her home in New York.[334]

Whatever the exchange between the two women, Howland felt wronged and Miner, guilty. To Sayles J. Bowen and his wife, Miner claimed diminished responsibility on the grounds of her own mental instability, adding that Howland had "misconstrued her motives." Bowen interpreted Miner's conduct as foul temper rather than insanity and hoped that her work as a medium would improve her disposition. "If the spirits can so far control her as to cause her to govern her temper and that loose unruly member of hers properly, the world will have lost nothing when they take the guardianship of her."[335]

In her letters, Howland condemned Miner and defended her own decision to leave. Washingtonians gossiped about the quarrel, and Bowen, who had been one of Miner's supporters, turned against her completely. He reported to Howland that there was peace in the nation's capital, but it would not last. "We expect again to see the hatchet uplifted, not against the sons or daughters of *Noah*, but of *Ham*, and when the strife begins, depend upon it, there will be weeping and wailing and pulling *wool* till one or the other party is annihilated."[336]

Jonathan Dennis wrote Samuel Rhoads an alarmed letter, lamenting Howland's departure and warning the Philadelphian that Miner had begun to make contracts for the construction of a school building. Rhoads, though equally concerned at the loss of Howland's services, assured Dennis that Miner could make no contracts without the approval of the trustees. But Rhoads's reply did not put Dennis's mind at rest. He went out to the school to determine the nature of Miner's plans for the future and was told that construction would commence as soon as blueprints were ready.[337] Howland now informed Rhoads that, according to reports from Washington, Miner planned not to build a school with the money she had collected but rather a dwelling house for herself with a small school building attached. Surely, observed Howland, this was not the purpose for which the school's supporters had donated money. Although Howland admitted that Miner had never actually told her of her intentions, she claimed to have seen plans for a dwelling house rather than a school.[338] However, in Miner's papers the only building plans are for the construction of a schoolhouse.

Rhoads was naturally distressed at the unfortunate turn events had taken. He had spent so much time working to make Miner's dream a reality, never faltering in his support even when he suffered from her eccentricities. But now he criticized Miner for having driven Howland from the school and gave Howland his sympathy and understanding: "I trust thou wilt not permit the unpleasant termination of thy engagement at Washington to rob thee of the satisfaction which should result from thy disinterested, and I have no doubt, successful effort to improve the condition of the abused colored people."[339]

According to Howland, Miner's greed was destroying the school. Upon her return, she began charging pupils a flat rate of $1.50 a month, much more than many of the girls' parents could afford. As proof that Miner was overcharging her pupils, Howland cited the fall in enrollment to fourteen within one week of the new policy.[340] Howland's experience in Washington had convinced her of the need for a school for black children, but she believed that Miner was not the person to run it. She had visited the Cook School, operated by George Cook after the death of his father, and found it inadequate in every way. Although the school had been in existence for twenty

years, there were no maps, no blackboards, and no library. Therefore, Howland suggested that people wishing to advance the cause
of black education in the District might better give their assistance
to Cook rather than to Miner.[341]

One of Howland's Washington friends corroborated the reports
of the steady decline of Miner's school. Matilda Jones did almost all
the teaching, while Miner was busy with "the spiritual circles of our
city." The school was dying for lack of attention:

We understand that the colored people are getting very much dissatisfied
and that all of the best scholars are leaving the school. They say, "We have
none but a colored teacher and we might just as well get up a school of our
own as to pay the price we do to Miss Miner." This is too true and I would
not be surprised at all if next winter found the school house without a
scholar, unless indeed, a change is effected.[342]

Miner apparently was obsessed with the construction of a new
building on the school property, and gossip continued to report that
she constantly referred to the proposed structure as "my house."
Washingtonians concluded that the schoolhouse would never be built
as long as Miner controlled the property, for her relations with the
Philadelphia Quakers had deteriorated to "*quasi* warfare." The Philadelphians were desperate to rid themselves of the trusteeship, but
had been unable to find anyone willing to assume responsibility,
though, as we have seen, Benjamin Tatham finally filled that place.
Sayles J. Bowen advised Miner "to get married and then her husband
could do what she desired for I did not believe any one else could
or would."[343]

In 1859 Miner approached Martha B. Briggs, a black woman who
had taught in Massachusetts and Rhode Island, proposing that she
assume responsibility for the school. Briggs refused on this occasion,
but years later became the first black principal of the Miner Normal
School.[344] Miner did not return to Washington in the fall of 1859,
which left Matilda Jones to begin the school year as the sole teacher.
The older pupils lamented that they were forced to work "pretty
much alone,"[345] but eventually Miner did appear and spent at least
part of her time teaching. When Jones left for Oberlin in February
1860, two of the older students became Miner's assistants. There
were few pupils, so the girls had time for "both studying and teach-

ing," as well as learning to operate the sewing machine that Miner had brought to the school.[346] For Miner had added to the burdens of teaching and spiritual work that of selling sewing machines.

The school that Miner had opened with such high hopes in 1851 had deteriorated considerably by 1860. In March of that year Benjamin Tatham, the trustee of the property, believed that Miner had closed the school entirely and rented out the house.[347] In fact, Miner was living there alone, and one night in May someone set fire to the building, an eventuality that Miner had feared ever since she had come to Washington. About one o'clock in the morning, the sound of "crackling fire" awakened her, which she knew meant trouble, for no fire had been lit in the stove that day. When she opened her bedroom door, she smelled smoke. She dressed hurriedly and rushed to the front window screaming "Fire!" with what she described as "awful fury." Then she ran for water, screaming all the while, until eventually the neighbors heard her and came to her aid. One of them climbed on the roof and extinguished the flames there, but when Miner returned to her room, she found the curtains and "a quantity of waste papers" burning. Within a half hour the fire was out. The moon was bright and the night "still & lovely," which had made the fire easier to control. Miner believed that if she had slept five minutes longer, it would have been too late. She felt relieved that she lived alone and had not had to waste time awakening other people. "The fire was introduced by an incendiary between the clapboard & lathing, & had burnt much between them before bursting out." Miner wrote: "For the last year the ruffians had been so quiet, I tho't they had given me up." She had underrated them, however, and it had been a narrow escape, "giving one the idea that the angels watch over us when we sleep."[348]

After the fire, Miner left Washington once again, this time on a business venture to sell sewing machines that took her to Chicago and as far west as the Mississippi River.[349] While Miner was traveling in the Middle West, Emily Howland wrote to Emma Brown in Oberlin, suggesting that she apply for the position of teacher at Miner's school. Somewhat reluctantly, Brown agreed. "I do not like or respect Miss M," she wrote, "Yet I owe her an eternal debt of gratitude."[350] It is not clear what disagreement had taken place between Miner and her prize pupil, but apparently Brown accused

Miner of saying cruel, unkind things about her. Before leaving for Oberlin, Brown had declared that Miner, who "would scruple to say anything," had lost the support of people in Washington because of her vicious tongue. Consequently, Brown felt unable to work in the same school as her former teacher, although she decided to write to Samuel Rhoads to discover Miner's plans. "I shall never teach there while she has anything to do with it."[351]

Nonetheless, Brown understood the nature of her debt to Miner: "I should not have been here [in Oberlin College], I might have remained in ignorance forever if it had not been for her instrumentality."[352] This, indeed, was precisely Miner's place in the history of education, for in spite of her idiosyncracies, she had the vision and the tenacity to create a successful school for black girls. Although she irritated and alienated almost everybody she worked with and was a thorn in the side of her supporters, no one could deny that she had acted while others merely talked.

In the spring of 1861 Miner returned to Washington to tie up any loose ends in preparation for her final departure. She rented the school building, indicating that she had given up any hope of continuing the school. Over the years Miner had collected books, maps, globes, "philosophical and chemical and mathematical apparatus, and a great variety of things to aid in her instruction in illustrating all branches of knowledge." When she rented the schoolhouse, she stored all these educational materials in one of the small cabins on the property. During the war they were "damaged by neglect, plundered by soldiers," so that what eventually remained was of little value.[353] It has been suggested that the danger of invasion during the war hastened the final closure of the school,[354] but it is more likely that Miner at last concluded that she could find no one willing to take responsibility for the school's operation. She herself had lost interest in teaching and remained, as always, terribly poor. Surely the sewing machine business was further evidence of her continuing desperate need for money.

In the summer of 1861 Miner left for California.[355] The reasons behind her choice are not clear. She probably hoped to make some money and had maintained an interest in California since the days of Eliza Farnham's expedition. She may have wanted to get as far away as possible from a city tense with civil war, and it is possible that she nourished the faith that she would find new support for her school.[356] She must also have envisaged the possibility of gaining renewed strength in California's mild climate.

As we have seen, Miner set herself up in San Francisco as a "Sympathetic Clairvoyant" and magnetic healer. Her ministrations appear to have been successful, for she began to make money from her work. In 1862 she sent Benjamin Tatham two hundred dollars from her earnings, which demonstrated that she had not forgotten the school.[357]

While Miner was in California, people in the East wondered about the future of the school in Washington. Ednah H. Thomas, who had given Miner the first one hundred dollars to open the school, wrote to Howland inquiring for news about Miner and the school: "How stands the property thou & Myrtilla Miner once had possession of?"[358] A Washingtonian named Nancy Johnson, who had remained Miner's friend when others had deserted her, shared the hope of others that the school would be reopened. In the spring of 1862 she approached Bowen, who was working on Capitol Hill, and asked him to draft a bill and persuade Congress to grant the Miner school a federal charter. He drew up the charter at once, and when he asked for the names of the incorporators, Johnson listed herself, Benjamin Tatham, Miner, and Bowen. Bowen refused to have his name associated with that of Myrtilla Miner, and after "a lengthy and earnest conversation on the matter," he erased his name from the list of incorporators. Bowen finally decided to oppose a federal charter under any circumstances and wrote to Howland: "I have not thought it my duty to interfere with matters under the control of *spiritualists* as this concern is evidently to be."[359]

In spite of Bowen's opposition, senators took up the cause of Miner's school and pushed through the federal charter. In 1860 Republicans in Congress had hoped to provide money for public schools in the District of Columbia, but the move failed because of Southern senators' opposition to black education. In the course of that debate, Senator Henry Wilson of Massachusetts had urged the importance of education for Negroes, citing the good work of Miner:

There is . . . a noble woman here in Washington teaching colored girls; and if the Senator from Mississippi [Jefferson Davis] and the Senator from Virginia [J. M. Mason] visited that school and saw the mental culture there, if they would not be proud of it, and thank God that these darkened minds were being cultivated by the efforts of philanthropy, I misunderstand these gentlemen altogether.[360]

In February 1863 Senator Wilson introduced a resolution in the Senate "to incorporate the institution for the education of colored youth in the District of Columbia."[361] Such was the magic of Miner's reputation in some circles that Congress, apparently freed from opposition by the secession of the Southern states, moved to give a charter to a school that did not exist. However, they reckoned without the Southerners that had remained in Congress, loyal to the Union, but antagonistic to black education. Senator J. W. Grimes of Iowa, chairman of the District of Columbia committee, and Senator John S. Carlile of Virginia debated the incorporation. Carlile, though an opponent of secession and one of the architects of the state of West Virginia, denied the right of Congress to interfere in education in any form. In his opinion, there was no legitimate reason for Congress to enter into any scheme for the education of blacks. According to Carlile, the sole justification for government involvement in education was assuring the intelligence of voters; he trusted that the United States had not yet reached the point of allowing blacks to vote. Education was a private matter better left to parents. "Why not leave to private enterprise, to the promptings of parental affection, the power of educating the children?" said Carlile. He could see no reason why Congress should make the education of Negroes its business.

Senator Grimes, on the other hand, thanked God that he came from a section of the country with "nobler and loftier sentiments" regarding education. In Iowa people believed that education was necessary "to elevate the human race." But he pointed out that the purpose of the federal charter was simply to protect the property that had been bought some years before; the government would not have to spend one cent.

Senator Lot M. Morrill of Maine joined the debate. "Gracious God, sir, has it come to this, that in the American Congress, and at this late day, an honorable Senator shall rise here and enter his protest against a measure of public popular education?" As education was the mark of a civilized nation, he rejoiced that New England saw public education as "the first great duty of the State." Morrill was appalled that a senator should object to the instruction of Negroes. Surely the time had come to allow Negroes to be educated if they could find the means. Morrill said:

Whether now or hereafter there is to be a system of public education for the negro by the United States Congress or by the States, I trust that from this time forth it will never occur in the Congress of the United States that it is thought proper or expedient to raise an objection against private individuals educating the negro if they choose to do so.

The bill passed and became law on March 3, 1863,[362] one day before Miner's forty-eighth and next to last birthday. She was thus assured that her work would continue, if official approval could help.

In spite of his opposition to the charter, Bowen was anxious to see the school reopen. He discussed the issue with people in Washington, and "with a single exception," they agreed that Lucy Mann, Anna Searing, and Emily Howland should operate it. Bowen proposed this scheme to Howland: "You three have the confidence and good will of the entire population here, white and colored, and Miss M. is obnoxious to all, save one or two, over whose eyes she had managed to pull the wool so thick that they cannot see her as she is." Although the time seemed right, the scheme could not be implemented without Benjamin Tatham's approval. As it turned out, Tatham would not give his permission, for he was pledged, according to Bowen, "to do nothing in that line nor permit any thing to be done till instructed by her Majesty. So it must lie over till the 'spirits' move her to return from California."[363] No one in Washington knew what Miner was doing or what plans she had for the future. In the fall of 1862 the United States government requisitioned the schoolhouse as a hospital for ex-slaves afflicted with smallpox,[364] so that, for the time being, no one could take any action to reopen the school.

Meanwhile, out in California Miner was enthusiastically seeing the sights. In 1863 she took a harrowing trip into the mountains, traveling on a mule over narrow, hazardous trails. Miner clearly relished the danger and discomfort, writing, "I was all chafed and mauled and pummeled, so that I could not move without groaning for pain for many days and nights, but was *glad* all the time."[365] The following year she visited Petaluma, where she suffered a serious accident. Miner loved to ride very fast, and so one of her friends, while taking her for an outing, drove his "fine span of black ponies" at top speed. But the light buggy overturned at a corner, throwing Miner out with great force. Her right hip was bruised badly in the accident, making her very lame. "I was compelled to keep my bed," she wrote, "until I became very nervous from inaction, suffering from congestion of the whole right side and fever, until it culminated last week in a profuse hemorrhage of the right lung, which reduced me very low." Eventually she was up, "slowly moving about, leaning upon a cane," but felt that the accident had destroyed all the good effects of her stay in healthy mountain air. Although she had been feeling "agile and strong," she had now become very weak. "My aspect," she wrote, "is that of a hopeless consumptive." She wrote of her death, anticipating that she would follow antislavery activists Owen Lovejoy and Joshua Giddings to the grave. "We have all worked well, and I shall find company with whom I can still work to great advantage 'on the other side of Jordan.' "[366] Although the fall from the buggy could not have caused tuberculosis, the blow and consequent lengthy stay in bed might have aggravated an already existing condition.[367] At any rate, Miner had been unwell all her life, and now was suffering from a mortal illness.

Her only hope for recovery was a sea voyage, and since she longed for home, she decided to take ship for the East Coast. Such a voyage involved sailing from San Francisco to Panama, crossing the isthmus, and then sailing from the Atlantic coast of Panama up to New York. It was an undertaking to exhaust the strong and healthy; for Miner it must have been a terrible ordeal. Somehow she survived and for a while stayed with friends in New York. Then she moved to Washington, arriving there in December 1864.[368] A rather macabre story appeared in a newspaper, reporting that when friends arrived at the railroad station to meet Miner, she was not on the train. Inquiring of station personnel, the friends learned that "a dying woman was in a car that had been dropped off the train." They finally traced her to the suburbs and found her alone in a railroad car. After lifting her from the car and carrying her down some steep banks, they took her to the home of a friend. According to the newspaper story, Miner rallied enough to ask after a particular teacher in the city, saying, "I want her to open the school before I die." The newspaper reported that as a result of her urging, the school was reopened, but in fact this did not happen.[369]

Miner was taken to the home of her friend Nancy Johnson, where she lingered for ten days, coughing incessantly, but when she could catch her breath, she talked about her plans for the future. She conversed with her "invisible friends," the spirits, and seemed "very happy in such communion." She died on December 17, 1864, at the age of forty-nine and was buried in Oak Hill Cemetery, with the Reverend William Henry Channing, pastor of the Unitarian Church of Washington, conducting the funeral services. The coffin was opened in the vault:

She looked so natural and so beautiful. It seemed as if she were only sleeping. The long, brown curls from one side had fallen partly over one cheek and lay across the throat. A strange and lovely sight, never to be forgotten, by those who witnessed it.[370]

On December 31 two of her friends—or former friends—went to the cemetery and had the coffin placed in "a very deep brick grave & sealed up."[371]

In reporting her death, *The National Anti-Slavery Standard* praised her founding of the first school for free black children in the nation's capital, "when her heroic benevolences subjected her to mob violence and to social insult." The *Washington Daily Morning Chronicle* and the *Daily Times* of Washington also mentioned her death.[372] In the decade of the 1850s it had seemed to many people nothing less than a miracle that Miner had been able to establish a school for blacks in Washington. The real miracle is that the school, which had not functioned since 1860, despite the federal charter, did not die with her.

The members of the board of the school as set up by Congress were Henry Addison, John C. Underwood, George J. Abbott, William H. Channing, Nancy M. Johnson, and Myrtilla Miner. After Miner's death, Johnson and Channing were the only members left who had even peripheral connections with the school. Channing had occasionally given Miner advice and encouragement, and Johnson, whose husband may have lectured on astronomy at the school, had remained Miner's faithful friend. It has been suggested that as Miner became more involved in spiritualism, she lost interest in her old friends and connections. While there may be some truth in this assertion, a more logical explanation may be that, having alienated so many of her old supporters, she was forced to look elsewhere for new ones.

With the war drawing to a close, Channing and Johnson again discussed reopening the school, probably with Lucy Mann in charge. But there was opposition to Mann on the grounds that she had "such active enemies who will thereby become enemies of the Miner School." Mann's supporters, however, insisted that the blacks of Washington and Georgetown favored her leadership. The New York Freedman's Society, which sought to take over the Miner property, erect a new building, and open their own school, presented an even more formidable obstacle to reopening the Miner school. The society seemed too powerful to stop, and alternative schemes were therefore formulated. One of these plans proposed acquiring a piece of land from the War Department and moving the house already standing on the Miner property to the new location, where Mann could then begin the school.[373] Since Miner had always stressed—and everyone else agreed—that the house was totally inadequate as a school, such a plan seemed farfetched.

For a while the board served simply as the guardian of the increasingly valuable school property. They did not reopen the school, both because of disagreement concerning the teacher and because the District now boasted a public school for black children, with Emma Brown as one of the teachers. Before long, however, the need for a training center for black teachers became obvious. General O. O. Howard, head of the Freedmen's Bureau, approached the trustees of the Miner school and offered them $30,000 from the bureau's building fund for the establishment of a college for black girls.[374] For reasons not now known, the offer produced no results. Miner had originally planned for the creation of a normal school, and her early acceptance of a more elementary level of education had stemmed from her perception of a need. Nevertheless, she had never lost sight of her eventual goal of a school where black women would learn to be competent instructors and examples for their pupils to emulate. The destruction of slavery and the development of black education demonstrated the wisdom and foresight of Miner's plan, even though she herself had not been able to implement it.

In 1867 Congress chartered Howard University in Washington, and two years later the university established a small normal department for the training of teachers. In 1871 the Miner Corporation decided to lend its support to Howard's program, and as the result of an agreement between the two, the Miner trustees and the Howard administration assumed joint control of the normal department. The arrangement proved unsatisfactory, however, and in 1875 the trustees dissolved the contract and leased a building for the operation of its own school, naming it Miner Normal School.[375]

The new school planned to offer an education equal to that of the best normal schools of New England. A New Englander, Mary Smith, became principal, and the Miner trustees encouraged the most advanced teaching methods.[376] The school held a memorial service for Miner and hung her portrait in the building. In the speeches that formed part of the ceremony, people talked of the affection that her pupils had felt for her. John Mercer Langston, who would later be a member of Congress from Virginia, "spoke very eloquently to the young men and women, urging them to bear in mind the fact that at present the entire colored race [was] . . . on trial."[377]

In 1872 the trustees of the Miner Corporation decided to sell the land that Miner and the Philadelphians had bought in 1854. They made a substantial profit, receiving $40,000 for the original $4,300 investment. The trustees set up the Miner Fund, and with a portion of the money acquired another lot in the District, at Seventeenth and Church Streets, N.W., where they erected the Miner School building, and in 1877 transferred the Miner Normal School to its new quarters. The stated purpose of the school was the training of teachers for the black children of the District.[378] Miner had envisaged the training of teachers for black children throughout the United States and in Africa as well, but if her spirit was watching over the new school, the actions of the Miner Fund trustees must have gratified her, as William Henry Channing said in his speech at the dedication of the new school: "If Myrtilla Miner's spirit was permitted to be present at the opening festival of her 'normal school,' she must have felt herself blessed beyond her highest hope by such a marvelous triumph." Channing discussed Miner's accomplishments at length, mentioning particularly her courage:

How little did I dream when, years and years ago, at Rochester, I met, one evening, a young, keen-eyed, thin-cheeked, pallid, yet elastic and fire-souled girl, of slight figure, and seemingly frail in health, and heard her scheme of organizing a school for black children . . . of what wonderful success her magnanimous efforts were to achieve.[379]

When Frederick Douglass spoke, he told of his attempts to discourage Miner from undertaking her project, and of his delight that she had persevered without him. When he had finished his speech and was sitting down, he turned to Channing and said, with deep emotion: "That this scene should actually happen in Washington; that . . . I, a fugitive slave from Maryland, should be here in my present position, when we look back upon the past, seems absolutely miraculous." Channing felt that Douglass "seemed bowed with awe, as well as gratitude."[380] *The Woman's Journal*, which had called Miner "one of the heroines of the irrepressible conflict" because of her work "in the humble walks of the lowly," used the dedication of the new building as an occasion to write about Miner and her great contribution to "the future of the colored race."[381]

The spacious new building provided the normal school with more space than it required, and consequently it rented to the District government the two unused floors, using the income to avoid depleting the capital of the Miner Fund. An agreement that female graduates of the public high school would be admitted to the Normal School worked well. In 1879 the Miner school became semipublic through an agreement that the Miner trustees and the board for public schools in the District would jointly control the establishment. The Miner Fund would pay all expenses, the Miner trustees would nominate the principal and her assistant, but the nominations would have to be confirmed by the public school board. In 1887 the Miner Fund withdrew its support of the Normal School, and from that time on the school was an entirely public institution.[382] In 1914 the Miner Normal School moved into a new building on Georgia Avenue, adjacent to Howard University. There were many suggestions for a new title, but the name Miner persisted, to the "satisfaction of the Negro community."[383] Miner Normal School became Miner Teachers College in 1929, and in 1955, following Supreme Court decisions outlawing segregated schools, Miner merged with Wilson Teachers College to become District of Columbia Teachers College.[384] The name Miner School disappeared as a result of the merger, and in 1975 it was further removed from the memory of Washingtonians, when the District of Columbia Teachers College merged with Federal

City College and Washington Technical Institute to create the University of the District of Columbia.[385] Miner Elementary School in northeast Washington is the sole reminder of Myrtilla's struggle for black education in the District of Columbia.

In the meantime, the Miner Fund had benefited from careful stewardship. Since they were no longer responsible for the financial support of the normal school or the teachers college, the trustees felt that they should provide funds for other educational purposes. In 1887 they bought a building that housed the first kindergarten for black children in Washington, which was named the Miner Institute. The Miner Fund provided scholarships for students at Lincoln University in Pennsylvania, Hampton Institute in Virginia, and Howard University. It supplied funds to settlement houses in Washington and to the National Training School for Women and Girls. One of its most important donations was $20,000 for the Myrtilla Miner Memorial Library at Miner Teachers College, enabling that institution to become a member of the American Association of Teachers' Colleges.[386] In 1940 the fund was officially dissolved, with its assets divided between Lincoln University and Hampton Institute.[387]

In the ninety years since Miner had resolved to establish a school for black girls in Washington, great changes had taken place. Emancipation had become a reality, and blacks had seen their great hopes of accomplishment frustrated. Yet, through it all a few people remained true to Miner's vision: Black children should have so sound an education that people could never claim that Negroes could not learn. Miner's faith in education was profound, and she was willing, with all her frailties, to face danger and discomfort to demonstrate the truth of her convictions. She herself gave up the struggle, but she had stimulated sufficient enthusiasm in others to guarantee that it would continue. Although her name is largely forgotten even in the District of Columbia, she performed a great service for the black people of the city and of the country as a whole.

Myrtilla Miner made many enemies in the course of her lifetime. She aroused the bitter hatred of Emily Howland and her friends, estranged her former pupil Emma V. Brown, and alienated Samuel Rhoads and the Friends of Philadelphia. But after her death, as the years passed, people largely forgot her difficult personality and remembered instead her bravery in opening the school in Washington and standing firm in her faith in education in the face of threats, violence, and arson. Although she was impatient, arrogant, and opinionated, she was also fearless, tenacious, and full of ideas. She reflected the discontent of nineteenth-century women with the life to which they were relegated and loudly proclaimed the injustice of woman's position in society. Paramount to her thinking was her belief in education as the liberator of the oppressed. She therefore sought to insure a level of educational opportunity that would grant freedom and equality to the exploited. It was a noble ideal, and if she did not always live up to that ideal, she never lost sight of it. Throughout her life she was restless and dissatisfied, but she used her discontent constructively in the creation of a school that proved an enduring benefit for many people.

NOTES

1. Lester Grosvenor Wells, "Myrtilla Miner," *New York History*, 24 (July 1943): 359–60; manuscript biography of Miner, p. 6, Myrtilla Miner Papers, Manuscripts Division, Library of Congress (hereafter referred to as Miner Papers).

2. Myrtilla Miner to "My dear father," December 10, 1845, Miner Papers.

3. Ibid.

4. Miner, School essay, undated, Miner Papers.

5. Ellen M. O'Connor, *Myrtilla Miner: A Memoir* (New York: Arno Press and the New York Times, 1969), pp. 10–11.

6. Ibid., p. 12; Wells, "Myrtilla Miner," p. 361.

7. O'Connor, *Miner: A Memoir*, p. 10.

8. Miner wrote a letter to her father, dated November 8, 1839, describing her first days at the seminary, but the catalogue of the seminary lists her as a student only for the year 1841. Muriel L. Block to L. G. Wells, May 24, 1941. Both are in Miner Papers.

9. Samuel W. Durant, *History of Oneida County, New York, with Illustrations and Biographical Sketches of Some of Its Prominent Men and Pioneers* (Philadelphia: Everts and Fariss, 1878), p. 228.

10. Quoted in Muriel L. Block to Wells, May 24, 1941, Miner Papers.

11. Miner to Seth Miner, January 27, 1840, Miner Papers.

12. Dr. Robert H. Fennell, Jr., to J. Pacheco, March 18, 1980, April 2, 1980.

13. Miner to Seth Miner, January 27, 1840, Miner Papers.

14. Miner, undated, unsigned essay, Miner Papers.

15. Miner, undated essay, Miner Papers.

16. Miner to Seth Miner, March 28, 1840, Miner Papers.

17. Listed in seminary catalogue for 1841. Muriel L. Block to Wells, May 24, 1941, Miner Papers; Miner to Seward, December 24, 1842, William H. Seward Papers, University of Rochester Library, Rochester, New York (hereafter referred to as Seward Papers).

18. Miner to Seward, December 18, 1841, Seward Papers.

19. Seward to Miner, December 27, 1841, Miner Papers.

20. *Special Report of the Commissioner of Education on the Condition and Improvement of Public Schools in the District of Columbia* (Washington: Government Printing Office, 1871), p. 207 (hereafter referred to as *Special Report of the Commissioner of Education*); George Washington Williams, *A History of the Negro Race in America*, 2 vols. (New York: G. P. Putnam's Sons, 1883; reprint ed. New York: Bergman Publishers, 1968), 2:197; Wells, "Myrtilla Miner," p. 361.

21. Miner to Seward, December 24, 1842, Seward Papers.

22. *Rochester Daily Advertiser*, October 11, 1843, January 1, 1844, June 28, 1844, August 5, 1844; Blake McKelvey to L. G. Wells, December 16, 1941, Miner Papers.

23. E. G. Miner to M. Miner, December 17, 1843, Miner Papers.

24. Seward to Miner, January 29, 1844, Miner Papers.

25. Seth Miner to M. Miner, March 26, 1844, Miner Papers.

26. E. G. Miner to M. Miner, March 31, 1844, Miner Papers.

27. E. G. Miner to M. Miner, May 3, 1844, Miner Papers.

28. E. G. Miner to M. Miner, February 18, 1844, Miner Papers.

29. Fanny to Miner, July 22, 1844, Miner Papers.

30. Amanda H. M. to Miner, October 13, 1844; Achsa Miner to M. Miner, November 15, 1844, Miner Papers.

31. S. Atwater to Miner, October 27, 1844, Miner Papers.

32. Ibid.

33. Seth Miner to Achsa Miner, February 14, 1845, August 19, 1845, Miner Papers.

34. Miner to "My dear father," December 10, 1845, Miner Papers.

35. "William Bentley Fowle," *Dictionary of American Biography*, 20 vols. (New York: Charles Scribner's Sons, 1980), 6:561–62.

36. William B. Fowle to Miner, June 23, 1846, Miner Papers.

37. O'Connor, *Miner: A Memoir*, pp. 14–15.

38. Maria to Miner, February 13, 1847, Miner Papers.

39. Phares advertised his school as being located in Whitesville, Mississippi, but when the state legislature incorporated the school in 1854, it stated that the school was in Newtonia, Mississippi. An examination of nineteenth-century maps of Mississippi seems to show that Whitesville later became Newtonia. Advertisement of Newton Female Institute, 1846, Miner

Papers; "An Act to Incorporate Newton College," *Laws of the State of Mississippi, Passed at a Regular Session of the Mississippi Legislature in the City of Jackson, From 2nd of January to 30 of March, 1854* (Jackson: Barksdale & Jones, 1854), pp. 457–58.

40. R. M. Church to Miner, August 31, 1847, Miner Papers.
41. Miner to Phares, March 5 [1847?], Miner Papers.
42. Achsa Miner to M. Miner, April 9, 1847, Miner Papers.
43. G.W.C. to Miner, May 30, 1847, Miner Papers.
44. Miner to Seward, December 25, 1850, Seward Papers.
45. Miner to Phares, July 26, 1847, Miner Papers.
46. Miner to Seward, January 1, 1848, Miner Papers.
47. Miner to Gerrit Smith, December 16, 1848, Miner Papers.
48. Gerrit Smith to Miner, January 10, 1848, Miner Papers.
49. [Achsa] Miner to M. Miner, April 23, 1848, Miner Papers.
50. Miner to Seward, December 25, 1850, Seward Papers.
51. Testimonial, D. L. Phares, May 31, 1848, "The School for Colored Girls, Washington, D. C.," in O'Connor, *Miner: A Memoir*, p. 9.
52. Memo from Trustees, Friendship Academy, Miner Papers.
53. L. G. Wells, manuscript biography of Miner, Miner Papers.
54. Achsa Miner to M. Miner, December 4, 1849; Report from Standing Committee of Regents, January 24, 1851, Miner Papers.
55. S. G. Miner to M. Miner, July 26, 1850, Miner Papers.
56. Miner to George and Louisa, September 28, 1850, Miner Papers.
57. Maria to Miner, May 10, 1849, Miner Papers.
58. L. M. Carpenter to Miner, January 18, 1853, Miner Papers.
59. Statement by Miner, undated, Miner Papers.
60. *Special Report of the Commissioner of Education*, p. 207.
61. Miner to Seward, December 25, 1850, Seward Papers; Seward to Miner, January 7, 1850, Miner Papers.
62. Miner to Gerrit Smith, February 11, 1850, Miner Papers.
63. Miner to Gerrit Smith, February 17, 1850, Miner Papers.
64. Undated statement by Miner, Miner Papers.
65. O'Connor, *Miner: A Memoir*, pp. 21–24.
66. Octavius Brooks Frothingham, *Memoir of William Henry Channing* (Boston: Houghton Mifflin and Co., 1886), p. 404.
67. John F. Cook to Miner, July 31, 1851, Miner Papers.
68. Miner to Mrs. E.D.E.N. Southworth, May 16, 1851, Miner Papers.
69. Southworth to Miner, August 23, 1851, Miner Papers.
70. Sadie Daniel St. Clair, "Myrtilla Miner: Pioneer in Teacher Education for Negro Women," *Journal of Negro History*, 34 (January 1949):33.
71. Miner to Mrs. Ford, February 15, 1851, quoted in O'Connor, *Miner: A Memoir*, pp. 25–26.

72. Ibid., pp. 26–27.

73. Miner to "Dear Friends," undated, Miner Papers.

74. Undated paper, Miner Papers.

75. J.[?] Bigelow to Miner, October 21, 1851, Miner Papers.

76. Constance McLaughlin Green, *Washington: Village and Capital, 1800–1878* (Princeton: Princeton University Press, 1962), p. 181.

77. Constance McLaughlin Green, *The Secret City: A History of Race Relations in the Nation's Capital* (Princeton: Princeton University Press, 1967), p. 48.

78. Frederick Douglass, *My Bondage and My Freedom*, ed. Philip S. Foner (New York: Dover Publications, 1969), pp. 145–47, 155.

79. M. B. Goodwin, "Schools of the Colored Population," *Special Report of the Commissioner of Education,* pp. 200–202.

80. Charles A. Harper, *A Century of Public Teacher Education: The Story of the State Teachers Colleges as They Evolved from the Normal Schools* (Westport, Conn.: Greenwood Press, 1970), pp. 43–44.

81. Ibid., p. 58.

82. Unsigned, undated statement, Miner Papers.

83. *Special Report of the Commissioner of Education*, p. 207.

84. J. N. Cary to Miner, November 21, 1851 and November 23, 1851, Miner Papers.

85. *Special Report of the Commissioner of Education*, p. 207.

86. Miner to Seward, December 15, 1851, Seward Papers.

87. A. S. Barnes & Co. to Miner, n.d., Miner Papers.

88. Miner to Hannah, May 17, 1852, Miner Papers.

89. This lengthy exchange is described in an undated, unsigned statement that Miner prepared in response to a request from H. B. Stowe for information about the origin of the school. Miner Papers.

90. *Special Report of the Commissioner of Education*, p. 207.

91. Frothingham, *Memoir of William Henry Channing*, pp. 404–5.

92. Miner Papers.

93. "A Democrat" to Fillmore, undated, Miner Papers.

94. This work was published in Philadelphia by Merrihew and Thompson Printers in 1844.

95. *See* Ruth Ketring Nuermberger, *The Free Produce Movement: A Quaker Protest Against Slavery* (Durham, N.C.: Duke University Press, 1942).

96. Rhoads to Miner, December 15, 1851; Rhoads to Miner and Inman, December 27, 1851; Rhoads to Miner, January 6, 1852, Miner Papers.

97. Rhoads to Miner, January 10, 1852, Miner Papers.

98. Ibid.

99. Ibid.

100. Ibid.

101. Rhoads to Miner, April 15, 1852, Miner Papers.

102. Rhoads to Miner, May (day illegible), 1852, Miner Papers.

103. Rhoads to Miner, April 15, 1852, Miner Papers.

104. Ibid.

105. Rhoads to Miner, May 1852, June 9, 1852, Miner Papers.

106. Rhoads to Miner, July 7, 1852, Miner Papers; Miner to Hannah, May 17, 1852, quoted in O'Connor, *Miner: A Memoir*, p. 38.

107. Rhoads to Miner, July 7, 1852, Miner Papers.

108. Thomas Williamson to Miner, October 16, 1852, Miner Papers.

109. Rhoads to Miner, November 4, 1852, Miner Papers.

110. Taylor to Miner, November 20, 1852; Rhoads to Miner, November 21, 1852, Miner Papers.

111. Rhoads to Miner, March 17, 1853, Miner Papers.

112. Rhoads to Miner, February 21, 1853, Miner Papers.

113. Rhoads to Miner, February 2, March 9, 1853, Miner Papers.

114. Rhoads to Miner, April 26, 1853, Miner Papers.

115. Rhoads to Miner, May 13, 1853, Miner Papers.

116. Rhoads to Miner, September 8, 11, 1853, Miner Papers.

117. Rhoads to Miner, September 22, 23, 1853, Miner Papers.

118. Miner to Rhoads, September 24, 1853, Miner Papers.

119. Miner to Rhoads, September 25, 1853, Miner Papers.

120. Rhoads to Miner, September 26, 1853, Miner Papers.

121. Miner to Stowe, October 1, 1853, Miner Papers.

122. Unsigned, undated statements, Miner Papers.

123. Unsigned, undated statements, one in Miner's writing, Miner Papers.

124. George E. Tingle, undated testimonial; Miner to M. Robinson, April 2, 1853, Miner Papers.

125. Unsigned document, partly in Miner's writing, December 1852, Miner Papers.

126. Miner to Cecil, undated; Miner to M. Robinson, April 2, 1853, Miner Papers.

127. W. C. Howard to Miner, March 7, 1853; unsigned, undated statement; Miner to Robinson, April 2, 1853, Miner Papers.

128. Unsigned, undated statement, Miner Papers.

129. Cecil to Miner, January 28, 31, February 3, 7, 9, 1853; and Miner to Cecil, April 8, 1853, Miner Papers.

130. E. N. Horsford to Miner, March 5, 1853, Miner Papers.

131. Miner to Treichel, April 8, 1853, Miner Papers.

132. Rhoads to Miner, March 9, 1853, Miner Papers.

133. Robinson to Miner, April 1, 1853, Miner Papers.

134. Horsford to Miner, February 10, 1853, Miner Papers.

135. Horsford to Miner, April 10, 28, May 1, 21, June 9, July 15, 1853, Miner Papers.

136. Cecil to Miner, February 3, 22, May 7, 1853, August 5 [no year], Miner Papers.

137. Miner to Cecil, April 8, 1853, Miner Papers.

138. Miner to Cecil, August 1, 1853, Miner Papers.

139. Miner to Cecil, September 5, 1853, Miner Papers.

140. Miner to Robinson, April 2, 1853, Miner Papers.

141. Miner to anon., 1853, quoted in O'Connor, *Miner: A Memoir*, pp. 45, 47–48.

142. Rhoads to Miner, February 25, 1854, Miner Papers.

143. *Special Report of the Commissioner of Education*, p. 208.

144. Miner to anon., 1853, quoted in O'Connor, *Miner: A Memoir*, p. 46.

145. Miner to anon., May 3, 1854, quoted in O'Connor, *Miner: A Memoir*, pp. 50–51.

146. *Special Report of the Commissioner of Education*, p. 208.

147. Unsigned, undated statement in Miner's writing, Miner Papers.

148. Miner to anon., May 3, 1854, in O'Connor, *Miner: A Memoir*, p. 51.

149. Unsigned, undated statement, Miner Papers.

150. Miner to anon., May 3, 1854, in O'Connor, *Miner: A Memoir*, p. 51.

151. Rhoads to Miner, July 6, 1854, Miner Papers.

152. Rhoads to Miner, July 6, November 18, 1854, Miner Papers.

153. Rhoads to Miner, December 20, 1854, Miner Papers.

154. Address by Miner, "The School for Colored Girls," printed in O'Connor, *Miner: A Memoir*, with separate pagination, pp. 3–4.

155. Ibid., pp. 4–6.

156. Lizzy Snowden to "Kind Friends," March 10, 1852, Miner Papers.

157. Lizzy Snowden to "Dear Teacher," April 6, 1853, Miner Papers.

158. L. F. Dewey to "My dear young friends," May 2, 1853, Miner Papers.

159. Mary Brent to "My Teacher," May 14, 1853, Miner Papers.

160. O'Connor, *Miner: A Memoir*, p. 113.

161. Maria Therr [?] to "Dear Teacher," May 17, 1853, Miner Papers.

162. Matilda A. Jones, "The Widow & her Children," March 15, 1854, Miner Papers.

163. Nancy Waugh to "Dear Teacher," July 10, 1854, Miner Papers.

164. M. A. Beckett to "Dear Teacher," July 12, 1854, Miner Papers.

165. Marietta T. Hill to "Dear Teacher," July 5, 1854, Miner Papers.

166. Matilda A. Jones to Miss Dewey, June 25, 1855, Miner Papers.

167. Ibid.

168. *Normal School for Colored Girls, Washington, D.C.* (Albany: C. Van Benthuysen's Print, 1858), pp. 13–14.

169. Julia Augusta A. to "My Dear Teacher," January 26, 1853; Matilda A. Jones to Miss Dewey, June 25, 1855; M. Miner to Newton Miner, March 15, 1852, Miner Papers.

170. Miner, "The School for Colored Girls," pp. 7–8.

171. Ibid., p. 8.

172. Testimonial of Dewey, January 27, 1853, of Channing and Sampson, January 7, 1854, Miner, "The School for Colored Girls," pp. 9–10, 12.

173. Testimonial of E. N. Horsford, December 28, 1853, Miner, "The School for Colored Girls," p. 11.

174. Miner to Newton Miner, March 15, 1852; M. E. Ford to Miner, June 29, July 5, 1852, Miner Papers.

175. Miner, "The School for Colored Girls," p. 7.

176. *Special Report of the Commissioner of Education*, p. 210.

177. L. Mann to Miner, September 1855, October 13, November 13, December 31, 1855, Miner Papers.

178. Stowe to Miner, November 8, 1855; Anna Smith to Miner, December 3, 1855; E. Davison to Miner, July 24, 1857, September 30, October 30, October 27, 1857, December 15, [1857], Miner Papers.

179. Miner to M. Burleigh, October 17, 1856, Emily Howland Papers, Cornell University Library, Ithaca, New York (hereafter Howland Papers, Cornell).

180. Florence Woolsey Hazzard, "Emily Howland," *Notable American Women*, 2:230; Emily Howland to Miner, October 28, 1856, Miner Papers.

181. Howland to Miner, December 14, 1856, May 17, June 25, 1857, Miner Papers.

182. Howland to Miner, October 26, 1856, February 17, 1857; Miner to Howland, June 23, 1857, Miner Papers.

183. Rhoads to Miner, April 12, December 3, 1857, Miner Papers.

184. *National Anti-Slavery Standard*, December 12, 1857.

185. M.C.W. to E.W.O., January 13, 1857 [?], Emily Howland Papers, Sophia Smith Collection, Smith College, Northampton, Mass. (hereafter referred to as Howland Papers, Smith).

186. M. J. Burleigh to E. Howland, January 11, 1858, Howland Papers, Cornell.

187. Miner to Howland, February 9, April 14, 1858, Howland Papers, Cornell.

188. Howland to Ramabai, April 1888, Howland Papers, Smith.

189. Brown to Miner, February 8, June 20, 1858, Miner Papers.

190. Miner to Howland, August 20, 1858, Howland Papers, Cornell.

191. Brown to Miner, May 9, April 11, 1858; Howland to Miner, December 5, 1858, Miner Papers.

192. Miner to Howland, August 20, 1858, Howland Papers, Cornell.

193. E. H. Valentine to Howland, October 22, 1858; Miner to Howland, December 5, 1858, Howland Papers, Cornell.

194. Howland to "Dear Folks at Home," October 24, 1858, Howland Papers, Cornell.

195. Howland to Miner, December 5, 1858, Miner Papers.

196. Emily Howland Notebook, entries for November 29, December 6, 1858, copy in Miner Papers.

197. *National Anti-Slavery Standard*, April 14, 1853.

198. Rhoads to Miner, March 17, 1853, Miner Papers.

199. "Testimonial to Mrs. Stowe, and what shall be done with it," *National Anti-Slavery Standard*, July 23, 1853.

200. *Frederick Douglass' Paper*, April 7, 1854.

201. *National Anti-Slavery Standard*, April 8, 1854.

202. *Frederick Douglass' Paper*, September 1, 1854.

203. S.A.M. Washington, *George Thomas Downing: Sketch of His Life and Times* (Newport: Milne Printery, 1910), esp. pp. 17–18.

204. George T. Downing to "Dear Douglass," December 4, 1854, *Frederick Douglass' Paper*, December 22, 1854.

205. Rhoads to Miner, January 13, 1855, Miner Papers; Rhoads to Douglass, January 6, 1855, *Frederick Douglass' Paper*, January 12, 1855.

206. Nancy Day to George T. Downing, June 8, 1855, Miner Papers.

207. Unsigned, undated paper, Miner Papers.

208. Atwater to Miner, January 18, 1852, Miner Papers; *see also* Mary Bowen to Harriet Underhill, November 14, 1846, Sayles J. Bowen Papers, Manuscript Division, Library of Congress (hereafter referred to as Bowen Papers); *Normal School for Colored Girls, Washington, D.C.*, p. 17; Horsford to Miner, January 24, 1854, Miner Papers.

209. H. B. Stowe to Miner, November 5, 1855; Miner to Rev. J. Murray, February 11, 1856, Miner Papers.

210. William H. Beecher to Miner, March 13, 1856, Miner Papers.

211. Rhoads to Miner, March 25, 27, April 5, 1856, Miner Papers.

212. Lyman Beecher Stowe, *Saints Sinners and Beechers* (Indianapolis: The Bobbs-Merrill Co., 1934), pp. 138–43; *see also* Milton Rugoff, *The Beechers: An American Family in the Nineteenth Century* (New York: Harper & Row, 1981), pp. 194–96, 415–17.

213. W. H. Beecher to Washington Normal School for Colored Girls, July 1856, Miner Papers.

214. Rhoads to Miner, July 29, 1856, Miner Papers.

215. "Circular," December 1856, signed W. H. Beecher, Miner Papers.

216. *The Boston Journal*, April 18, 1857, as quoted in *The National Intelligencer*, May 6, 1857.

217. Allen C. Clark, "Walter Lenox, the Thirteenth Mayor of the City of Washington," *Records of the Columbia Historical Society* 20 (1917):167–93.

218. *The National Intelligencer*, May 6, 1857.

219. Grace Greenwood, "An American Salon," *Cosmopolitan* 8 (February 1890):437–47.

220. *The National Era*, May 14, 1857.

221. L. D. Gale to Miner, June 3, 1857, Miner Papers.

222. W. H. Beecher to Rhoads, September 14, 1857, Miner Papers.

223. Statement in Miner's writing on the bottom of L. D. Gale's advertisement for work, Miner Papers.

224. L. D. Gale to Miner, May 5, 1857, Miner Papers.

225. Gale to Miner, May 20, 1857, and June 3, 1857, Miner Papers.

226. Statement by Gale, October 1, 1857, Miner Papers.

227. Rhoads to Miner, July 31, 1857, Miner Papers.

228. Beecher to Rhoads, September 14, 1857, Miner Papers.

229. Rhoads to Miner, February 17, March 3, 1856, Miner Papers.

230. Constitution in Miner Papers.

231. Rhoads to Miner, July 15, July 31, 1857, Miner Papers.

232. Rhoads to Miner, December 3, 1857, Miner Papers.

233. Sayles J. Bowen to Miner, November 7, 1858, Miner Papers.

234. Rhoads to Miner, July 14, 1859, Miner Papers.

235. Ibid.

236. Ibid.

237. Bowen to Julia Barker, December 6, 1857, Bowen Papers.

238. Williamson to Bowen, August 30, 1859, Miner Papers.

239. Bowen to Miner, January 10, 1860, Miner Papers.

240. Tatham to Miner, December 2, 1859, January 7, 1860, Miner Papers.

241. Bowen to Miner, July 11, 1860, Miner Papers.

242. Tatham to Miner, March 30, 1860, Miner Papers.

243. Tatham to Miner, May 24, 1860, Miner Papers.

244. Tatham to Miner, August 28, 1860, March 15, May 6, 1861, Miner Papers.

245. Tatham to Miner, March 29, 1861, Miner Papers.

246. Tatham to Miner, July 20, 1861, Miner Papers.

247. Miner to "My dear father," December 10, 1845, Miner Papers.

248. *Special Report of the Commissioner of Education,* p. 209.

249. L. M. Carpenter to Miner, January 18, 1853, Miner Papers.

250. Miner to M. Burleigh, October 17, 1856, Howland Papers, Cornell.

251. Miner to "My dear father," December 10, 1845, Miner Papers.

252. Stowe to Miner, November 8, 1855, Miner Papers.

253. Miner to "My dear brother," October 5, 1856, Miner Papers.

254. Miner to M. Burleigh, October 17, 1856, Howland Papers, Cornell.

255. E. E. Colfax to Miner, May 11, 1857; Eliza Gale to Miner, December 17, 1856, Miner Papers.

256. M. C. Horsford to Miner, December 14 [?], 1853, Miner Papers.

257. W. H. Channing to Miner, May 14, 1858, Miner Papers.

258. Interview of L. G. Wells with Robert Goff and Marian Goff Pond, collateral descendants of Myrtilla Miner, September 6, 1941, Miner Papers.

259. See, for example Rhoads to Miner, July 6, 1854, Miner Papers.

260. S. Atwater to Miner, October 27, 1844, Miner Papers.

261. Joel Shew, *The Cholera, Its Causes, Prevention, and Cure, Showing the Inefficacy of Drug-Treatment, and the Superiority of the Water-Cure, in This Disease* (New York: Fowlers and Wells, 1849); Ronald G. Walters, *American Reformers 1815-1860* (New York: Hill and Wang, 1978), p. 154.

262. Evelyn Giammichele and Eva Taylor, "Elmira Water Cure: Silas and Rachel Gleason and Their 'Tavern for the Sick,' " *The Chemung Historical Journal* 12 (December 1966):1535–41.

263. *The Water-Cure Journal and Herald of Reforms, Devoted to Physiology, Hydropathy, and the Laws of Life* was published by the same company that had a "Phrenological Cabinet" in New York; quotation in O'Connor, *Miner: A Memoir*, p. 112.

264. "Phrenological Character of Miss M. Miner," June 28, 1860, Miner Papers.

265. Achsa Miner to M. Miner, July 9, 1848, Miner Papers.

266. Achsa Miner to M. Miner, August 1848, Miner Papers.

267. Achsa Miner to M. Miner, November 17, December 10, 1848, July 21, 1849, January 6, 1850, Miner Papers.

268. Achsa Miner to M. Miner, May 21, 1850, February 28, 1850, Miner Papers.

269. Achsa Miner to M. Miner, April 28, 1850, Miner Papers.

270. Achsa Miner to M. Miner, May 21, 1850, Miner Papers.

271. Cholera morbus, also known as "summer complaint," should not have been fatal. Dr. R. H. Fennell, Jr., to J. Pacheco, September 14, 1980; Achsa Miner to M. Miner, June 16, 1850; Sara Eddy to Miner, July 16, 1850; Mary Atwater to Miner, July 21, 1850, Miner Papers.

272. Miner to George and Louise, September 28, 1850, Miner Papers.

273. Interview of L. G. Wells with Robert Goff and Marian Goff Pond, September 6, 1941, Miner Papers.

274. Undated notes in Miner's writing, Miner Papers.

275. Miner to "My dear brother," October 5, 1856, Miner Papers.

276. E. Gale to Miner, July 18, 1855, Miner Papers.

277. R. Laurence Moore, *In Search of White Crows: Spiritualism, Parapsychology, and American Culture* (New York: Oxford University Press, 1977), pp. 7–8, 15; Michael Flusche, "Antislavery and Spiritualism: Myrtilla Miner and her School," *The New-York Historical Society Quarterly* 59 (January 1975):170.

278. L. M. Carpenter to Miner, January 18, 1853, Miner Papers.

279. Celia to M. Miner, n.d., Miner Papers.

280. E. N. Horsford to Miner, June 20, 1858, Miner Papers; H. Augusta Dodge, ed., *Gail Hamilton's Life in Letters*, 2 vols. (Boston: Lee and Shepard, 1901), I:233–34.

281. Nelly T. O'Conner to Miner, April 17, 1859; Sister Nell to Miner, September 5, 1861, Miner Papers.

282. Clippings from San Francisco newspapers in Miner Papers.

283. C. Browne [?] to Mrs. Celia Albe, February 11, 1865, Miner Papers.

284. Miner to "My dear brother," October 5, 1857; Miner to "My dear father," December 10, 1845, Miner Papers.

285. S. R. Howland to [Emily Howland], March 3, 1882, Howland Papers, Cornell.

286. M. C. Horsford to Miner, December 14 [?], 1853, Miner Papers.

287. Eliza [Gale] to Miner, November 24, 1855, Miner Papers.

288. Eliza [Gale] to Miner, September 28, 1855, Miner Papers; *Boyd's Washington and Georgetown Directory Containing a Business Directory and an Appendix of Much Useful Information* (Washington, D.C.: William H. Boyd, 1853), p. 91; Rhoads to Miner, April 15, 1852; Thomas Williamson to Miner, October 16, 1852, Miner Papers.

289. L. D. Gale to Miner, May 5, 1857; A. E. Gale to Miner, June 19, 1857, Miner Papers.

290. Jonathan Dennis to Emily Howland, July 31, 1858; Gulielma Breed to Emily Howland, November 12, 1860; J. Dennis to Emily Howland, May 2, 1859, Howland Papers, Cornell.

291. C. Browne [?] to Mrs. Celia Albe, February 11, 1865, Miner Papers.

292. Rhoads to Miner, February 8, 1854; interview of L. G. Wells with Robert Goff and Marian Goff Pond, September 6, 1941, Miner Papers.

293. Maria to Miner, May 10, 1849, Miner Papers.

294. Printed, Broadside of California Association of American Women, February 2, 1849, Miner Papers.

295. Notation on "Articles of Agreement" of California Association of American Women, Miner Papers.

296. Maria to Miner, February 13, 1847, Miner Papers.

297. Undated letter signed "Pillsbury's Patient," in Miner's writing, Miner Papers.

298. Unsigned, undated paper in Miner's writing, clearly July 4, 1850, Miner Papers.

299. O'Connor, *Miner: A Memoir*, p. 117.

300. S. T. Martyn to Miner, January 25, 1847, Miner Papers.

301. O'Connor, *Miner: A Memoir*, p. 118.

302. *The Una: A Paper Devoted to the Elevation of Woman* 2 (February 1854):218.

303. Miner to Seward, December 18, 1841, Seward Papers.

304. Miner to Seward, December 24, 1842, Seward Papers.

305. Seward to Miner, December 28, 1842, Miner Papers.

306. Seward to Miner, January 16, 1843, Miner Papers.

307. Maria to Miner, May 10, 1849, Miner Papers.

308. Undated, unsigned paper in Miner's writing, Miner Papers.

309. Ibid.

310. Ibid.

311. "Henry Barnard," *Dictionary of American Biography*, 1:621-25; Sadie Daniel St. Clair, "Myrtilla Miner," p. 32.

312. Molly to Miner, February 22, 1847; Passmore Williamson to Miner, April 5, 1856, Miner Papers.

313. Unsigned, undated paper in Miner's writing, Miner Papers.

314. *See*, for example, Miner to Brents, May 8, 1855, Miner Papers.

315. Eliza Gale to Miner, August 10, 1855, October 18, 1856, Miner Papers.

316. Horsford to Miner, January 24, 1854, Miner Papers.

317. Miner to Rev. J. Murray, February 11, 1856, Miner Papers.

318. Statements for Miner's pupils, January 16, 31, 1859, Miner Papers.

319. Statement for Miner's pupils, January 10, 1859, Miner Papers.

320. M. C. Horsford to Miner, December 14 [?], 1853, January 24, 1854, Miner Papers.

321. Mary Mann to Frederick Douglass, March 3, 1852, *Frederick Douglass' Paper*, March 25, 1852.

322. Dr. B. Ayer to Miner, April 8, 1855; P. Williamson to Miner, May 15, 1855; E. G. Gale to Miner, August 2, 1855; Ayer to Miner, April 2, 1856; Williamson to Miner, April 5, 1856; L. B. Mann to Miner, December 31, 1855; Williamson to Miner, May 19, 1856, Miner Papers.

323. Emma Brown to Miner, June 20, October 7, 1858, Miner Papers.

324. Emma Brown to Miner, February 8, 1858, Miner Papers.

325. Brown to Miner, May 9, June 20, 1858, Miner Papers.

326. Matilda Jones to Miner, April 30, 1858, Miner Papers.

327. Jones to Miner, April 30, 1858, Miner Papers.

328. M. P. Dascomb to Miner, January 26, 1860, Miner Papers.

329. Oberlin College, *Alumni Register: Graduates and Former Students Teaching and Administrative Staff 1833-1960* (Oberlin, Ohio: Published by the college, 1960), pp. 16, 22.

330. Winfield S. Montgomery, *Historical Sketch of Education for the Colored Race in the District of Columbia, 1807–1905* (Washington, D.C.: Smith Brothers Printers, 1907), p. 20; Isabel Howland to L. G. Wells, June 24, 1941, Miner Papers.

331. A. E. Gale to Miner, January 18, 1861; undated note by L. G. Wells, Miner Papers.

332. M. A. Jones to Miner, September 24, 1861, Miner Papers.

333. Note by L. G. Wells, Miner Papers.

334. Howland to "Dear folks at home," February 2, 1859; Mary H. Thomas to Howland, March 28, 1859, Howland Papers, Cornell.

335. Bowen to Howland, September 17, 1859, Howland Papers, Cornell.

336. Bowen to Howland, April 14, 1859, Howland Papers, Cornell.

337. Rhoads to Dennis, April 14, 1859; Dennis to Howland, May 2, 1859, Howland Papers, Cornell.

338. Howland to Rhoads, April 27, 1859, Howland Papers, Cornell.

339. Rhoads to Howland, April 14, 1859, Howland Papers, Cornell.

340. Howland to Rhoads, April 27, 1859, Howland Papers, Cornell.

341. Ibid.

342. Gulielma Breed to Howland, June 9, 1859; Bowen to Howland, September 17, 1859, Howland Papers, Cornell.

343. Bowen to Howland, September 17, 1859, Howland Papers, Cornell.

344. Bernard H. Nelson, *Miner Teachers College: The First Century 1851–1951: The Biography of a School* (n.p., 1953), pp. 32–33.

345. Bettie [Browne] to Howland, October 4, 1859, Howland Papers, Cornell.

346. [Browne] to Howland, February 18, 1860, Howland Papers, Cornell.

347. Benjamin Tatham to Miner, March 30, 1860, Miner Papers.

348. Miner to "Dear Friends," May 13, 1860, Miner Papers.

349. Gulielma Breed to Howland, November 12, 1860, Howland Papers, Cornell; A. E. Gale to Miner, December 3, 1860; Miner to "Dear Brother," March 13, 1861, Miner Papers.

350. Brown to [Howland], November 29, 1860, Howland Papers, Cornell.

351. Brown to Howland, November 19, 1859, Howland Papers, Cornell.

352. Brown to [Howland], November 29, 1860, Howland Papers, Cornell.

353. *Special Report of the Commissioner of Education*, p. 209.

354. St. Clair, "Myrtilla Miner," pp. 42–43.

355. Mary to Miner, August 21, 1861; E. S. Miller to Miner, August 27, 1861, Miner Papers.

356. Montgomery, *Historical Sketch of Education*, p. 40.

357. Miner to "My blessed brother N & Wife," December 9, 1862, Miner Papers.

358. Ednah D. Thomas to Howland, March 24, 1863, Howland Papers, Cornell.

359. Bowen to Howland, May 31, 1862, Howland Papers, Cornell.

360. Henry Wilson, *History of the Rise and Fall of the Slave Power in America*, 3 vols. (Boston: James R. Osgood and Company, 1874), 2:578–83; quote on 2:582.

361. U.S. Congress, Senate, Senate Resolution 536, *The Congressional Globe: Containing the Debates and Proceedings of the Third Session of the Thirty-Seventh Congress* (Washington, D.C.: Congressional Globe Office, 1863), p. 1018 (February 17, 1863).

362. Ibid., pp. 1325–26, (February 27, 1863), p. 1499.

363. Bowen to Howland, May 31, 1862, Howland Papers, Cornell.

364. E. Brown to Howland, September 23, November 22, 1862 (postscript to November 19 letter), Howland Papers, Cornell.

365. O'Connor, *Miner: A Memoir*, p. 124.

366. Ibid., pp. 125–26.

367. Dr. Robert H. Fennell to J. Pacheco, March 18, April 2, 1980.

368. O'Connor, *Miner: A Memoir*, p. 126.

369. Unattributed clipping, without date, in Miner Papers.

370. O'Connor, *Miner: A Memoir*, pp. 126–29.

371. C. Browne [?] to Mrs. Celia Albe [?], February 11, 1865, Miner Papers.

372. *The National Anti-Slavery Standard*, December 24, 1864; *Washington Daily Morning Chronicle*, December 19, 1864; *Daily Times*, December 20, 1864.

373. Eliza P. Peabody to Howland, March 9, 1865, Howland Papers, Cornell.

374. *Special Report of the Commissioner of Education*, p. 211 n; Nelson, *Miner Teachers College*, p. 25.

375. Nelson, *Miner Teachers College*, pp. 32-33.

376. *Washington Chronicle*, December 16, 1876.

377. Ibid.

378. William Lincoln Brown, *The Miner Fund Board of Trustees and its Seventy-five Years of Semi-Public Service* (Washington, D.C.: The Institution for Education of Colored Youth, 1938), p. 2.

379. Frothingham, *Memoir of William Henry Channing*, p. 404.

380. Ibid., p. 405.

381. *The Woman's Journal*, September 27, 1873, December 1, 1877.

382. Nelson, *Miner Teachers College*, pp. 37–40.

383. Ibid., p. 92.

384. Ibid., p. 185.

385. U.S. Congress, House of Representatives, 93rd Congress, *Hearings Before the Subcommittee on Education of the Committee on the District of Co-*

lumbia . . . to Authorize the University of the District of Columbia . . . (Washington, D.C.: Government Printing Office, 1974), pp. 128–29.

386. Brown, *The Miner Fund*, pp. 2–13.

387. Elmer Stewart to L. G. Wells, April 17, 1941, Miner Papers.

Bibliography

MANUSCRIPT COLLECTIONS

Bowen, Sayles J. Papers, 1846-1892. Manuscripts Division, Library of Congress, Washington, D.C.

"Christ Church, Norfolk City, Vestry Minutes, 1828-1905." Virginia State Library, Richmond, Virginia.

Garrison, William Lloyd. Papers. Boston Public Library, Rare Book Room.

Howland, Emily. Papers. Cornell University Library, Ithaca, New York.

———. Papers. Sophia Smith Collection, Women's History Archive, Smith College, Northampton, Mass.

Miner, Myrtilla. Papers. Manuscripts Division, Library of Congress, Washington, D.C.

Seward, William H. Papers. University of Rochester Library, Rochester, New York.

PUBLIC DOCUMENTS

House Petition No. 48, January Session, 1886, Connecticut State Library, Hartford, Conn.

Journal, Acts and Proceedings of a General Convention of the State of Virginia, Assembled at Richmond, on Monday, the Fourteenth Day of October, Eighteen Hundred and Fifty. Richmond, Va.: W. Culley Printer, 1850.

Laws of the State of Mississippi, Passed at a Regular Session of the Mississippi Legislature in the City of Jackson, from 2nd of January to 30 of March, 1854. Jackson: Barksdale & Jones, 1854.

Public Statute Laws of the State of Connecticut, 1833, Revised as of 1838, Hartford, Conn.: 1839.

The Seventh Census of the United States: 1850. Washington, D.C.: Robert Armstrong, 1853.

Special Report of the Commissioner of Education on the Condition and Im-

provement of Public Schools in the District of Columbia Submitted to the Senate June, 1869, and to the House, with Additions, June 13, 1870. Washington, D.C.: Government Printing Office, 1871.

State Supreme Court 10 Conn. 339. "Crandall against the State of Connecticut in Error."

U.S. Congress. House of Representatives. 93d Congress. *Hearings Before the Subcommittee on Education of the Committee on the District of Columbia, House of Representatives 93rd Congress on Implementation of the Decree of Judge Joseph C. Waddy of Aug. 1, 1972, on Special Education, in Hills v. Board of Education and on H.R. 15643 to Authorize the University of the District of Columbia May 29 & 30, 1973, and July 1 & 3, 1974.* Washington, D.C.: Government Printing Office, 1974.

U.S. Congress, Senate. Senate Res. 536. *The Congressional Globe: Containing the Debates and Proceedings of the Third Session of the Thirty-Seventh Congress.* Washington, D.C.: Congressional Globe Office, 1863.

NEWSPAPERS

American Beacon, Norfolk, Virginia.
Connecticut Courant, Hartford, Connecticut.
Daily Express, Petersburg, Virginia.
Daily Southern Argus, Norfolk, Virginia.
The Daily South-Side Democrat, Petersburg, Virginia.
Daily Times, Washington, D.C.
Frederick Douglass' Paper, Rochester, New York.
Freeman, New York City.
Genius of Universal Emancipation, Greeneville, Tennessee, and Baltimore, Maryland.
Independent, New York City.
The Liberator, Boston, Massachusetts.
National Anti-Slavery Standard, New York City.
National Era, Washington, D.C.
National Intelligencer, Washington, D.C.
New-York Daily Times, New York City.
New York Herald, New York City.
The Non-Slaveholder, Philadelphia, Pennsylvania.
Pennsylvania Freeman, Philadelphia, Pennsylvania.
Richmond Enquirer, Richmond, Virginia.
Rochester Daily Advertiser, Rochester, New York.
The Una: A Paper Devoted to the Elevation of Woman, Providence, Rhode Island.

The Unionist, Brooklyn, Connecticut.
Washington Daily Morning Chronicle, Washington, D.C.
The Water-Cure Journal and Herald of Reform, Devoted to Physiology, Hydropathy, and the Laws of Life, New York City.
The Women's Journal, Boston, Massachusetts.

BOOKS

Bailey, Philip James. *Festus: A Poem*. Boston: Routledge, 1845.
Barnard, John, and Burner, David, eds. *The American Experience in Education*. New York: New Viewpoints, Franklin Watts, 1975.
Benson, Clarence H. *A Popular History of Christian Education*. Chicago: Moody Press, 1943.
Berlin, Ira. *Slaves Without Masters: The Free Negro in the Antebellum South*. 2d ed. New York: Vintage Books, Random House, 1976.
Boyd's Washington and Georgetown Directory Containing a Business Directory and an Appendix of Much Useful Information. Washington, D.C.: William H. Boyd, 1858.
Brown, Letitia Woods. *Free Negroes in the District of Columbia 1790-1846*. New York: Oxford University Press, 1972.
Brown, William Lincoln. *The Miner Fund Board of Trustees and Its Seventy Years of Semi-Public Service*. Washington, D.C.: The Institution for Education of Colored Youth, 1938.
Cremin, Lawrence A. *American Education, The National Experience, 1783-1876*. New York: Harper & Row, 1980.
————. *The American Common School: An Historic Conception*. New York: Teachers College, 1951.
Curti, Merle. *The Social Ideas of American Educators*. New York: Charles Scribner's Sons, 1935.
Dictionary of American Biography. 20 vols. (1928-1936) and 7 supplements (1944-1981). Published under the auspices of the American Council of Learned Societies. New York: Charles Scribner's Sons.
Dodge, H. Augusta, ed. *Gail Hamilton's Life in Letters*. 2 vols. Boston: Lee and Shepard, 1901.
Douglass, Frederick. *My Bondage and My Freedom*. Edited by Philip S. Foner. New York: Dover Publications, 1969.
Douglass, Margaret. *Educational Laws of Virginia. The Personal Narrative of Mrs. Margaret Douglass, A Southern Woman Who Was Imprisoned for One Month in the Common Jail of Norfolk, Under the Laws of Virginia, for the Crime of Teaching Free Colored Children to Read*. Boston: John P. Jewett and Co., 1854.

Du Bois, W. E. Burghardt. *The Negro Common School*. Atlanta: Atlanta University Press, 1901.

Durant, Samuel W. *History of Oneida County, New York, with Illustrations and Biographical Sketches of Some of Its Prominent Men and Pioneers*. Philadelphia: Everts and Fariss, 1878.

Farish, Hunter Dickinson, ed. *Journal and Letters of Philip Vickers Fithian, 1773-1774: A Plantation Tutor of the Old Dominion*. Williamsburg, Va.: Colonial Williamsburg, Inc. 1943.

Fletcher, Robert Samuel. *A History of Oberlin College From its Foundation Through the Civil War*. 2 vols. Oberlin, Ohio: Arno, 1943.

Foner, Philip S. *Frederick Douglass*. New York: Citadel, 1964.

———. *History of Black Americans*. 3 vols. Westport, Conn.: Greenwood Press, 1975-1983.

———, ed. *Life and Writings of Frederick Douglass*. 2 vols. New York: International Publishers, 1950.

Forrest, William S. *Historical and Descriptive Sketches of Norfolk and Vicinity, Including Portsmouth and the Adjacent Counties, During a Period of Two Hundred Years*. Philadelphia: Lindsay and Blakiston, 1853.

———. *The Norfolk Directory for 1851-1852: Containing the Names, Professions, Places of Business, and Residences of the Merchants, Traders, Manufacturers, Mechanics, Heads of Families, Etc.* Norfolk, Va.: n.p., 1851.

Frothingham, Octavius Brooks. *Memoir of William Henry Channing*. Boston: Houghton Mifflin and Co., 1886.

Fuller, Edmund. *Prudence Crandall: An Incident of Racism in Nineteenth Century Connecticut*. Middletown, Conn.: Wesleyan University Press, 1974.

Good, Harry G., and Teller, James D. *A History of American Education*, 3d ed. New York: Macmillan, 1973.

Green, Constance McLaughlin. *The Secret City: A History of Race Relations in the Nation's Capital*. Princeton, N.J.: Princeton University Press, 1967.

———. *Washington: Village and Capital, 1800-1878*. Princeton, N.J.: Princeton University Press, 1962.

Grimké, Archibald H. *William Lloyd Garrison*. New York: Funk, 1892.

Harper, Charles A. *A Century of Public Teacher Education: The Story of the State Teachers Colleges as They Evolved from the Normal Schools*. Westport, Conn.: Greenwood Press, 1970.

Helen Eliza Garrison, A Memorial. Cambridge, Mass.: Riverside Press, 1876.

James, Edward T., James, Janet Wilson, and Boyer, Paul S., eds. *Notable American Women 1607–1950: A Biographical Dictionary*. 3 vols. Cambridge, Mass.: Harvard University Press, 1971.

Kennedy, William Bean. *The Shaping of Protestant Education: An Interpretation of the Sunday School and the Development of Protestant Educational Strategy in the United States, 1789-1860.* New York: Association Press, 1966.

Larned, Ellen D. *History of Windham County, Connecticut.* Worcester, Mass.: Printed by C. Hamilton, 1874-1880.

Litwack, Leon F. *North of Slavery: The Negro in the Free States, 1790-1860.* Chicago: University of Chicago Press, 1961.

Mabee, Carleton. *Black Education in New York State from Colonial to Modern Times.* Syracuse, N.Y.: Syracuse University Press, 1979.

McElroy, A. *McElroy's Philadelphia City Directory for 1865.* Philadelphia: Sherman and Co., 1865.

McGinnis, Frederick A. *The Education of Negroes in Ohio.* Wilberforce, Ohio: Curless Printing Co., 1962.

May, Samuel J. *The Right of Colored People to Education, Vindicated. Letters to Andrew T. Judson, Esq., and Others in Canterbury, Remonstrating With Them on Their Unjust and Unjustifiable Procedure Relative to Miss Crandall and Her School for Colored Females.* Brooklyn, Conn.: Advertiser Press, 1833.

————. *Some Reflections of Our Anti-Slavery Conflict.* Boston: Fields, Osgood & Co., 1869.

Merrill, Walter, ed. *The Letters of William Lloyd Garrison.* Vol. I (1822-1835). Cambridge, Mass.: Harvard University Press, 1971.

Montgomery, Winfield S. *Historical Sketch of Education for the Colored Race in the District of Columbia, 1807-1905.* Washington, D.C.: Smith Brothers Printers, 1907.

Moore, R. Laurence. *In Search of White Crows: Spiritualism, Parapsychology, and American Culture.* New York: Oxford University Press, 1977.

Nelson, Bernard H. *Miner Teachers College: The First Century, 1851-1951: The Biography of a School.* N.p., 1953.

Nuermberger, Ruth Ketring. *The Free Produce Movement: A Quaker Protest Against Slavery.* Durham, N.C.: Duke University Press, 1942. Historical Papers of the Trinity College Historical Society, Series XXV.

Normal School for Colored Girls, Washington, D.C. Albany, N.Y.: C. Van Benthuysen's Print, 1858.

O'Connor, Ellen M. *Myrtilla Miner: A Memoir.* New York: Arno Press and the New York Times, 1969.

Rugoff, Milton. *The Beechers: An American Family in the Nineteenth Century.* New York: Harper & Row, 1981.

Shew, Joel. *The Cholera, Its Causes, Prevention, and Cure, Showing the Inefficacy of Drug-Treatment, and the Superiority of the Water-Cure, in This Disease.* New York: Fowlers and Wells, 1849.

Sillen, Samuel. *Women Against Slavery*. New York: International Publishers, 1952.
Stowe, Charles Edward. *Life of Harriet Beecher Stowe Compiled from Her Letters and Journals*. Boston: Houghton Mifflin & Co., 1889.
Stowe, Lyman Beecher. *Saints Sinners and Beechers*. Indianapolis, Ind.: The Bobbs-Merrill Co., 1934.
Tappan, Lewis. *Life of Arthur Tappan*. New York: Arno, 1970.
Thayer, George B. *Pedal and Path: Across the Continent Awheel and Afoot*. Hartford, Conn.: Hartford Evening Post Association, 1887.
Tucker, George Holbert. *Norfolk Highlights 1584-1881*. Norfolk, Va.: The Norfolk Historical Society, 1972.
Tyler, Alice Felt. *Freedom's Ferment*. New York: Harper & Row, 1944, 1962.
Walters, Ronald G. *American Reformers 1815-1860*. New York: Hill and Wang, 1978.
Washington, S.A.M. *George Thomas Downing: Sketch of His Life and Times*. Newport: Milne Printery, 1910.
Welter, Rush. *Popular Education and Democratic Thought in America*. New York: Columbia University Press, 1962.
Wertenbaker, Thomas J. *Norfolk: Historic Southern Port*. Durham, N.C.: Duke University Press, 1962.
Williams, George Washington. *A History of the Negro Race in America*. 2 vols. New York: G. P. Putnam's Sons, 1883. Reprint. New York: Berman Publishers, 1968.
Wilson, Henry. *History of the Rise and Fall of the Slave Power in America*. 3 vols. Boston: James R. Osgood and Company, 1874.
Wolf, Hazel Catherine. *On Freedom's Altar: The Martyr Complex in the Abolition Movement*. Madison: University of Wisconsin Press, 1952.
Woodson, Carter Godwin. *The Education of the Negro Prior to 1861: A History of the Colored People of the United States from the Beginning of Slavery to the Civil War*. New York: G. P. Putnam's Sons, 1915.
Yates, Elizabeth. *Prudence Crandall: Woman of Courage*. New York: Dutton, 1955.

JOURNALS

Bunkle, Phillida. "Sentimental Womanhood and Domestic Education, 1830-1870." *History of Education Quarterly* 14 (Spring 1974): 13-30.
Clark, Allen C. "Walter Lenox, the Thirteenth Mayor of the City of Washington." *Records of the Columbia Historical Society* 20 (1917): 167-93.
Conway, Jill K. "Perspectives on the History of Women's Education in the

United States." *History of Education Quarterly* 14 (Spring 1974): 1-12.

Crandall, Prudence. "Letters." *Journal of Negro History* 18 (January 1933): 80-84.

Flusche, Michael. "Antislavery and Spiritualism: Myrtilla Miner and her School." *The New-York Historical Society Quarterly* 59 (January 1975): 149-72.

Garrison, Wendell Phillips. "Connecticut in the Middle Ages." *Century Magazine* 30 (September 1885): 780-86.

Giammichele, Evelyn, and Taylor, Eva. "Elmira Water Cure: Silas and Rachel Gleason and Their 'Tavern for the Sick.'" *The Chemung Historical Journal* 12 (December 1966): 1535-41.

Greenwood, Grace. "An American Salon." *Cosmopolitan* 8 (February 1890): 437-47.

Mattingly, Paul H. "Educational Revivals in Ante-Bellum New England." *History of Education Quarterly* 11 (Spring 1971): 39-71.

Riley, Glenda. "Origins of the Argument for Improved Female Education." *History of Education Quarterly* 9 (Winter 1969): 455-70.

St. Clair, Sadie Daniel. "Myrtilla Miner: Pioneer in Teacher Education for Negro Women." *Journal of Negro History* 34 (January 1949): 30-45.

Small, Edwin W., and Small, Miriam R. "Prudence Crandall, Champion of Negro Education." *New England Quarterly* 17 (1944): 506-29.

Southall, Eugene Portlette. "Arthur Tappan and the Anti-Slavery Movement." *Journal of Negro History* 15 (April 1930): 162-97.

Trachtenberg, Leo. "The Canterbury Tale." *Negro History Bulletin* 12 (March 1949): 123-30, 143.

Vinovskis, Maris A., and Bernard, Richard M. "Beyond Catharine Beecher: Female Education in the Antebellum Period." *Signs: Journal of Women in Culture and Society* 3 (Summer 1978): 856-69.

Wells, Lester Grosvenor. "Myrtilla Miner." *New York History* 24 (July 1943): 358-75.

Wormley, G. Smith. "Prudence Crandall." *Journal of Negro History* 8 (January 1923): 72-80.

Index

About the Authors

PHILIP S. FONER is Professor Emeritus of History at Lincoln University in Pennsylvania. His books include the first three volumes of *History of Black Americans* (Greenwood Press, 1975 and 1983), and *American Socialism and Black Americans* (Greenwood Press, 1977), among many others.

JOSEPHINE F. PACHECO is Associate Professor of History and Director of the George Mason Project for the Study of Human Rights at George Mason University in Fairfax, Virginia. She is the author of *O Problema do Racismo nos Estados Unidos* and the editor of *The Legacy of George Mason*.